P9-CRF-998

THE HUGUENOTS

Fighters

for God and Human Freedom

GASPARD DE COLIGNY
Admiral of France
1572

OTTO ZOFF

THE Huguenots

FIGHTERS FOR GOD AND HUMAN FREEDOM

LONDON

GEORGE ALLEN & UNWIN LTD

First published in Great Britain in 1943

Translated by

E. B. ASHTON

and

JO MAYO

THE PAPER (AND BINDING) OF THIS BOOK CONFORMS TO THE AUTHORIZED ECONOMY STANDARD

Printed in Great Britain by
Billing and Sons Ltd., Guildford and Esher

CONTENTS

Contents

A LIST OF ILLUSTRATIONS

1

AN INTRODUCTION

IN THE War for American Independence, men of English stock fought beside the sons of French, Dutch, German, and Swedish settlers. Yet an eighteenth-century American named Van Zandt usually hailed from around New York; one named Schmidt from New Jersey, upstate New York, or Pennsylvania; one named Gulbransson from Delaware. Each had his general locality but for one non-English strain, the French, who were spread, however thinly, throughout the Thirteen Colonies.

French names are prominent in Revolutionary history. Many were Carolinians: General Francis Marion, the "Swamp Fox," dreaded by the Redcoats; Henry Laurens, Hancock's successor as President of the Continental Congress; Gabriel Manigault, who gave a quarter of a million dollars for the prosecution of the war and, at seventy-five, helped fight off a raid on Charleston by the side of his fifteen-year-old grandson. Some were New Yorkers like John Jay, first Chief Justice of the Supreme Court; or Pennsylvanians like Washington's good friend John Bayard, whose Second Battalion of Philadelphians was complimented by the general for gallantry, after the battle of Princeton; or Virginians like John Sevier, frontiersman,

Indian-fighter, and first Governor of Tennessee. Others came from New Jersey, like Elias Boudinot, who, as President of the Congress, signed the French alliance and, as Secretary for Foreign Affairs, the peace treaty with Britain. Some came from Massachusetts, like Governor James Bowdoin and Paul Revere. North or south, seaboard town or inland plantation, wherever the white man had settled one met Americans whose grandfathers or great-grandfathers had emigrated from France.

Another fact stands out. In 1776, their territorial dispersal notwithstanding, there were virtually no bearers of French names to be found among the Loyalists. Coincidence? Hardly. There was an influence at work, an old and strong inner compulsion which ranged the French on the side of freedom and progress, against authoritarian rule and reaction. To them, as to the sons of the Puritans, the Revolution meant but a renewal of an earlier struggle. They, too, saw in America a haven, perhaps more than any other Colonial group, because it had proved itself to be a refuge from as cruel a persecution as was ever visited on a religious and political minority. For those Colonial Americans with French names were children of Huguenots.

Their fathers arrived in this country during a period of more than a century. They settled Charlesfort (now Port Royal, S.C.) in 1562, which was wiped out by the Spaniards a few years later, and founded New Rochelle in 1688. Between, they returned to South Carolina in 1568; came to Virginia, under Lord De La Warr's flag, in 1610; to New Amsterdam with the Dutch in 1623; to Delaware around 1660. They were in Pennsylvania before Penn arrived in 1681; and finally, in one mass flight from the great persecutions under Louis XIV, they came to New England in the 1680's. They generally arrived in poor, little ships, only good enough for folk unwanted in their own country. They were backed by no government; it was their own from which they fled. They brought few possessions: most everything of theirs had found its way into the coffers of His Most Christian Majesty, the King of France. But they did bring memories of a civil war waged for decades with unspeakable bestiality, with no quarter given or asked, that made an Indian raid seem tame. And they brought the qualities which had enabled them to survive that ordeal: courage, tenacity, an unshakable trust in God, and a rarely equaled readiness to die for their convictions. This was no mean equipment for pioneers.

In America, their story was like that of all other first settlers. It was a story of heat and blizzards, of clearing forests and wrestling with the soil, of crop failures and disease, of alternately trading and fighting with the Indians. It was the old, ever-new story of America's youth, alike in its essentials from Jamestown to New Amsterdam, from Plymouth Rock to the Friends' properties along the Delaware.

The French were perhaps not as peace-minded as the Quakers, for they came from a war-torn land, often directly from army camps or cities under siege or cities already taken and sacked. Their ships' companies were militarily organized. The men wore steel vests and heavy helmets and carried halberds and arquebuses. When they reached land, they took the cannon from their vessels and dragged them along by hand, over the narrow forest trails, choosing to abandon their most prized household goods rather than their artillery. They never encamped overnight without posting guards, and had trumpets to wake them, to sound the signal to march after morning services.

On the other hand, though often of noble birth, the Huguenots lacked the proud aims of an Oglethorpe or Raleigh. They were not out to found an empire but to find a home. They did not wish to lord it over any man, white or red. Their faith forbade it, for as followers of Calvin they believed that all men are equal. Wherever religious, social, or political issues arose in Colonial America, Huguenot voices were heard on the side of tolerance. Accepting evil and misfortune as the will of God, they were able always to keep up their spirit of *camaraderie*. They were honest and plain-spoken. Their ancient slogan, *Foy d'un Huguenot*, points to a man who never breaks his word.

It is not surprising that within a very few generations they rose to a position of influence out of all proportion to their number. Nor is it surprising that today a million Americans are proud of their Huguenot ancestry. Huguenot descendants have remained prominent in the life of this country. One need only mention the La Follette family in politics, and the Lamar family in the field of law. But in three hundred years the face of this country has changed; more, probably, than that of any other on earth. Not much remains that will tangibly connect any present-day Americans with their forefathers, however the latters' memory or tradition may be cherished.

Not much that is tangible is left of the Huguenots, either. Some yellowed parchment, some simple buildings of stone or pieces of furniture, carved before Duncan Phyfe was born; a few songs, sad or gay; family prayers in antique French, handed down from grandparents to grandchildren. And stories—stories which sound at first like all pioneer tales until somehow an odd twist appears, to give them a flavor all their own. Stories like that of Catherine Du Bois, seized by the Esopus Indians with her three little children and held for months in a tepee on the bank of Shawangunk Kill. One evening in September she began to sing.

> "*By the rivers of Babylon, there we sat down, yea, we wept when we remembered Zion.*
> *We hanged our harps upon the willows in the midst thereof.*
> *For there they that carried us away captive required of us a song; and they that wasted us required of us mirth, saying, Sing us one of the songs of Zion.*"

As she sang, the savages stood about the clearing, motionless. They had ordered her to sing before, but in vain. Now they listened rapturously to the soft, sad voice, lost to all other sound till suddenly, from the edge of the forest, dogs barked and shots rang out from white men's muskets . . .

And Louis Du Bois took his wife and children home to Wiltwyck, which today is Kingston, N.Y. But not for long; when Catherine told him of the Indians' fertile land, he went back and purchased a large tract from the tribe, for which he and his and nine other Huguenot families were duly granted patents by the Colony's first English Governor. And on this tract now stands the town of New Paltz.

Although a Frenchman's love of country is renowned, he is surprisingly quick to adapt himself to other lands and customs when it is necessary. No matter how foreign the surroundings, he will not be a stranger long. The Huguenots soon felt at home here. They fast became good colonials, eager to forget what lay behind them. And yet, along with the basic toughness which they shared with all American pioneer groups, they held on to a number of plainly French traits which came to be of great value to the growing nation. Into the still largely unexplored, sinister wilderness, into the first primitive settlements they brought an air of refinement. They brought the love of beauty, the art of making life a joy. With a Frenchman's taste and his sense of quality, every Huguenot naturally became a messenger of civilization.

In their houses, rooms were bright and full of sunlight but the light was never glaring, for it was dimmed by thin, translucent parchment when glass could not be afforded and by curtains of fine linen. The parchment windows were softly tinted, often painted in delicate patterns. Instead of sand or rushes, rugs were spread on the floors, made from bits of worn clothing, usually oval-shaped and with dark blue and pale pink as the dominating colors. On the mantels over fireplaces, huge enough to roast whole sides of beef, pieces of simple pottery stood. Furniture was low and comfortable; tiny chairs, built as if for children, stood before the hearth. Deep chests lined the walls, great unwieldy mortars lay beside the tongs, and a whetstone lay under the table. Always, somewhere, there was unspun flax hanging as a token that the house should never lack what future generations need. There were odd little cradles with gabled roofs of solid wood over one end, as though the babies had been kept outdoors in rain and snow; and artfully fashioned spinning wheels that were often man-high and had to be run by heavy cranks. When they turned the wheels, the Huguenot women sang, not only dark songs of their grim religion, but dance tunes as well, that went with the bagpipe.

How deep then, on those amiable Gallic natures, was the imprint of their fathers' trials? There is no way of telling. They wanted to forget, and so far as mere memory goes they succeeded. It is rather as if a curtain had been dropped once they had left Europe, concealing in its folds all but the shadows of a great past. Yet there were reminders of another kind: their faith, to which they clung as determinedly before every new temptation as their fathers did before the stake; their beautiful language; the little things, customs, manners, likes and dislikes, which are always more difficult to shed than national allegiances; their pride in a history of their own, in a land to whose history they were contributing. They might forget that that pride was rooted in a tradition they had brought with them, but the Huguenot descendants would never have played the part they did here had their ancestors not lived through an age of dread and glory.

When we lift the curtain behind those first French Americans, we come upon a grandiose pageant. White plumes flutter from huge helmets; swords and lances gleam; the thunderous beat of innumerable hoofs resounds. Soft, sultry music of mandolins is heard in gardens, on the banks of the Seine or the Loire, by the loveliest of the charming women of the realm in tremendous hoop skirts—although the great King Francis I had forbidden hoop skirts at his court because too often they were used to hide a deadly weapon! Dagger and poison, *billets-doux* sent by Italian servants who are slippery as eels, doors battered down by assassins, Cardinals in robes of satin and velvet who translate Virgil at night and in the morning attend a princess's *levee* . . . And through it all, above it all, the monotonous, faith-drunken battle hymn of the Huguenots:

Je me couche sans peur,
Je m'endors sans frayeur,
Sans crainte je m'éveille;
Dieu, qui soutient ma foi,
Est toujours près de moi
Et jamais ne sommeille.

Non, je ne craindrai pas,
Quand j'aurais sur les bras
Une nombreuse armée;
Dieu me dégagerait,
Quand même on la verrait
Autour de moi campée.

2

PRELUDES OF EVIL

BY THE agreement of historians, the Huguenot age refers to a period of approximately one hundred years during which France was in a state of civil war. The main point at issue was the fate of French Protestantism; so the Huguenot wars—the books count at least five—are generally labeled religious wars. If such they were, they began without cause, and ended, save for two million deaths, without result, leaving the Catholic and Reformed faiths in about the same position as before swords were drawn.

The label does not fit. History knows no purely religious wars. At that time, too, there were other issues at stake, social, economic, and political in nature—issues which were settled in that crimson century. Their solution made the France we know in history; that which as kingdom, empire, republic, always remained one nation in different garbs. This France was cemented, if not created, in the blood and tears of the Huguenot wars.

In the Middle Ages, all Christian countries were much alike. The feudal structure and code which they all shared, and the pervasive influence of a single, well-organized, international church, made them a genuine "family of nations." The rules were the same for a Teutonic Knight or a Hispanic one, for a merchant from Venice or one of the Hansa; a Frenchman could—and on occasion did—become King of England and begin to rule without having to learn anything new.

With the break-up of feudalism and centralized Christianity, this system ceased to work. The several member countries of the medieval family were cast adrift, as it were, put on their own, to sink or swim according to their individual merits. Some, like the once powerful Holy Roman Empire, which turned into a mere shell containing a motley lot of sovereign states, could not meet the test. Those that survived were led along different paths by their varying circumstances. The national character which England got from sailing the seven seas; which was fashioned for Russia by the ukase of Peter, the autocrat; which Prussia derived from her poverty and which, in time, the United States was to glean from its giant size and wealth; in short, the character that a nation must form to endure in modern history, this, for France, originated in a welter of domestic strife. For the fact that this strife, on the surface, was largely over the theological interpretation of Holy Communion, no better reason than historic accident has yet been advanced. It was pure chance that brought the issues to a head in France just after Luther, in Germany, broke away from Rome.

Under Francis I, of the House of Valois, France had regained its place in the world and re-established its authority over the restive, autonomy-seeking barons. It also had breathed deeply of the explosive spirit of the Italian Renaissance. A new France had come to life, baffled, itself, by the change. The outer and inner contraction, the clouded vision of the fustily passing Middle Ages gave way. The dominant Church was replaced by the sovereign state, prescribed belief by skeptical thought, unworldly bonds by the enjoyment of a deep, inexhaustible, fearfully beautiful world.

The high-living, fast-loving, prodigal monarch who was not given to brooding, who acted only on impulse, whose sun-burnt skin, laughing eyes, buoyant step had so little in common with his bigoted ancestors, paid small attention at first to clerical and other protests. It is said that in his insatiable urge to keep active and prove himself he often broke sixty lances a day in tournaments; and so he also wished his people to live: challenging the old, denying the past, ringing in the bright and gay new age. He opened the doors wide to the Italian spirit and to the study of classic literature and art. Leonardo da Vinci, whom he personally brought from Milan, and Benvenuto Cellini were his high-salaried guests. He gathered a circle of scientists around him. Clément Marot, the bard of the French Reformation, became his poet laureate. All Italian emigrants were welcome at his lavish court—the King felt that he was not doing them as much of a favor as they were doing France.

Rapidly the scholasticism of the universities yielded to free science. Gothic towers and redoubts were torn down. Foreign artists, pursued with envy by the native ones, created magnificent castles of a new architecture: huge Chambord, the Château St. Germain-en-Laye, last but not least Fontainebleau. The King supported anything if only it was new, and not ecclesiastic or prudish. The vogue for filigree work, hunting festivities, mythological plays, glass-blowing and cabinet-making; public mockery of the Sorbonne and impudent display of concubinage—all go back to the same source. The old faith was broken; what takes its place is skepticism. One used to pray with eyes shut or lowered; now one opens them, wonders, and sees.

A fight against abuses in the Church ensued, as in Germany. Causes were pondered: the pointless wealth of the Church and its orders, the ignorance and immorality of the clerics, and their neglect of ministerial and educational tasks. Arch-dioceses, dioceses, abbeys, and priories—the higher dignities which in effect make up the Church—were the preserve of a *jeunesse dorée* who drained the taxes from their sees and lived, unworried over duties, in Paris. If the lord does not tend to business, why should the liege? The parson bolstered his income by acting on the side as doctor, druggist, courtier, farmer; often he did not set foot in the parish house for years. He named as assistant the vicar who took the parish on a sort of lease—but he, too, usually preferred the temporal whirl and left the care of school and hospital to servants.

Once embarked on, criticism reached no end. Discrepancies in the social framework began to be questioned. Even the most unpolitical-minded noticed that this was an age of royal ascendancy; that nation and sovereign had reached a peak of power, supported by strong and self-confident cities, well-organized in guilds; that France was moving toward a unity which made for success in business. And should one not share in this vaunted progress? Must one stay in poverty, dirt and sweat? Were the abuses in the Church alone responsible? Or was something wrong with a Christianity which everyone professed and no one practiced?

Strikes broke out, which would not have been dared under medieval constraint. On May 1, 1539, the typographers' assistants in Lyon walked out, complaining that they had not enough to eat although the shop owners in one year had doubled their capital. They were obliged to handle 3350 sheets a day while the typographers of Paris reasonably maintained that even 2630 sheets were too many. They demanded that wages and the number of apprentices be arbitrated by boards equally composed of employers and employees. In reply, Francis I abolished the workers' right to organize.

But there was no abolishing discussion, pamphleteering, and strikes. Questioning increased daily, and Church and monarchy had no answer. Somewhere it had to be, but where?

They found it in Scripture.

A bishop stands at the threshold of the French Reformation: Guillaume Briçonnet, Comte de Montbrun, Bishop of Meaux, and once Francis's Ambassador to the Holy See. What he brought back from Rome was the *protest*. What he found at home was disorder in his own diocese. Under Luther's impact he began to institute reforms, and to receive a group of like-minded thinkers—Farel, Lefèvre d'Etaples, Miguel d'Aranda, Gérard Roussel. Around them another circle took form, consisting, strangely enough but symptomatically, of artisans. Noblemen began to appear in time, and then a boatman, a village school-teacher. Seen at Briçonnet's house, as his guests, were weavers, paperhangers, carpenters, fullers.

When he attempted to end the scandals in his see by commanding his parsons to live in their parishes and not in Paris, an accusation of heresy was conveniently brought against him. He answered in sermons, and made the revolutionary point that men should bring their hearts to God, not their purses. The astonishment in Meaux was great. The bishop's church was thronged, and the peasants flocked in from the countryside.

The movement stirred one province after another. It was still chaotic. In Lyon a few burghers joined to get in touch with the Reformed leaders in Switzerland. The monks in Annonay declared in a body for Luther, one of them having been to Germany and told of the peasants' unrest there. More manual workers joined the movement. They protested against the high church levies, and also against the big profits of their masters and their own long hours of work. There was another strike. The authorities countered with arrests, which served to solidify the discontent. When the Inquisition took a hand, the universities of Bourges, Poitiers, and Orléans published protests. To Orléans came German students, who translated Luther's writings for private groups. In Toulouse three professors were prosecuted for heresy and fifty suspects, rounded up in house-to-house raids, were taken to jail. In Noyon and Bordeaux, scientists, teachers, priests, noblemen were arrested, and also some peasants, although not many of these. But in Paris no mention is made of priests and nobles; the Sorbonne describes the straying sheep as "only foolish people in small circumstances: cobblers, tailors, and such . . ."

In France, as in Germany, England, and the Netherlands, the first Protestants were good Catholics taking a stand against the rot of churchly and monastic morals, and against the extremes of the scholastic method. All they wanted was a substantially devout faith, obedient to the teachings of the Bible, true to the Word of God. They even feared for the authority of the Church and the stability of the hierarchy. They roamed through the land, preached and prayed. The man who might be called the patriarch of the French Protestants, Master Jacques Lefèvre of Etaples, was of a Franciscan gentleness and, though he had forsworn the saints, had not the heart to pass their pictures without kneeling. And he was afraid of Purgatory, the existence of which he denied.

The civil wars, which would put their cruel stamp upon the period, began with protest meetings, disputations, local riots. Not one of the astrologers who were so much in fashion at the time divined that four coming generations were to drown in blood and misery. The first hint came in 1520, when Luther's Theses were officially condemned by the Sorbonne.

The Sorbonne was the spearhead of the orthodox battle line. Founded in the thirteenth century by Robert de Sorbon as a modest community of impecunious teachers, it had become the top-ranking school of divinity, not in France alone but in the world. It wielded a huge power. The treasures of its library were an eighth wonder; its teaching methods were considered unique and its faculty oracles. More and more often it was asked to arbitrate disputes; more and more often it thrust itself into disputes without being asked. Its verdicts, it was true, were not legally binding. But what judge would have dared to controvert them? Until 1520, for example, Luther was no more than an ecclesiastic nuisance. It took the action of the Sorbonne to transform him into a heretic, false prophet, and Anti-Christ.

For a century the Sorbonne had been a butt of ridicule

to educated people. With the decline of scholasticism its day of greatness had passed. But for the masses it was and remained the guardian of the faith; belittled by the few, it still was feared by all. Devout and obedient, it maintained the decrees of the Papal See, and was a peril to all intellectual progress. Before Luther, it had condemned Marsilius of Padua, persecuted Wycliffe and Huss, engineered the excommunication of Reuchlin. It was an implacable foe of the Renaissance. In the orthodox view, the writings of antiquity, the life-blood of the new civilization, could be perused safely only by ordained priests. Lest the study of the ancients breed heresy, the Sorbonne banned the teaching of Greek within its walls. And the man who wanted to learn Hebrew and read the Bible in the original courted death by fire.

Yet, stake and confiscations notwithstanding, so long as Francis I, this French Renaissance prince in the Italian style, gave vent to his own protestant leanings, the Sorbonne was kept in bounds. To offset it in its home bailiwick, Paris, he founded the Collège de France, where Greek and Hebrew were taught and lectures given in philosophy, medicine, and mathematics. At Court the Sorbonne was jeered as a den of reaction, a seat of learning frequented only by old women. This was especially so while Francis's sister Margaret lived at his court, the brightest and gayest figure of the time. Her *Heptameron*, a book of stories modeled after Boccaccio, has entranced millions up to the present day. Amiable, warmhearted, cultured, she was an excellent influence on Francis I. But much too soon she married the King of Navarre; leaving the glamorous Court and her glamorous brother for the distant little land of Béarn, so far from the great world and so near the Pyrenees, with their wolves and bandits.

There, in time, her castle of Nérac became a refuge at whose bounds the hatred of the Sorbonne stopped. She had a friendly, tacit understanding with her brother: out of regard for his position she did not openly confess to Protestantism, and he, amused by her strange predilection for taking life so seriously, let her do as she pleased. She extended aid to all who were no longer safe in France: Clément Marot fled to her, Lefèvre d'Etaples, Calvin. She protected Bonaventure Despériers, and wrote touching letters of admiration to Melanchthon. In her last writings she tried to reconcile classic philosophy with Christian teachings. Meanwhile, the King retreated step by step before the Church. Once he had called preachers of a Lutheran tinge to his Court; now they were dismissed under any pretext. It was one of these, Luther's ablest exponent in France, who became his first and most striking sacrifice to political expediency.

Louis de Berquin was Francis's great favorite. When the Sorbonne first managed his arrest on suspicion of heresy, he had to be released upon the Court's intervention. When the King, himself, became a prisoner of war in Madrid, after the luckless battle of Pavia, he was incarcerated a second time. Only Francis's return saved the quiet, God-fearing, fifty-year-old Berquin's life. Friends warned Berquin, urged him to emigrate, but he would not yield. He even challenged the syndics of the Sorbonne to a public debate, and said on that occasion that everyone, not only clerics, should read the Bible. That statement sealed his fate. The King, at the low ebb of his fortune, defeated by Spain (which held his children as hostages), surrounded by vassals in league with the enemy, dared not add the Pope to his other foes. He dropped his protégé, and Berquin died at the stake on April 17, 1529.

From that time on the King ceased to offer resistance. Never a man of strong convictions, he capitulated before the propagandistic assaults of the Sorbonne. Posters began to appear on the doors of churches and town halls in Paris, Rouen, and Meaux, cynically attacking Catholic tenets. The miraculous statue of Our Lady in the Rue des Rosiers was smashed to pieces and thrown into the gutter. When the people were seething ominously, the Sorbonne released a statement that the "unknown" miscreants were only too well known to the courts, that they were none other than the carriers of the new ideas. Worried, Francis went to Paris to calm the excited populace, and there found the dastardly placards hanging not only on church walls but in the Louvre, in the royal apartment itself. The machinery functioned smoothly. Next came the discovery of a Protestant plot, aimed, it was alleged, at nothing less than the murder of all Catholics at divine services. The Sorbonne produced no proof, but twenty-four persons were condemned to die by fire.

On January 19, 1535, a great procession to celebrate the executions moved from the Louvre to Notre-Dame. At its head walked the King, hatless and carrying a torch; behind him followed Queen Eleonore, their children, his mistress, Madame d'Etampes, the gentlemen and ladies of the Court. In the Cathedral Francis made a speech. "If my right arm," he exclaimed pathetically, "were infected with heresy I'd cut it off! And were one of my sons so depraved as to follow that devil's creed—with my own hand I'd offer him as a sacrifice to God Almighty!"

The Sorbonne had conquered.

The Church, confirmed in its power, could now safely drop whatever steps it had taken against the abuses within it. In fact, they were henceforth displayed with growing frankness. And if anyone thought that no increase in frivolity were possible, he was to be surprised after Francis's death, when his son, Henry II, ascended the throne.

This Henry had the right, under a treaty with Rome, to fill ecclesiastic benefices as he saw fit. It was a cheap and easy way to reward services rendered to the Crown by soldiers and politicians. True, students of divinity became rare in the French Church as a result, but this did not disturb the House of Valois. Warriors who had led their companies on foot lived sumptuously on revenues from abbeys; others changed their trades: yesterday soldiers or merchants, today they strutted in episcopal robes. Soon, merit was no longer so important as being on good terms with the royal mistress. The Duchess of Valentinois asked her lover to leave the distribution of Church offices to her; so now it was a concubine who made and unmade bishops.

The persecution of the dissidents kept pace with the decay of the Church. In 1547, the first year of his reign, Henry II set up a special court to fight the Lutherans. Calvinists were handled even more harshly. By 1549, seventy-two had fled from France to Geneva. In 1550 the number increased to 122, and in 1551 to 285.

But attack spurs defense. Among the ever harder pressed French Protestants, the Lutheran creed, which showed its followers a way to inner betterment but no method of maintaining themselves against the outer world, gave way to Calvinism. The great reformer, party leader, and statesman of Geneva had overshadowed the monk of Wittenberg. Under Calvin's cautious but dictatorially relentless guidance, the Reformation in France began to advance by strides.

Whole cities had already leaned toward it under Francis I, but then it had been a matter for the individual. Now those individuals united. Congregations sprang up in Normandy, in virtually all towns along the Loire. They adopted common constitutions and, eventually, the consistory of Geneva. To give their decrees legal force, they introduced regular meetings of deputies. Entire communities took up the practice of the Biblical life. Their back was turned upon the world; they hardly would have made trouble had they been left alone. But they were not left alone. They were martyred.

By 1558, according to a cautious estimate, the Protestants in France numbered 400,000.

3

KINGS AND CAPTAINS

HENRY II was his father's successor and exact opposite. His character did not fulfill the promise of his excellent appearance. He was tall and well-built, with regular features and lustrous brown hair. His bearing was dignified. His body had been trained since childhood. Twice weekly he rode to hounds, preferably after deer, galloping through the woods for hours, heedless of fatigue or danger; when a horse collapsed under him he jumped on a fresh one and rode on. Yet a glance into his eyes, dully regarding the world beneath heavy lids, showed what he really was: a colorless bureaucrat—well-meaning but untalented. He had begun his reign with the best intentions; before his coronation he had prayed that God might give him a long life if it would benefit his people, otherwise to let him die early. The prayer was granted. He died early.

At the age of fourteen he was married to Catherine de' Medici, whom we shall encounter in many stellar rôles on the terrifyingly illumined stage of this Court. But while Henry lived she was no more than an extra. Italian-born, she felt lonely among the unsympathetic French; it took her years to become acclimatized. Even as a girl she was not pretty. Her cheeks were too full as were her lips, and her chin was too short; soon she acquired a second one, and other fat that defied exercise. Only her eyes were remarkable and were described by her contemporaries as "oddly vivid." In fact, nobody liked her, with the exception of her father-in-law. She flattered Francis, and her merry wit amused him. She made him take her into the "*petite bande*," his private hunting group, where he enjoyed her daring horsemanship. She introduced the Italian custom of putting the feet on the saddle bow while riding, the reason being that she had very nice legs.

The man who paid the least attention to Catherine was her husband. At seventeen he fell in love with Diane de Poitiers, Duchess of Valentinois, who had the title of Madame la Sénéchale. Although she was twice his age and past her prime when he met her, he remained under her spell till he died. Diane was not pretty but made up cleverly; adept in the wiles of love and court life, sensuous, and shrewd. She knew how to handle this sleepy, taciturn fellow who was at ease only on horseback and whom people called "the leaden king." At Court, where she had arrived as a young widow, she advanced cautiously; but once sure of her domination over the King she overstepped all bounds of avarice.

The Queen was convinced that Diane had a love charm, some secret means of fanning Henry's desire. Both women displayed the utmost affection for each other—Diane procured healthy nurses for the royal princes and princesses, and Catherine addressed her in letters as "Ma bonne cousine et amye." Meanwhile, the *maîtresse* grew more powerful and no one paid attention to the Queen. The people cursed Diane's greed, but the few who might, perhaps, have altered the situation preferred to play up to the dangerous woman.

Henry, spurning the advice of his dying father, removed the incumbents from most Court and government posts and replaced them with men who had not enjoyed Francis's confidence. For instance, he brought back as Constable Anne de Montmorency, First Baron of the Realm, a talented wire-puller, able organizer, and inept soldier, who had graced that high office under Francis until he had fallen out of favor. At the start of his second career, the Constable was in his fifties but of unbroken strength. He was cold, calculating, ever bent on adding to his family power, and immensely wealthy—much wealthier than the King. He was a snob, a bully, and a boor. But if the state household somehow kept running on the brink of ruin, France had his strictness and hard work to thank for it.

What made Montmorency indispensable to Henry II was his political reliability. He was a blind slave of Church and Crown, equally a bigot about the lords of heavenly and earthly hosts. He never missed a prayer; every morning, whether at home or on horseback, hunting or with his troops, he told his beads. This habit gave rise to the adage, "Beware the Constable's rosary!" for during prayers he would command, on occasions: "Go hang this fellow! Cut that one down right away! Shoot the knaves before my eyes! Quarter the tramps who want another church than the King's—burn their villages down, start a blaze a mile wide!" And as Brantôme reports, who knew the gentleman and favored Catholicism, he never put the rosary out of his hands, for he would have deemed it a grave sin to postpone his devotions.

Yet actually the camarilla which aimed at the annihilation of the Reformed faith was not led by the Constable so much as by the House of Guise. One of France's most illustrious families—the ranking branch of the Lorraines, who traced their ancestry back to the old Frankish kings—the Guises were to play the main rôle in turning the French drama into a great tragedy. Francis I had never trusted them. He never let them gain influence in his Council, and constantly gave them new estates to add to their old ones so as to keep them away. They were too wily for his taste, too quick, too grasping. "Their spines don't bend when they bow," he used to say, "only when they stand straight."

The House of Guise was his greatest worry. On his death bed he warned his son not to bring any of them to Court. He took Henry's hand. "I can't breathe for fear you'll let them serve you. They can't serve anyone. They care as little for the King as for the faith, and least of all for the people. They'll sell out God and the Crown for a cheap honor. If you surround yourself with assassins, and treat them well, you'll be safer than in honoring a Guise. Mark my words, son. I beg of you, don't forget them!"

Henry promptly forgot. At his Court, advising and guiding him, we immediately find a famous pair of brothers: Francis of Lorraine, Duke of Guise, and Cardinal Charles of Lorraine.

Francis—*Le Grand Guise*—was one of the most successful generals of his time. He had élan, presence, ability, and luck. He was the kind of soldier who takes cities and women in turn—a master of the offensive. A wound had left him with a striking scar on the forehead, from which his nickname, the Gashed One, was derived. The King had a weakness for conquering types; far from being jealous, he was fascinated by the handsome, scarred young Duke. When Henry had made a deal for Metz with German Protestant princes, Guise's defense of that city, against the combined might of Spain and the German Empire under the dreaded Alva, made him the most popular man in France. To this swashbuckling hero, cheered by the masses wherever he appeared, the sleepy King, who never finished what he started, could not refuse his ear.

Francis brought his brother along with him to Court. Charles de Guise, a cardinal at twenty-three, resembled the older in ambition but, instead of war, he had chosen science as his field. He spoke most living languages, knew the ancient writers by heart, was at home in the politics of Europe, and delighted in glittering oratory. His residence in the archiepiscopal see of Reims was that of a brilliant, far-seeing prelate. He drained swamps and made them into lawns and gardens; he founded a university, a divinity school, a seminary, and a convent. He took his spiritual duties seriously, kept his parsons disciplined, and liked to preach. He abhorred the pleasures indulged in by the Renaissance clerical gentry, and retired annually to a monastery for religious meditation. As attractive as he was intelligent, he dominated every gathering; his learning and presence of mind gave him the last word in every dispute. But despite his superior talents, he was universally accepted as a man who must be handled with care. Although the most gifted statesman of his age, in a country shoulder-deep in trouble, no one wished to see him in power.

These, then, were the men around the throne. They grudged each other the breath of life, not to mention the King's favor. Soon, with all the vehemence of their youth, the two Guises turned on old Montmorency. They fought with rapiers, the Constable with a bludgeon. He found out too late that they had a powerful ally at Court in Diane de Poitiers, when they arranged the marriage of their third brother, the Duke of Aumale, to one of her daughters. The Constable countered and promptly proposed another match to Diane: between one of his sons and her granddaughter. But the Guises had a head start; and to make doubly sure, they arranged for young Francis, the King's first-born, to marry the heiress of Scotland, Mary Stuart, whose mother was their sister, Marie de Guise.

Thus the "King's rule" established by Francis I had been of short duration. The era of royal ascendancy was already all but forgotten, the power of government was again the toy of feudal cliques. And this reaction, which was nothing but a return to the Middle Ages, had yet to reach its peak.

There was one conspicuous exception to the noble families gathered round the Valois throne, rising and sinking in power according to chance, whimsy, and poor statecraft. The one family most closely related to the Blood Royal remained aloof. The House of Bourbon, although it had by achievements in war and peace constantly grown in stature, was denied the favor of the Court. Also at the head of this house stood two brothers: Anthony, Duke of Bourbon and King of Navarre, and Prince Louis de Condé. They saw themselves pushed aside by the Guises and felt it to be a particular indignity, for the Lorraines, in their eyes, were not Frenchmen. Scheming foreigners, they said, had elbowed out a family which should, by rights, have stood first after the King. But their complaints went unheeded. On the contrary, the King nursed a suspicion that those he slighted were bound to be his worst enemies.

Anthony de Bourbon was cultured, conciliatory, and charming. The calm with which he bore injustice won respect. He married Jeanne d'Albret, only child of King Henry of Navarre and of Princess Margaret; when his father-in-law died, he became titular King of Navarre. His residence was Nérac, Margaret's castle in Béarn, in the so-called *Landes*—flat, arid wastelands covered with heather and occasional oak and pine woods. The capital of the tiny domain was Pau, a crude small town with crooked streets and a view of the Pyrenees. The kingdom of Navarre itself had been lost in the quarrels with Spain.

This mediocre gentleman might well have been content with a life devoted to petitioning for his lost realm, and with wolf and fox hunting in between. But he was married to the daughter of Margaret Valois, who had inherited her mother's mind. Where gentle Margaret had only inclined toward the Reformation, Jeanne declared herself frankly. She became the great Protestant woman of her time; destined, in the course of a hard life, to be an ascetic martyr because of her convictions and to bear the greatest monarch France ever had, Henry IV.

By a strange coincidence, the two outstanding figures on opposing sides, during the first half century of the Huguenot Age, were women. And how revealing it is to compare them! At Court we find Catherine de Medici: fleshy, voluptuous, charming, clever; an accomplished liar and *intrigante*, as utterly lacking in principle as in morals—the perfect prototype of a group whose single aim was to hold on to its power and wealth. On the other hand there was grave Jeanne d'Albret, who would have been a saint had she been born a thousand years earlier. She was gaunt and bony, with a too high forehead and a long, hooked nose, but many called her beautiful. There was magic in her dark, patiently penetrating eyes. Her mode of living was of an early Christian simplicity; her reputation—despite rumors liberally thrown out by the Queen—was immaculate. She never compromised with her standards; affianced to Francis de Guise, then the most eligible young man in Europe outside of royalty, she broke the engagement when his brother took a harlot's daughter to wife. She and Catherine were born to hate each other. Their enmity was as natural as that of water and fire, a perfect symbol of the hatred that was rending France.

Jeanne had little of the Queen's lust for power. Only her deep feelings concerning her faith and family brought her into the field of public affairs at all. Even so, her participation was limited to counseling the men about her, to whom her bold spirit and unfailing trust in God were a deep inspiration. It was she who roused her husband out of his inertia and wakened his Protestant sympathies. He yielded easily to her advice, and it was his misfortune that she could not give him some of the steel in her soul.

His brother, Louis de Condé, was cast in a different mold. He was a fighter, a man whose mettle showed only in the face of peril and responsibility. At other times he was delightfully imaginative, a brilliant talker, and a lover of the best in life. His success with women was a constant danger—he could never get rid of them, and seldom tried to. Only when he had the opportunity to fight did he return to his other self; then he accepted any challenge at once and met it bravely to the end.

Like Anthony, he had been slighted in every way, and

ridiculed whenever he took his poverty to Court. He fought in all of Henry's wars and earned the reputation of an exceptional soldier, but his merits availed him nothing. Refused the commands which were his due, and put off with empty titles, without functions, Condé saw that the King would have nothing to do with his family. For a man of his type there was only one way to solve the issue: the Bourbons would have to battle for their rights. It was then that he realized the political possibilities of the Reformation, which his brother's wife so passionately espoused.

Condé revered Jeanne. She had converted him during long winter nights by the Nérac fireside, when they discussed and interpreted the language of the Gospels. To the ardent warrior it seemed like a gage flung at his feet: what a chance to risk one's life in a holy cause, and at the same time to regain one's proper place and influence! For while Condé many times proved his devotion to the new faith, it also doubtless fitted well into his other plans.

He and Jeanne were the moving spirits of the House of Bourbon. But the King of Navarre was its head. It was he who would have to take any effective action. So between them they pushed the languid Anthony forward step by step, until he was figurehead of the most serious menace to the throne.

The Protestant party came into being in 1558. By this time the movement had grown enormously, and many Reformed churches had sprung up. One of Calvin's close collaborators, Theodore Beza, went to France as missionary and sent back exultant reports: "God must plan great things for the flock, already the well of Geneva has begotten rivers!"

strong measures. The Constable was still in Spanish hands. The Duke of Guise, though back from Italy, was in the field again. He had succeeded brilliantly at Calais, taken it from the English, but another defeat in Flanders, at Gravelines, so depleted the French forces that all Guise could do was to keep the enemy away from Paris by daring thrusts at his flanks. He could not spare a man—much less an army such as would have been needed for a show of force against the Protestants.

Perhaps this was one reason why even the Guises were now ready for peace. Another reason may have been that France was milked dry. Under crushing and ever-increasing levies, the peasants were deserting the soil, and no brutality could squeeze enough out of the urban taxpayers to keep the troops in the field much longer. But with these drab prospects, Queen Mary of England died and was succeeded by Elizabeth, who proudly called herself "mere English" and saw no point in waging war for Spain's benefit. The Spaniards were tired, too, and uneasy about Protestant trouble in their own Netherlands. So peace—a peace of mutual exhaustion—was made at Cateau-Cambrésis. It has since become famous in history books, chiefly for the fact that everybody lost by it. England lost the Channel ports; Spain her "Three Bishoprics" of Metz, Toul, and Verdun; France her Italian sphere of influence and hope of breaking her encirclement by her Spanish-Imperial arch-foe.

This was 1559. And in the same year the Protestants held their first synod, in Paris.

4

CALVIN

NOT by accident has Calvinism been called the most logical and clearly thought-out of Christian denominations. No other has been built up by a Frenchman.

Calvin was a native of Picardy, a region which, far from Parisian vivacity and closer to the measured though still Gallic spirit of Flanders and Hainaut, most highly cultivates the perfect balance of common sense and passion. He was born at Noyon in 1509, studied for the ministry, became a chaplain in his home town when he was twenty, heard about the Reformation from a relative —Pierre Robert Olivétan, the first French translator of the Bible—and at once felt the need to spread his new-born knowledge. A love of the idyllic life, to which he often privately confessed, of "peace and quiet," was stifled by a sense of supreme duty.

For a lecture he gave at the Sorbonne, in 1533, he was suspected of heresy. He fled, through the window of his house, a few minutes before the police broke in. Like so many, he took refuge at Nérac, and there met Lefèvre d'Etaples, who impressed him deeply. He resigned his chaplaincy and made the final break with Catholicism in 1534. There followed a time of wandering and teaching, often under false names, in Poitou and Saintonge, and finally in the great Reformed center of Basel where, at the age of twenty-six, he wrote his monumental "Institutions." In 1536 he traveled to Italy, and on the return trip stopped in Geneva, where Farel—also a Frenchman and a member of that original Protestant group around Bishop Briçonnet—had set up a Reformed congregation. Calvin only wanted to greet Farel and be on his way, but Farel, sensing the youth's ability and realizing that he had found in him a man who could make his community into a state, threatened him with the wrath of God if he left. Calvin renounced "peace and quiet," forever. Out of sheer humility, he became the spiritual and temporal head of the little republic beneath Europe's highest mountains.

There, under his rule, it happened for the first time that the Roman Catholic Church was confronted with an equivalent instrument, a similar fusion of religious and political forces. Luther's "otherworldliness," which was roving, visionary, popular, German-romantic, basically naïve, was changed to a Latin, juridico-political science. Hard sense governed the republic of Geneva. Always completely aware, with the *clarté* of reason, Calvin not only enforced Calvinism in Geneva but sent it across the borders into foreign lands. From his study, in incessant activity which grudged itself a few hours of sleep, he led the disciples who labored for the doctrine in every country between Poland and Spain. His directions were absolute and unalterable, as he quickly grew to a sense of his superiority. The hardness of his procedure may seem shocking, even inhuman, but nothing else could have saved the Reformed faith from destruction.

The congregation of Geneva was subjected to the most

rigid discipline. Not only were the daily work of the individual and his fulfillment of religious duties placed under control, but his meals, dress, leisure, residence, and conversation were regulated, meted, judged. Reading matter was prescribed, as well as the bounds of pleasure; light music was banned, as naturally was gambling. In time, the ideas of what should be permitted and what should be forbidden to a Christian grew ever more harsh. Eventually, a smile on Sundays became punishable; a woman who had hummed a loose song at work was burned; public penance, before the assembled congregation, threatened those who repeated a joke about the Council; adulterers paid with their lives.

For vice and sin evoke the wrath of God, and therefore the government of man must strive to exterminate them.

The core of Calvin's teachings was the doctrine of predestination. That nothing is done by our own power, and only the free grace of God can save the sinner, is a fundamental recognition of all faiths which was exhumed by Luther after it had lain buried for centuries. Upon it Calvin built. The step he took beyond Luther was the conclusion logically drawn from this theory. For of God's counsel, which stands so high above our conception that it would be presumptuous to believe we might, with our poor human understanding, divine His intentions, there is only one thing which we know: that His omniscience has always, in all eternity, seen everything He was ever going to let happen. Also, it is written that by the grace of God alone can the soul be saved; man can do nothing toward his salvation, just as no act of the worm can affect whether it will be crushed or spared by the human foot.

On these two premises rises Calvin's fearful doctrine: *before* original sin, eons back, God must have decreed man's election or damnation, dividing mankind into two herds, the chosen and the reprobate. Once made, this decree must be unalterable; for were God to change it, would He not have foreknown that fact as well? Between us and the mystery lies a chasm so immense that we cannot even peer over its edge. Even so, our eternal fate is signed and sealed, and nothing we can do is capable of changing it. As Calvin put it: "Those of mankind that are predestinated unto life, God before the foundation of the world was laid, according to His eternal and immutable purpose and the secret counsel and good pleasure of His will, hath chosen in Christ unto everlasting glory; out of His mere free grace and love, without any foresight of faith or good works or perseverance in either of them or any other thing in the creature as conditions or causes moving Him thereunto, but all to the praise of His glorious grace." And again: "The rest of mankind God was pleased, according to the unsearchable counsel of His own will whereby He extendeth or withholdeth mercy as He pleaseth, for the glory of His sovereign power over His creatures, to pass by, and to ordain them to dishonor and wrath for their sin, to the praise of His glorious justice."

Thus angels and devils, virtue and sin, rest in God alone. For how could man—involved by original sin in eternal death, with animal reason that can never perceive the faintest trace of any of God's steps—raise himself out of guilt by his own power? And as all that is done is done by God's decree, the evil too is done after His will, and the sinners are His tools. Calvin states: "As for those wicked and ungodly men whom God as a righteous judge for former sins doth blind and harden, from them He not only withholdeth His grace whereby they might have been enlightened in their understandings and wrought upon in their hearts, but sometimes also withdraweth the gifts which they had and exposeth them to such objects as their corruption makes occasion of sin: and withal gives them over to their own lusts, the temptations of the world, and the power of Satan: whereby it comes to pass that they harden themselves even under those means which God useth for the softening of others."

Who, then, is elected? Only God knows. Nevertheless, He has given us something like a sign, at least a means to sense the fact of election: for since only the elect are able to do the bidding of Scripture, persevering unto the end, this ability is in itself a probable, even though sometimes deceptive, warrant. This is the argument with which Calvin refuted his opponents, who time and again maintained that his "immutable predestination" was bound to cause fatalism. What good, they asked, does it do man to struggle for spiritual betterment if he is irrevocably chosen or condemned already? But, Calvin answers, it is a fallacy that pious living could earn man a *right* to salvation. Man is utterly without right before God—who is always free to have condemned even the most pious for all eternity. It is true only that the pious life, that is to say the power to do good works, furnishes man with the probability of being of the elect. The good works are not the premise of salvation but the fruit of it.

Calvin was justified when, with the ire of the fanatic, he scorned the charge that his teachings induced fatalism and moral inertia. For if the moral effort is a sort of guarantee of the possession of grace, how inexorably must this terrible dogma drive the faithful forward on the path of virtue! Neither awake nor asleep can they ever be rid of the frightful fear of being mistaken, of not really being in that blessed state. An unsurpassed tension enters into their lives; the dread that their *certitudo salutis* might be deceptive spurs them on to ever firmer self-control, to ever greater efforts. But, on the other hand, how this certainty swells their pride! They, they alone, are of the elect—while around them the reprobate mass head for certain hell. It is like a private understanding between the small elite and the God they cannot fathom.

A new aristocracy took shape in this manner, an aristocracy of individuals thirsting after an exalted servitude. Life to them seemed stale unless it was spent slaving for the glory of God. One might call it "Life as Discipline." It was a noble life; for true nobility is recognized by its demands upon itself, by voluntarily assumed duties rather than by arrogated privileges. Nothing about this nobility was static or passive. It had to be perpetually gained anew, and could not be inherited.

This new sense of values, this blind surrender to the Divine pleasure, made the Calvinists indifferent to the trials they had to undergo. In their "certainty of salvation" martyrdom became an ecstasy of boundless joy.

JEANNE D'ALBRET
1560

Engraving 16th Century

THEODORUS BEZA, VESELIUS

5

THE COUNTER-REFORMATION BEGINS

IT HAS often been said that France and Spain mapped a joint campaign against heresy at Cateau-Cambrésis. It has never been proved; history shows only that with this peace the Counter-Reformation began. On the day it was signed, King Henry solemnly announced that he would now attend to his "religious tasks." What could he mean, under the circumstances, except that on the heels of foreign war would come a civil one?

The Protestants failed to take the hint. From all over the country they flocked to Paris for the first synod, boldly, almost officially. Their meeting had become necessary because of dogmatic differences within the movement. It was still in a nascent, chaotic state. They had no rules to draw on except the Geneva constitution—which was inapplicable because at Geneva church and state were one, while in France they were enemies. Yet the time for haphazard growth was past. Machinery was needed for the discipline preached by the master. Order had to be created if the gains which had been made were to endure.

On what dark roads, so far, had the Word reached France! Aside from Calvin's letters and writings, there were proclamations of frequently unknown authorship; theses often penned by provocateurs; Bible exegeses composed by dilettante laymen. Some of these were turned out at night in French country barns and cellars, others were smuggled in from Geneva. Merchants hid them in their bales. Booksellers bound them into other books with deceptively innocuous titles. Students who had traveled to Geneva to hear the master preach returned and passed on what they had received. Future teachers were already being trained in Geneva, but there were not nearly enough of them to fill the need.

All were menaced by the stake.

This first period of French Calvinism was alive with a naive, blind, and touching valor. Preachers moved from place to place, leading a miserable existence, with hardly enough clothing to withstand the rigors of the climate, hourly prepared to be seized and beaten to death. The pastor of Bayonne sailed with fishermen, to convert and save souls out in the Bay of Biscay. In Saintes two laborers got together to interpret the Bible to a dozen faithful on Sundays. There was also Bernard Palissy, a simple potter who gained adherents with primitive methods and who has left us a deeply moving story of the time. Often preachers, unable to find safety from their persecutors under a roof, slept in the woods, living on water and windfalls; for in many communities poverty was so great that they refused subsidies.

But always comforting and strengthening them were Calvin's letters. They were magnificent documents of Latin logic, full of hidden pity and an iron, relentlessly driving force. He maintained his vast correspondence with men and women in Germany, Switzerland, Spain, Italy,

Sweden, Poland, England, and the Low Countries, although he was not well and his strength was failing him. He counseled moderation and rejected all excesses. And in the early years of the movement there were hardly any; the Protestants were slaughtered like lambs, but their dead became martyrs and examples.

At the synod the representatives of seventy-two churches appeared. The most important subject on the agenda was the Creed, for which a draft of Calvin's was accepted as basis. It condemned Catholic tradition and referred exclusively to the Bible. Election by grace, after eternal, pre-mundane decree, was set up as dogma. The Lutheran concept of Holy Communion was definitely dropped—agreeing with the Catholics, it held that the body of Christ is actually one with the bread, received at once *with*, *in*, and *under* it for forgiveness of the sins. According to Calvin, the body and blood of Christ are truly shared, but in a *spiritual* sense. Not in and under, but *with* the bread is the body of Christ received: as the mouth receives the bread, the soul receives the Savior. *Quod cum pane et vino vere exhibeantur corpus et sanguis Christi vescentibus in coena domini.* It was the formula laid down by Melanchthon against Luther, and approved by Calvin as in accordance with his own; the formula on which was based the Augsburg Confession of 1530. Finally the synod agreed on the fundamentals of a constitution: all churches and pastors were equal, and the preachers were to be chosen by ballot.

Of course the synod only fanned the rage of the orthodox. But it must be said that not all of them were extremists. The *parlement* of Paris displayed an unmistakable tendency toward the mitigation of inhuman penalties. Its criminal division, the *Tournelle*—headed by two jurists of unquestioned authority, Séguier and Harlay—sentenced some boys who had admitted errant views about the Mass to banishment instead of to death, as the letter of the law required. This sentence stirred up a violent debate. Advocates of moderation in dealing with heresy soon became suspect themselves—and heresy in officials was tantamount to high treason. Eventually a session of the full *parlement* was called, to lay down a policy.

That session met in the Spring of 1559, at the same time as the Reformed synod. But its deliberations, though orderly, were less fruitful. Opinion divided strictly on lines of age. The older generation pleaded for stake and gallows while the younger held that accused persons should have six months in which to return to the fold and, if they continued in their errors, should be allowed to quit the country with their worldly goods. Tempers grew heated, and agreement moved ever further out of reach. Finally, when it was suggested that the issue be put to a general council, the wisdom of thus shifting the responsibility seemed evident to all.

On June 10, however, the King himself attended the *parlement* and the Protestants, taking heart, addressed a petition to him praying for toleration. The modest tenor of the document might even perhaps have permitted an acceptable outcome, if only the Reformed spokesmen had used diplomacy. They tried the opposite: from petitioners, they suddenly turned accusers. They thundered against the corruption in the Roman Church and complained that the vice and crimes of the Catholic clergy went unpunished, while the most pious men of Protestantism were hounded to death.

Henry rose, and curtly declared: "I see there are good and evil men here. We shall protect the good ones and make an end of the evil ones."

The two leaders who had talked most, Dufour and Anne du Bourg, were thrown into the Bastille. Lest the *Tournelle* pass too mild a sentence, the King ordered that it be shown to him before issuance. In addition, he sent a circular letter to all *parlements* and courts, spurring them to strong action regardless of cost and threatening lenient judges with punishment. He showed himself in his true colors: an avenger who has waited too long and must make up for lost time.

Paralyzing fear swept over the whole country. Clearly, the government was preparing a grand coup: the destruction of religious opposition in one blow. Some Protestants gave themselves up for lost; others armed for civil war. The police, those of Paris in particular, raided homes for weapons. Already the mob saw a chance to vent its lowest instincts: looting, arson, and murder followed on the heels of the new policy. What would the next day bring?

Fate took a hand.

A tournament was held in honor of the marriage of Henry's daughter, Elizabeth, to Philip of Spain, the widower of "Bloody Mary." The King himself took part, in black and white armor, the colors of the Duchess of Valentinois. He broke two lances with the Count of Montgomery, and when he wanted to try yet another joust Marshal de Vieilleville stepped forward. "Sire, you have shown enough of your skill; let me ride against Montgomery." The King insisted on his revenge; the Count had come close to unseating him on both occasions. "Sire," the Marshal pleaded, "for three nights I have dreamed of calamity!" Montgomery, too, asked to be excused. But the King insisted.

This time, the opponent's lance broke on Henry's visor and the splinters entered into his brain. He was carried unconscious from the field. The surgeons could not agree from which side the splinters had penetrated. In vain, four criminals were executed and their heads dissected; the doctors still did not know how to apply their findings to the royal case. The King died.

The Protestants received the news in awe, as a judgment of Heaven. In Geneva, they held services of thanks to God. Strange tales went from mouth to mouth: the blanket which in the turmoil was thrown over the King's bier was said to have borne a picture of Paul's conversion and, in large letters, the text: "Saul, Saul, why persecutest thou me?"

As honor guard, the two first soldiers of the realm stood by the bier: the Constable and his nephew, Admiral de Coligny, who had no idea how soon he was to head those who exulted over this corpse.

The Dauphin who suddenly became King was not yet of age, weak in body and mind, unable to make a decision, and wholly dependent on his mother who hated him because at fifteen, despite his debility, he had the constitutional right to govern. "A sorry kingdom, where children sit on the throne!" wrote the Ambassador of Venice. He was only too right.

Poor little Francis II was sinking daily. To breathe, he had to open his mouth wide; chronic inflammation of the middle ear made him hard of hearing. With shoulders too broad and too small a head, he looked like a misshapen doll. He dreaded his mother because he could never talk back to her; and for his wife, the seventeen-year-old Mary Stuart, he harbored something like love, because she shielded him as much as was in her power. But her power was so limited.

All indications are that Catherine eagerly awaited the death of this son. His brother, in line to succeed him, was only nine and would assure her the regency—her only goal. She felt her time had come. She was a mature woman now, obese and voracious, but also witty and clever; ten times as smart as all those who cooed around her and fancied themselves capable of ruling. Only she could rule, she alone! But after so many years of patience, she had to look on again while the two brothers Guise, exploiting the King's weakness and their position as uncles of the new Queen, seized the highest power of the realm.

There was the Duke, for instance. King Henry was not yet buried and already he took over the army. The Constable, its constitutional commander? He was harassed and thwarted, held in suspicion until at last he left the Court. Had he not opposed all anti-English plans? And now Francis, told that his marriage entitled him to it, assumed the name and arms of a King of England; for the Catholics Elizabeth was illegitimate and had no right to inherit. Montmorency was finished. The Cardinal of Lorraine quickly seized the financial administration; an ally of the Guises, Olivier, became Chancellor. The entire government lay in their hands.

This turn, of course, effectively dashed the hopes which the Protestants had built on Henry's demise. Their position became worse, if possible. Mitigation of criminal procedure was no longer discussed; triumphantly, the

Sorbonne branded such suggestions as heretical. Religious meetings were forbidden under penalty of death, a fate which also awaited anyone who harbored a suspect. It was not long before others as well felt the new hand. Taxes, already confiscatory, rose even higher. Fiscal departments became hotbeds of corruption—whoever sat next to the pot skimmed off the cream. Unrest stirred, not only in the villages, but in the towns where salaries fell in arrears and food grew scarce. The Cardinal was in the saddle now, with Papal favor holding hierarchy and orders in line behind him; and he who owned the church of France owned the state.

The Dowager Queen, frustrated in her larger ambitions, used this opportunity to get rid of Diane de Poitiers. She would have liked to avenge herself, thoroughly and with imagination, on the lady who had humbled her so long. But the Guises vetoed anything beyond banishment to the provinces. This was the end of the woman in whose honor, under the laws of chivalry, Henry II had died—not, however, before Catherine had deftly robbed her of her lovely manor of Chenonceaux.

A battle of intrigues began. To protect herself in all directions, Catherine maintained surreptitious contacts with the Protestants. Mutual distrust grew. The Guises—not without justification—feared that the Queen Mother might plot a *coup de main* against the young royal couple. Because Francis and his wife were not safe at St. Germain, the Guises took them in the depth of winter to Blois, where at least the castle had a moat. Catherine moved to Blois, too. The Guises did not dare to leave the castle. All watched each other like hawks, and everybody's retinue was in the pay of some one else.

Thus was the government administered for a fifteen-year-old King—each conspiring against the other, to the sole exclusion of those called to it by law: the Princes of the Blood.

The lines were sharply drawn now. The early skirmishes had revealed the conflict of interests. On one hand stood the Court and the Church: the old, hereditary powers, owning more than two thirds of the land and resources of France, representing the few great and very great families who did not propose to yield a tittle of their monopoly on political power. They owned the fields, the vineyards, the forests, the fisheries, the mines; they owned the tax and custom receipts, the military and the clerical benefices, and the fat jobs in the government and at Court. They controlled an army of either loyal or venal retainers, tenants, petty officials. As a last resort, there was the large mass of plain people, who had not yet learned to question authority, and whom they could stir up and turn loose against any desired target.

They viewed any demands made upon them as attacks on the Divine plan, and refused to notice any change in the times. But times had changed in spite of them. The growth of trade, the opening of markets overseas, the accumulation of money in cities and ports, these necessitated a new social order in which the *bourgeois*, who paid the taxes and did all the new work for the state, claimed equal rights. In his hands lay the capital he earned, and without it the King could no longer govern. When the feudal forces tried to keep him in dependency, he naturally allied himself with other groups who like him were disfranchised. These were the guilds, the lower clergy and lower nobility; even that part of the upper nobility which, for one reason or another, was not in favor at Court. It was thus that Bourbons, Princes of the Blood, came to head a party basically hostile to their kind. So it happened, too, that this party became consonant with the Reformation. As the conservatives invoked the certain protection of Rome, it was natural for the progressives to join together in an anti-Papist faith.

It was well understood at the time that the religious fight was equally a political one: if the egalitarian, class-dissolving Reformed tenets prevailed, the feudal sovereignties were done for. Likewise, the economic consequences were plain to those in power: what the *grand bourgeois* were granted today, the *petit bourgeois* might claim tomorrow and the peasants the day after. There was but one thing to do: choke the evil growth at the root.

6

A PLOT FAILS

BY 1560, the opposition had become organized. There were local uprisings. Transports of prisoners were ambushed. At times men were torn from the hands of the executioners. Out of such small actions grew a large, far-flung one: the plan for a *coup d'état*, aimed at a full reversal of national policy.

The conspirators saw the overweening Guise regime as certain to bring disaster upon the realm. Their plot was directed against the two brothers and their henchmen, not against the sacred person of the King. Their principal demands were the ousting of the Guises, toleration of the Protestant faith and convocation of the *States-General.* They sent emissaries to Geneva, but Calvin solemnly shook his head and warned: "Suffer, suffer—never use force!" However, many of his flock went along to France and battled by the side of their co-religionists. The King of Navarre and Admiral de Coligny strongly disapproved of the idea; and how the coup materialized has never been discovered. Even on the rack, the participants refused to name "higher-ups."

History shrouds the preparations for the affair with a strange, eerie light. We know that its soul was a nobleman from Périgord and one-time émigré in Geneva, named de la Renaudie, a reckless, brilliant adventurer who had lived so long on borrowed time that he did not mind risking his head. Gathered around him was a mixed company of lords and peasants, students, discharged soldiers, artisans, and volunteers from Geneva. It was to these men that the term "Huguenots" was first applied. Its origin has been variously traced: one explanation being that it stems from an early French King, a savage hunter, named Hugh, and therefore referred to a roving, riotous band. But while the Huguenots were called many bad names by their enemies, these hardly had so deep a feeling for ancient folklore. The more plausible derivation is from the German *Eidgenoss*—meaning oath-fellow—which the Swiss use to describe themselves to this day. On French tongues, the Swiss pronunciation of this word sounds much like "Huguenot"; and so the name is likely to have originated with the Frenchmen who tried to repeat the word with which the Swiss volunteers introduced themselves.

Renaudie organized the planned rebellion regionally. Operations were to start simultaneously in Gascony, Limoges, Normandy, Picardy, Brittany, in Champagne and Provence, provinces where the leading families were sympathetic to the movement. The main force gathered secretly in Nantes, while Condé, probably ignorant of its decisions, was in Blois with the King. It counted on him to speak for them, and, if they were refused admission, to open the gates to them.

In small groups, on separate roads, they rode to Blois. Such a movement of men, no matter how carefully organized, cannot be hidden from a government whose police functions properly. That of the Guises functioned very well indeed, and the brothers knew what was afoot long before the King, Catherine, or Condé did. Since Blois was an open town, they hastily decided to move the Court to Amboise, a mighty fortress on the bank of the Loire, whose walls and towers overlook the Touraine countryside, which could withstand a siege if necessary.

When the news became known, the entire Court was in panic. The boy King repeatedly burst into tears. He asked again and again what he had done to hurt his people, and begged to be allowed to hear their complaints. "I don't know what this is about," he told the Guises, "but I understand enough to know that it is your fault and not mine." The Queen Mother, after the first shock, also favored conciliation. She knew very well that, once a shot was fired, a woman would no longer have anything to say.

The Guises bided their time. One day when Catherine was in the park with her ladies they brought a messenger before the King who told him that the rebels were past Blois and marching in strong formation on Amboise. He was told that they were well-armed and shouting threats against His Majesty, which was enough for Francis. Desperately now, he begged the Duke of Guise to accept the post of Governor-General with full powers, which the Duke had wanted from the very first.

The Queen Mother, when informed of what had happened when she left her son alone for an hour, had a fit. She screamed like a mad woman, exhausted her store of vulgar Italian oaths, and physically attacked everyone who came into her presence. When she was somewhat calmer, she went to see the King in his chambers. She found the cautious chancellor, Olivier, with him, unwilling to sign the decree. Having been politically associated with the Guises, he knew that such authority in their hands meant bloodshed.

He looked to Catherine for support, but, curiously and unexpectedly, it was she who argued the Duke's case most strongly. Why, within an hour, she had changed her mind in this way, no historian of the period has tried to explain. Probably it seems stranger now than it did then, for every one who knew Catherine was content to observe that unprincipled individuals are likely to behave surprisingly. She stormed; helpless with fear, the King cried; the Duke of Guise may, for emphasis, have added a few words of his own. In any event, Olivier's objections were no longer heeded. He affixed the Great Seal of France to the appointment, which a Court official anxiously pressed upon him.

Francis de Guise had made his plans before. The castle gate, leading into the park, was walled up. A company of musketeers was put behind the main gate. Messengers went to the loyal commanders in the region, ordering them to patrol all roads that the rebels might use, and the Count of Sancerre was sent out to reconnoiter. Not least of all, Condé was rendered harmless by being placed in command of the King's body-guard. This last was a masterly stroke. It was an honor to which Condé could not object, and at the same time it tied him to the person of the King, who made no move without Guise's permission, and thus put him also under the surveillance of reliable men. It was even better than locking the Hugenot Prince into a cell.

When Renaudie arrived at Amboise with his troop, he asked for safe conduct. If granted, he and some of his men would lay down their arms, go before the King, and personally beg him for freedom of conscience. From the castle walls came jeering refusal. Then he asked to speak to Condé, and was told that the Prince was busy. Renaudie wavered. For his little band to assault Amboise would be suicide. He knew now that the Guises had been warned in time and that royal troops were probably converging upon him, so he retreated. His troop avoided several ambushes, but when he finally ran into a superior force, led by Seigneur de Pardaillan, he attacked. It was a brave try for volunteers, amateur soldiers, who were pitted against old veterans. The latter yielded, and Renaudie sought out the enemy leader, killed him with a thrust of his sword through the visor, and then dropped, himself, his side torn by a musket shot fired by Pardaillan's page. This was the end for the band of brave men, none of whom survived.

Another troop, led by Mazère, fell into an ambush of the Count of Sancerre, and was captured. The Gascon contingent, under Baron de Castelnau, took quarters in the Château Noyze. When the Duke of Nemours appeared with the royal musketeers, he was permitted, as a man of honor, to enter the château for a parley before opening hostilities. On his pledged word that no one who surrendered to him would be punished, fifteen noblemen followed him to Amboise, where they were thrown at once into dungeons and put to the torture.

The Duke of Nemours was outraged when he saw his promise dishonored by the Guises, but Olivier told him a King was not obliged to keep his word to rebels. The fifteen died as assailants of His Majesty, and the Duke of Nemours fell into melancholia.

The uprising was over. Those who were not dead were condemned to die: one to be hanged, another to be beheaded, a third to be drowned, a fourth to be quartered.

The executions took place with ceremony on the public square of Amboise. Outside the castle, stands and benches were erected for the spectators. The town could not accommodate the curious who gathered from near and far for the joyous occasion, close to ten thousand of whom had spent the previous night in the open fields.

The day began with services in all churches of the town. When the condemned men were led to the place of execution, escorted by a company of the King's Guards, a few Dominicans, scurrying alongside, tried even at the last moment to convert them. But not one paid any heed. They went to their deaths singing Clément Marot's psalm:

Dieu, tu nous as mis à l'épreuve
Et tu nous as examinés,
Comme l'argent que l'on épreuve
Par feu tu nous as affinés.

A few days later, when the trees were still decorated with the bodies of the hanged and many posts with severed heads, including that of the brave Renaudie, an old, impoverished Calvinist nobleman, named d'Aubigné, rode through the town with his eleven-year-old son. They were poorly-clad and had eaten scant food on their long journey. The old man reined in his horse on the gruesome spot, and said: "My son, you shall not spare your head, any more than I shall spare mine, to avenge these valiant ones! If you spare it, you shall be accursed!"

The boy, his lips pale and unable to speak, raised his hand in solemn oath.

7

VOICE OF THE PEOPLE

VENGEANCE swept the country. Rebellion flared up and was stamped out. Yet the gallows at Amboise caused an upsurge of the Reformation. Venerable force of an idea, heedless of the suffering of its vessel, the body! The executions took place in March, but in May, in that very town which still harbored a specially reinforced royal garrison, the heretics paraded psalm-singing, and tore the gallows down.

Like a fatal illness which no operation can stop, which only breaks out more violently at other points, the infection spread over the body of France. The provincial governors reported that armed bands, on foot and on horseback, were seen here and there, emerging from the dark and vanishing into it. As if there had been no avenging terrorism, the Reformed Provincial Synod of Normandy and Brittany met publicly at Caen. At Rennes, a central committee of Calvinist nobles was set up. At Rouen, the Corpus Christi procession started a street fight that grew into a three-month civil war. In a town as small and unimportant as Dieppe, the Protestant congregation increased at a rapid rate, because the pastors had no fear of holding open meetings in broad daylight. On a single day eight hundred members came for communion. In the south, Lyon, Nîmes, Montauban, not to mention smaller hamlets, declared themselves Protestant communities. Mayors and priests were helpless to counteract the flood.

What good is an arsenal if the weapons are rusty? For any forceful action the Guises would have had to be certain of their tools. But the movement had seized every class. What, to give but one example, was the use of ordering a clean-up in Guyenne, when the Governor was Anthony of Navarre, the recognized head of the entire Huguenot party? The county clerk, the policeman, the pastor, the teacher—none could be sure of the others. Those engaged in illegal activities had refined their methods. The secret groups had learned to guard against spies. Besides, there was not enough money for the large-scale bribery that would have been necessary.

The royal power had dwindled at an incredible rate. Barely a year of Guise rule was sufficient to let the land fall apart again into provinces menaced by revolt. Gone was King Francis's authoritarian centralization, that astonishing unity welded out of talent, caprice, and bravado. Opposition was everything.

Catholics and Royalists, too, stood in opposition. Of course, the bulk of it was made up of poor, little people; but the proscription lists named pastors as well as judges, doctors as well as apothecaries, innkeepers, farmers, merchants, small businessmen, students, laborers. Everywhere nobles were more in evidence than before; their better education and larger purses made them leaders. The Guises were not only anti-Protestant, they also stood in the way of any attempt on the part of the lower nobility to gain independence of the higher, and to ease the tax burden.

One may regret that the religious idea was tied up so early with political and personal interests. But when or where would that not have been the case?

What did the opposition want? Beyond doubt, a "new order." What did they demand? First and most vociferously, the restoration of the old "order of Estates." A paradox? Only a superficial one.

The Middle Ages had divided all people into three "Estates." They were the clergy and nobility—the two which in England, for example, found parliamentary representation in the House of Lords—and the commonalty, consisting of the remainder of free men. The three Estates made up the body of a nation. They represented it before the King, who was its head. They balanced the feudal structure which, based on real property tenure, tended to overlook the existence of people other than the royal liege lord and his land-holding vassals. In France, the Estates were organized in thirty districts, each one of which sent three deputies, one from each Estate, to the national assembly of the *States-General*. In theory, the *States-General* was to meet at regular intervals; and consent was required for tax levies and important decisions on national policy. But up to Henry II's death, in 1559, it had not been in session for seventy-five years.

The French "constitution," like that of England until this day, was an unwritten compound of time-hallowed institutions and inherited, often illogical, sometimes directly conflicting, rights and privileges. But without power to enforce it, a man's right was a dead letter. The Kings, for instance, saw no purpose in setting up the *States-General* as a sounding-board of criticism. Of the Third Estate, the urban bourgeoisie had, under Francis I especially, become the King's ally against the feudal powers. It relied on this alliance and on the walls of its towns for the protection of its interests, rather than on any national parliament; and the rest of the commoners—peasants, small town folk, urban workingmen—found themselves disfranchised without much ado, and without recourse. The same was true of the lower nobility and clergy. Outnumbering the rich and mighty, they would have captured many seats in the *States-General;* but they could not convoke the assembly.

The ranking few preferred to make their influence felt in other ways. One of these, grown out of the feudal past, derived from their wealth in land. Originally, fiefs had been granted by the Crown only in exchange for continued fealty and war service. But in the course of time this had been all but forgotten; and now, whenever the King needed the great baronial families for anything, he had to pay blackmail in the form of more land. With less and less French soil remaining at the sovereign's disposal, the vassals ran their domains like independent principalities. The greatest of them—like the Lorraines or Savoys, or those Angevins who were Kings of England at one time—were not averse to making use of their French holdings against the interests of France, in a game of international power politics. Another, even more effective, instrument in their hands was the King's Council. Though appointed by the monarch, its members had to be drawn from the ranks of prelates, high nobility, leading officers and jurists; and insofar as this rule did not insure their selection, tradition then gave the chief feudal families the right to be permanently represented on it.

The Council, for all practical purposes, was the government. It had no fixed meeting place but always stayed with the King's person. When he traveled, it traveled with him. It prepared laws and decrees for the royal signature. It controlled the judiciary and assisted the sovereign in his function as a judge of last resort. It approved the appointments of ministers and other high officials, such as the Chancellor who was the King's executive aide and the Constable who was the commander-in-chief of his armed forces. And with the tasks of government continually expanding, it was from the Council that the first French specialized administrative agencies derived their functions.

The oldest of these were the *chambres des comptes* (courts of exchequer) and the *parlement* of Paris. While other regions, too, soon had *parlements*, that of Paris remained the most important. They were organs of the royal will, clothed with the attributes of the King's Council. They reflected the struggle which went on in the higher body, between the Crown and the great lords, where the latter fought any attempt at centralization, any restriction of the privileges granted them centuries before under different conditions, and the royal officials tried just as assiduously to whittle down and destroy the baronial rights.

As in every period of transition, the old powers had lost their reason for existence, before the young and vital ones had found their form. Less than a hundred years earlier, feudalism had fulfilled its function, with the coalition of King and *bourgeois* preventing it from overstepping its bounds. Now feudalism was an empty formula, as empty as the universal, international dominion of the Pope, while the idea of the *nation*—whether under democracy or royal absolutism—was yet unconceived. The last reigning Valois, vacuous figures dominated by a self-centered mother, and hardly worthy of the name of kings, abandoned the *bourgeois* alliance because they did not realize its worth. The great vassals raised their heads, as servants not of the state, however, but only of their own interests. Regionalism was rampant in politics, law, and culture, and the central authority, trembling for its own position, was unable to enforce even a semblance of order. It was anarchy grown permanent; thus it was only natural for the opposition to clutch at the straw of the last remembered method of harmonious procedure: the Estate system.

After the events of Amboise, the situation was as follows. Although the House of Guise had dealt the opposition a hard blow and insisted on the merciless prosecution of all rebels caught in the act, in general it was forced to moderate its policy. The Cardinal, in fact, had found it necessary to grant a pardon and amnesty to all who had solemnized communion and baptism according to the ritual of Geneva. Even those men who had shown their intention of participating actively in the coup were promised forgiveness if they refrained from further opposition. Jails filled with men and women arrested on mere suspicion were opened everywhere. It was also deemed advisable to reach an understanding with Condé, now as before regarded as the chief conspirator. He was relieved of his position as commander of the Guards, which had only confined him, and allowed to remain at Court or travel where he pleased.

The Prince, to be sure, did not trust the pacific atmosphere and the Queen Mother's honeyed, artificial demeanor. She talked with him as though he were the one man in France who understood her, and while he was susceptible to such siren songs if they emanated from the lips of young and pretty damsels, in this case he maintained complete reserve. It was not always easy, for the lady, although she was fat, had a great deal of charm. She was jovial, witty, excelled at repartee, loved song and music as he did, and could shed copious tears at will. Condé, despite her fascination for him, felt more in danger after the offer of lasting reconciliation than before. If he stayed at Court he might disappear overnight, without a trace. To leave, on the other hand, would be an admission of guilt. He thought it over; then, being a soldier, decided to pass from defense to attack.

He appeared in the King's Council in a violent temper. In strong words, he complained of the treatment accorded him and asked assurances against a repetition of it. The faces of the Guises froze; the Duke may even have laughed. Condé gripped his sword and defied anyone who doubted him. Never, not for a second, he protested, had he planned an attack on the King or the Queen Mother! The Duke changed his tune. His reply was an equally fine piece of acting. He was convinced, he said, at the bottom of his heart, that the Prince was the most loyal man of the century, and any one who thought differently would have to fight a duel with him, de Guise.

Thus the Court's impotence took the form of conciliation. But this did not prevent ecclesiastic, financial, and political troubles from rising hourly. The situation seemed beyond repair. The King, harassed, egged on, reviled in pamphlets, deceived by his retinue, anxious, sick, and ignorant, called a conference of his supreme advisers at

Fontainebleau. All the Marshals of France, the members of the Order of St. Michael and the councilors of the highest commissions, were summoned. That most massive of royal castles saw a gathering of great lords such as had not taken place since Francis I's time. On August 16, 1561, the Constable made his entrance with his relatives and an entourage of eight hundred horsemen.

The meeting was opened by the King. In a speech with almost human accents the pitiable boy asked for sincere advice. The Chancellor described the disease that had seized the realm, and the chief ministers talked about finances and military matters. Suddenly, without having been scheduled to address this first session, Admiral de Coligny left his seat, walked up to the King, and handed him two Protestant petitions. The King gave them to a secretary, who read them aloud. The petitioners averred that their purposes were peaceful and lawful and their faith conformed to the Gospel, and asked the King for a church, or at least a suitable place in every hamlet for prayer, sacrament, and sermon.

There was nothing unusual about this. What was unusual was that the Admiral, the highest soldier in the realm after the Constable, immediately took the floor for the petitioners, declared their demands justified and that it was the duty of the King to re-establish true worship of God and to safeguard his subjects from abuses. Most unusual was that the King not only listened, but promised to consider the matter. This, in the eyes of his people, was sensationally important. Did not the French monarchy rest on the premise of the "Most Christian King," on the oath, taken by every monarch upon his accession, to guard the laws of the Catholic Church and to destroy all heresy? Was it not monstrous enough for the Admiral to make himself the heretics' advocate without the King's nodding his head in their direction?

A new era began with this meeting. The Middle Ages were over. Subjects were debated at Fontainebleau which could not have been discussed before. And as though Coligny's action had inflamed the others, one opposition speaker now followed another. The Bishop of Valence deplored the corruption of justice and the immorality of the clerics. He demanded a national council that would replace weapons of force with those of the spirit. The Archbishop of Vienne, advancing toward the ministers with raised fists, shouted that their kind of government was a fraud, utterly incapable of doing justice to the times. Everywhere in Europe, wherever you looked, he told them, forms of popular representation were in effect. Would they never be reintroduced in France? It was a rotten state of affairs, controlled by rotten men and rotten institutions! He even hinted that provinces might secede if laws continued to be enforced without first having been passed by the *States-General.*

Coligny took the floor in behalf of the Protestants for a second time, a few days later. Originally, he said, it was his intention to submit petitions with signatures, but time was short. He could state that in Normandy alone he was able to gather fifty thousand names. Then he formally made three demands: an end to all persecutions, Church reform, and a council. Once more summing up the complaints of previous speakers, he analyzed the situation of the state. It was an evil thing, he said, to bring up the young King in distrust of his people; the love of the French for the House of Valois was undying, only the ministers were hated.

This blow struck home, and Duke Francis leaped to his feet. The boyhood friends, Francis de Guise and Gaspard de Coligny, Catholic and Protestant, stood face to face. Two swords were loosed in their scabbards. Bystanders interposed.

The opposition won out. A royal edict convoked two national assemblies: the *States-General* for December, and a council of the French clergy for January.

It was on a hopeful note that the conference at Fontainebleau drew near its close. Perhaps the two assemblies, temporal and spiritual, would bring freedom of thought. Perhaps the financial measures they would adopt would benefit the people. Perhaps men might yet be free to pray according to the dictates of conscience. And the Catholics hoped that the Church would now reform in earnest.

Already, while the notables were still in session, new ideas and trends revitalized the land. Pamphlets found their way from house to house. Discussions assumed the form of public debate. A new Chancellor, L'Hospital, known as a man of peace, was appointed by the King in place of Olivier, and rumors circulated, "on the very highest authority," that the Guises had met in him not only their match but their master and that their exclusive power was broken once and for all. Even Cardinal de Guise, when he was compelled to give his consent to the assemblies, complained to the Papal Nuncio that the game was lost for the time being.

False, ever again false hopes of a people! Passionate

oratorical denunciations had found a more or less kindly hearing, but nothing more happened. Bows had been made, to the right as well as to the left, but who could tell if those in the seats of the mighty were not already working on some kind of deal? Besides, what good could *States-General* and council do if the executive power remained in the hands of the Guises?

It was Calvin again who saw most clearly. Like others, he rejoiced over the enforced convocation of the assemblies as a Guise defeat; but of the actual meetings he only expected a new and more glorious victory for the Court. To forestall it, he sent his faithful Beza on the perilous trip to Béarn, by way of the turbulent provinces, to strengthen the King of Navarre and the Prince of Condé in their resistance. He warned them not to be taken in by meaningless resolutions, and that it was senseless to make agreements with the Guises. Until they were destroyed, the forces of reaction would always find a way out; the King had to be compelled to call a new government. Calvin advised the Bourbons to join with the nobles of Provence, Languedoc, and Normandy in a large-scale demonstration, whose effect would be to deter the enemy from new bloodshed.

Thus an oppositionist uprising was prepared, which by a show of power sought to avoid civil war. The Huguenots were certain that right would always prevail, that faith in the right would give them power. Any military move by Navarre, which would attract all the enemies of corruption, was bound without actual fighting to fell the Guises, whose position had been undermined for months.

The greatest danger to the enterprise was not the enemy but its own head. Whereas Calvin's intentions, as interpreted by Beza, were unequivocal, the King of Navarre was far too amiable to be consistent. He made ten decisions a day, so as not to be forced to execute a single one. He boasted of his impending march on Orléans, and laughed heartily, imagining how quickly the camarilla would scatter to the four winds. He was incessantly active, organizing, giving orders and taking them back. "A hundred times he changes his mind," Calvin complained in a letter.

Just when the notables at Fontainebleau prepared to go home, an incident occurred which gave matters a sudden, frightening turn.

La Sague, an intimate of the King of Navarre, who had attended the conference for him, departed for Béarn. With him he took letters and messages from the Constable, the Admiral, and others. He got as far as Etampes, and was caught.

It all happened very quietly. In the dark of night, in silence, except for the clatter of hoofs, he was brought to Orléans. Hurriedly the correspondence he carried was examined. It was disappointing, nothing but private communications. He was questioned. *Had he other, oral messages?* He played dumb, knew of nothing. All right, there was always the torture chamber. Led into the dreaded place, he quickly confessed: the Prince of Condé, at the head of the oppositionists, intended to march on Orléans and oust the Guises. *Was the King of Navarre a party to this?* La Sague did not know, but volunteered the information that Paris and several other cities were to be occupied. *Was this with or without the Constable's assent?* He was not sure. But the regency which was to replace the Guises would consist of Montmorency, Condé, and Navarre. *Was that all?* Yes, that was all. But with another hint of the torture, La Sague, deathly pale, and staring at the thumbscrews, added a final confession: if certain of the seized letters were wetted, all he had said would appear there in invisible ink.

At last the Guises discovered a tangible foe. There, finally, was a crime, great and irrefutable, against which all the royal forces could be mobilized in full justice. It was a day of joy. Conference followed conference in the most private circle of the King, the Queen Mother, the Chancellor, the Guises, and their trusted aides. The notables left Fontainebleau, ignorant of what was brewing. The Constable rode off with his pompous train. The Admiral retired to his castle at Châtillon.

An excited season, this autumn of the year 1560. The ferment in the country was sensed even by the dainty ladies-in-waiting, whom Catherine always had around her in large numbers and whom she led into *affaires d'amour* with gentlemen who might drop a possible word of secret machinations. There was paralyzing insecurity; daily some new turn in events; a curious mixture of espionage and heroism. In addition, a new upsurge of Protestantism. In Brittany there were public meetings, defying all prohibitions, the founding of new churches, the arrival of preachers. There were street battles in Dauphiné. A thousand persons, heavily armed, gathered for the Lord's Supper in Anjou. In the Cévennes, General Villars had to use force to disperse the Huguenots. He razed their castles, and the woods were full of the persecuted; but as soon as the soldiers moved on, they returned and services were resumed.

The date set for the *States-General* drew nearer. The provincial deputies were called to Orléans for October;

the King with his entourage and the chief officials were already there. The quarters in the town began to fill up; the several committees held preparatory conferences. It seemed, however, as though the displeased Princes of the Blood meant to absent themselves. They still sat in Béarn. One knew at last what to think of them. Their presence was requested in personal letters from the King which they answered politely but found ever new reasons to ignore.

Condé was not suspicious by nature but he could see that no good lay behind such invitations, just when the plotters caught at Amboise and Lyon were being tortured and executed. He was for staying away from Orléans, but Navarre, always relying on his diplomatic skill to find some amiable way out, thought otherwise. The two brothers had heated discussions. "If we stay away," Anthony contended, "there'll be no more mention of government reform. Why, then, have we been fighting for it all these years? And what will happen to us when the Guises have the upper hand again, now that they have the papers of that traitor, La Sague? I don't have to tell you. The point is, we must be heard for once."

His councilors and friends agreed. Only Jeanne d'Albret, his wife, raised her voice in warning: "No, you mustn't go to Orléans; stay, I beg you! None of your reasons matters beside the fact that there both of you are in danger of your lives."

Two royal emissaries appeared, one after the other—first Count de Croussol, then Marshal de Saint-André—to explain that the venerable body had been called, at enormous cost, above all to hear the complaints of the Princes of the Blood. Should government reform be considered without their participation? Should a decision about the Reformation be reached while they were hunting in Béarn? Impossible. It was an insult to the King and to the *States-General*, if the Premier Princes—the heirs to the throne if the Valois should become extinct—acted as if the whole thing was no concern of theirs.

Thus the three Bourbons—for the third brother, the quiet, harmless Cardinal Charles, came along—journeyed to Orléans. However, that sly old fox, the Constable, who despite his bigoted Catholicism was also involved more or less as an active foe of the Guises, put less faith in the professed peace. He accepted the invitation with thanks, but time and again found ways to delay his departure. Once, he got as far as Paris but, dreading the last lap to Orléans, suddenly came down with influenza, gout, and neuritis, and had to go back home quickly to take a cure. Fully recovered, he set out a second time and noticed to his chagrin that his great age could no longer stand the strain of travel, and that after one day of it he always needed three days' rest before continuing.

But at Orléans, Marshal de Thermes had ridden forth with a few squadrons of cavalry, to give the Bourbons the escort due their rank. At the same time, he hurriedly occupied all roads with troops, for his orders were to prevent a possible about-march of the princes at any cost. Meanwhile, the Guises were working at full speed: they jailed the county judge of Orléans on a charge of sympathizing with the Huguenots, and also the Prior of Chartres. They would have liked to seize Coligny's brother, Chevalier d'Andelot, but he had preferred to go to the farthest corner of Brittany, whence if need be, he could flee to England. The Admiral himself had already arrived in Orléans—voluntarily, gravely, silently, and as a matter of course. Although he had so surprisingly spoken for the Protestants at Fontainebleau, his prestige was still high. Observing quietly, he refused to commit himself.

The Princes were received at Orléans with the iciest reserve. Highest lords of the realm, they found the gates closed, were forced to dismount outside, and were led by way of a side door into the royal presence. There a bitter argument ensued. The poor, sickly boy, who called himself His Majesty and really was as helpless as a beaten child, screamed loud accusations he had learned by heart, to which Condé replied fearlessly. Before he had finished, the King ran out of the room and commanded the captains of the guard to seize the Prince.

Condé was led into a building with walled-up windows and double doors. Cannon were mounted outside. Day and night, he heard the steps of the guards. His brother was assigned quarters in the royal palace, where the Queen Mother visited him, tearfully protesting that all was the Guises' fault: she herself was quite innocent of the events. Before entering the room, though, she had given orders for Navarre's secretary to be thrown into prison and his letters and papers seized. Despite attempts to keep them secret, news of these incidents spread fast. And the Constable, again spending a few days of rest some miles from Paris, had a worse attack of gout than ever.

The *States-General* was opened with a solemn procession. Then, the Chancellor made a speech in the King's presence, enumerating the various points on the agenda. He also read a summary prohibition by the Cardinal against bringing questions of religion into the debate. It caused crest-fallen silence. Along with the preliminary talks, the trial of the Princes of the Blood began. One had witnesses from Amboise and Lyon, but the Prince of Condé stubbornly refused to answer the charges, contending that only the *parlement* had the right to try him. The Council pondered for a long time, and finally announced that in case of further refusal he would be declared guilty. Condé yielded to force, and the trial got under way.

The country hardly dared breathe. And still the Queen Mother tried to mediate, for with the Guises' enemies out of the way, she and the King would have to do as they were told. Daily she conferred with Admiral de Coligny and his brother, Cardinal de Châtillon, about a way to save the Princes. But the verdict quickly came: Condé was found guilty of rebellion and sentenced to be beheaded before the royal palace at the formal session of the *States-General.*

The execution was put off a few days, for it was still hoped to catch the Constable in the same trap. Besides, new evidence had been uncovered, sufficient also to indict the King of Navarre, for whose trial Condé was needed as a witness. Everything was going according to plan. A better effect than the execution of two Bourbon princes on the same day was hard to be imagined.

The King bore the strain with difficulty. Let come what might, so long as he did not have to watch the execution. On its eve he trembled from head to foot, and decided to go hunting and not return till everything was over. Then, while he was being shaved, he fainted. The servant who caught him thought he was dead, laid him on the bed, and ran out, screaming. An hour passed before Francis regained consciousness. But it was only a dim consciousness. He grew weaker from minute to minute. A fistula in his ear, from which he had suffered since childhood, seemed to have reached the brain.

The terror and tumult were indescribable. The palace shook with the noise. The Guises urged the Queen Mother to have the sentence against Condé carried out immediately, while the King was still alive, and were even in favor of having Navarre executed, although the proceedings against him had hardly begun. For when the King was dead everything would have to be postponed, according to law, and Heaven only knew what would happen later.

The Queen and L'Hospital delayed the decision. Catherine, liar extraordinary, unsurpassed in this respect in many centuries, even spread a rumor that her son was recovering. Actually, Francis had already lost his voice and was no longer able to take liquid nourishment. On December 5, he died.

He left not only the court but all of France in disorder and misery. At his death-bed the parties stood, armed to the teeth, stalking each other like wolves; the least word or accident would bring the swords into play. In every room, on staircases, in stables and servants' quarters, behind the shrubbery of the gardens, intrigue went on. King Charles IX, the brother of the deceased, was eleven years of age! Who was to govern for him?

The Salic Law stated clearly that the regency belonged by right to the Princes of the Blood; as to the joint right of the Queen Mother, the jurists disagreed. But would it be possible to hand the regency over to men convicted of high treason a few days before? And again, under the law, the *States-General* had to decide. But law—right—what outdated prejudices! It was the military that mattered. Whose side would it take?

The military knew least of all what it should do. So the terror grew. And yet to many the King's death was a relief. For the Huguenots it was salvation. Suddenly, more unexpectedly than ever, their God delivered them for a second time.

Coligny, too, had stood at the King's death-bed, not a muscle moving in his gaunt, ascetic face. When Francis had drawn his last gasping breath, the Admiral turned to those present and said, aloud: "Gentlemen, the King is dead; that teaches us to live."

Without waiting for what would follow, he went to his quarters, accompanied only by his friend, Fontaines. The December cold was grim. He had great logs put on the fire and sat before it silently staring into the flames, the inevitable tooth-pick between his lips. He was so absorbed that he did not notice when the soles of his shoes began to char. Fontaines called him a few times, in vain; only when he grabbed his shoulders and shook him and shouted his name, did Coligny look up. "Fontaines, Fontaines," he said, "a week ago we would both have been glad to get off with the loss of one leg. Now we have to buy a pair of shoes. You must admit that is cheap."

The King is dead; that teaches us to live. In those hours by the fireside, while the dense, thick, heavy snow fell in the dark night and the boy King lay on his gorgeous, useless bed, with his brain eaten away, deserted by all his courtiers, in those hours Coligny made his decision and set his course.

8

THE ADMIRAL OF FRANCE

A FEW hours from the Loire, in a valley cut into the undulating plain by the river Loing, lies the little town of Châtillon. A castle, the residence of the Seigneurs de Châtillon, overlooks the countryside. Here, in the year 1519, Gaspard de Coligny was born.

The Châtillons, or Colignys, as they were properly called, originally came from the region of Bresse, in the Jura mountains; a region which, incidentally, is not very far from Geneva. From their manors in the Jura they derived the names of Coligny, Andelot, and Fromente, borne, respectively, by the several male members of the family. Only the eldest always called himself Châtillon after their new domain in central France. Gaspard's father had acquired fame and fortune in the service of Francis I, and had definitely assured the position of his house by marrying Louise de Montmorency, the future Constable's sister.

He rose to the rank of a Marshal of France, and died early. The good luck of his three boys was not so much that they were his sons as that they were the Constable's nephews. Massive, unscrupulous, Montmorency pushed them into careers. When he did not quite know how to utilize the Cardinal's hat given him by Pope Clement VII, he passed it on to the sixteen-year-old Odet. Thus Gaspard, the second, became temporal head of the house and Seigneur de Châtillon; and his younger brother Francis, Sieur d'Andelot.

It is unnecessary to relate in detail Coligny's early life, spent solely in military pursuits. His rise was too rapid to be ascribed to nepotism. His ability, both as army leader and as civilian administrator, was beyond doubt. Regulations issued by him and known as *Les Ordonnances de l'Amiral* became the basis of French army discipline; Brantôme credits them with having saved a million lives and fortunes. In 1552 he was appointed Admiral: an exalted office, laden with honors, powers, and functions, everything but that of leading a navy. For France had no navy. To be Admiral meant to be able to make bold maritime plans; whether they would be executed was another question. It also meant to stand next to the Constable, on the steps of the throne.

Sickly from childhood, Coligny was often forced to take lengthy sojourns at Châtillon. There his wife kept him company. She was Charlotte de Laval, daughter of a Breton count, whom Coligny loved as a child and waited for until she was deemed old enough to marry. We know little about her—and yet much. She was his comrade; shared the struggles he had with himself as well as with the world; braced him when he came to the point of announcing his conversion, for she had been a Calvinist before him.

In Châtillon, Coligny divested himself of his uniform. There he led the life of a wealthy landowner whose estate was as well-organized as his department, and later, when religion filled his heart, he became the patriarch of the congregation, not only praying with them but preaching to them. He rebuilt his paternal castle in the sumptuous style of the Renaissance. He read and loved the poets of his time: Ronsard and Clément Marot, protégés of his brother Odet, who by then was Archbishop, Count-Bishop, Cardinal, and Peer of France. The French Renaissance was at its height then, disciplined, strict: Ronsard's poems, the architecture of the Louvre, the castles of Chambord, Blois, St. Germain-en-Laye, the park of Fontainebleau, the work of painters and sculptors, miniaturists, printers, goldsmiths, gardeners, and embroiderers.

But meanwhile the drab and senseless war with Spain dragged on, the war which was not to end until Cateau-Cambrésis. The country was impoverished, the exchequer empty. But the French were not the only ones to tire of war: an armistice was concluded at Vaucelles, in 1556. Within two years, Henry II was to break it at the inducement of the Guises, but now Gaspard de Coligny was chosen to travel to the Spanish Netherlands and receive the oath of the enemy sovereign.

It was a great day, for the sovereign was Charles V, Lord of the Universe. With a splendid train the Admiral entered Brussels. The Emperor was ill with gout, longing already to exchange his Imperial robes for a monk's habit in San Juste near Madrid; but his son, King Philip, went to Mass with Coligny and at the altar of the palace chapel swore to the treaty. As with everything in that age, the scene was a grotesque mixture of dignity and comic barbarism. The representatives of two great powers stood before the Cross and took the oath. Meanwhile, Brusquet, the French King's popular court jester, ran wild among the faithful and scattered money from his pockets, making fun of the Spaniards' parsimony. Sinister King Philip turned in indignation; but the sight of the jester made him laugh so hard that he had to steady himself at the altar.

A few days later, Emperor Charles received the Admiral. The room was hung with black cloth, and the sick monarch sat on a black chair behind a black table. He replied politely to the formal address; then, kneeling, Coligny handed him a letter from his King, which the Emperor's gouty fingers could not open. He smiled sadly at his own decrepitude and bade Coligny rise. In a low, almost tender voice, with a touch of humor in his eyes, he started a conversation about the French Court which might better be called a bit of discreet gossip. He praised Montmorency as a great general, put him on a plane with himself and Alva; he was equally interested in what Diane de Poitiers was up to just then. And all the time the jester bawled his tasteless jokes.

This was a dignitary's life as desired and respected by the period: measured, cavalier, thoroughly Catholic. How then—and when—did Coligny turn Protestant?

Legend has it happening after the fall of St. Quentin, when he sat for two years, a prisoner of war, in the Flemish castle of Lécluse. When Henry II, over his protests, broke the truce in defiance of all vows, Coligny handed in his resignation. But the King, more obstinate than ever after many failures, insisted on his leading the army of Picardy. Coligny's defense of St. Quentin against the Spanish siege ranks with France's greatest deeds of glory. He surrendered only when the enemy had entered the town over its leveled walls. He was taken to Lécluse, where he is said to have read the *Livres de Genève*, and in his disgust with the King's perjury to have turned from the French official religion.

We cannot tell. We know only that his brother, Andelot, had been active in the Reformation for some time and had taken every opportunity to try to convert Gaspard. He adored his elder brother, never wanted to leave him, and always sought to emulate his soldierly virtues. He was an able officer but choleric; he saw enemies where there were none and was always too quick with his sword. He also came upon the new faith as a prisoner of war, in Milan. When he was freed in 1556, after five years, he succeeded Gaspard as Colonel-General of Infantry, but even then he spent most of his time with his brother, protecting him and yet dependent upon him. Does it matter whether it was really he who sent Coligny the *Livres de Genève?*

In any event, while the prisoner of Lécluse wrestled with himself and his conscience his wife had already taken the great step. Charlotte de Laval-Coligny corresponded with Calvin; his letters, counting her among the elect, comforted and sustained her, and, above all, directed her as to how to shield her husband from the Court's influence when he returned. She was as humble as a medieval nun; as tenacious as her countrymen, the Breton peasants. She knew that her husband's character would not permit him to remain half-way between two parties. He would never shirk a clean decision. And she also knew that he was a supreme egoist, bound to force his person, and a cause he had embraced, into one.

When he had returned to Châtillon Coligny found his

wife imbued with the faith. They stayed awake nights, talking. To Charlotte, Catholicism was nothing more than idolatry and superstition: "Throw it off! Get rid of it!"

He reminded her first of what confessors had to suffer. "But if you are prepared in your heart to take this fate upon yourself—torture, even death . . ."

She interrupted him eagerly. She had weighed everything, tested herself ever again; nothing could deter her. Persecution had always been the lot of the faithful, and would remain so until the end of time.

Thus husband and wife looked into their own and each other's hearts.

Soon afterwards, in the little town of Valleville, the Admiral attended a secret service. Before communion, he stepped in front of the congregation, begged them not to take offense at his weakness, and asked the preacher to instruct him in detail about the sacrament. He heard Calvin's doctrine, knelt, prayed, gave thanks for his conversion, and was accepted into the fold.

Portraits of this great man show an extremely long, gaunt face, one that might have been put into a vise and squeezed into angular shape, one that had no flesh on the cheekbones. The nose was long and narrow, the lips too thin and unsensuous. The face was framed by short, blond hair and a loose beard. Furrows lined the forehead and temples, and ran sharply from the wings of the nose to the corners of the mouth. They betrayed premature aging, illness from youth on, a man who had spent himself early. The gray eyes probe but do not reflect; absorb everything, painfully, slowly, without fire, without joy. The patrician features do not conceal the slow flow of the blood, or the fact that here determination was no gift of nature but the product of perseverance.

Coligny was a mysterious compound of sober realism, abstract thought, and unworldly dreaming. In him, grim, easily provoked ambition was paired with sensitive humility. He was a courtier and a hermit, a man of battle and of prayer. But what predestined him to leadership was his power of finding the highest courage in the greatest misfortune. He rose in the very moment of a fall. None of the Court's intrigues could break him. As soon as one illusion was shattered, he clung to the next. He was a realist who fed on dreams.

His greatest dream was colonization. His roving spirit, plagued by evil premonitions, embraced these vague, romantic ideas which involved so much good sense. Did he know that sooner or later, despite all temporary reconciliations, the Protestants' only salvation would be flight overseas? Did he understand that distant continent which was as yet but rumor and legend? Did he perhaps figure out quite soberly that across the Atlantic were lands and resources in plenty, removed from Europe's many prejudices?

In July, 1555, an expedition under his patronage sailed for Brazil. An expedition of this kind was the riskiest of ventures. Did Coligny decide on it to "spread the glory of the French name, to create trade routes which would add to the wealth of France, finally, not to leave that continent wholly to Spain"? These were his officially announced reasons, and surely he, a great patriot, found them important enough. But even more decisive might have been his wish to give his persecuted co-religionists a lasting haven, where they would be able to live and worship according to their convictions, without fear. What a prospect!

Coligny entrusted the leadership of the expedition, with the title of Vice-Admiral, to a daring adventurer, Nicholas Durand de Villegagnon, who in the preliminary conferences had posed as a warm friend of the Reformation. The emigrants—men, women, and children—numbered barely a hundred. The Protestants were probably in the minority, for anything else would have made the government suspicious of the enterprise.

After a hard crossing, their two ships reached the beautiful bay on which Rio de Janeiro lies today. They settled on an island in it, which they fortified and named Fort Coligny in honor of their patron. But Villegagnon was not competent to deal with the inevitable lack of food and water, loneliness, nostalgia, quarrels, crime, and religious dissension. On the contrary, he showed himself now for what he was: an opportunist who, not without reason, had brought with him some of the worst criminals from the Paris jails. When theological disputes arose among the settlers, he took the side of the Catholics, and soon began to persecute the Protestants with the cruel methods they had known at home. He even passed death sentences for heresy, and had some of the Huguenots, whose fate Coligny had placed in his hands, cast into the sea. When there was no more hope for the colony, he sailed back to France, leaving a handful of helpless settlers in Fort Coligny. A year later they were attacked by Portuguese fanatics and slaughtered.

The dreadful report caused the Admiral deepest anguish. But the very next day he was again seen bent over maps which had been drawn, with whatever skill or knowledge, of the American continent. The old plans had failed. New ones had to be made.

9

A BAD YEAR

HOW thoroughly everything had been changed by the King's death became apparent when the *States-General* at last met formally in that December of 1561. No one bothered about the Cardinal of Lorraine's injunction against the mention of religious matters. One knew that liberties could be taken. Of the four now sharing power, only the Cardinal held to the old authoritarian policies. But even he was no longer able to enforce them.

The Queen Mother, finally at the goal of her ambitions, was most interested in standing well with everyone and being bound to no one. What a robust animal nature! All her children were sickly, and in the physicians' opinion each had carried the germ even at birth: pitiable heirs to the blood of their grandfather Lorenzo who had acquired the dread disease, the scourge of the century, in Paris. But Catherine herself, what did she care? She triumphed over her heritage, year by year seeming to become stronger and more full-blooded.

The third in the government, Anthony of Navarre, though by nature amiable and conciliatory, could hardly forget from one day to the next that only a short while before—how long ago was it?—he was to have been beheaded in honor of the *States-General.* Embittered and stubborn, he protested against every resolution adopted by his enemies and co-regents. As for the fourth, the Constable, it was becoming more apparent every day that he was growing old.

What a state France was in! A boy King; the government headed by a woman to whom the common weal meant nothing and who was still a stranger in the land; the leaders feuding and the people in revolt.

The Queen Mother worked slowly, hurried nothing; she never lost sight of her goal: a compromise between the parties, which would increase her power. She had grown fatter, had a double chin, breathed with difficulty—but her charm remained. She knew how to pick her aides. There was Marshal de Saint-André, aligned with the Guises but reasonable enough to respect the Bourbon princes, too. There were the Duchess of Montpensier, the King of Navarre's best friend, and many others. There were also her little fifteen-year-old ladies-in-waiting, often three hundred in number, exquisite beauties, who were delighted to go to bed with gentlemen if by so doing they could do their mistress a favor.

Thus the face of French politics, hard and determined the day before, quickly turned into a grinning grimace. The same Prince of Condé whose execution was to have been the occasion for a great festival now was acquitted and given a seat in the Council. The prior of Chartres was freed, too. And Admiral de Coligny, the Chancellor, and the Bishop of Orléans formed a triumvirate with moderate tendencies. Still, the Guises had only been checked—by no means crushed.

What was the use of attempts at conciliation if religious

tension continued? The Protestants utilized the new situation to hold public services. At Calvin's door in Geneva, French emissaries crowded each other, asking for preachers. A new edict, very mild in tenor, prohibited action against them while at home or in the homes of friends. But in direct contradiction of this conciliatory royal attitude, the *parlement* of Paris forbade all gatherings to solemnize the sacraments in a non-Catholic form, under penalty of confiscation or death. Confusion as before. Would it never end?

It had to end. Things could not go on as they were.

The great Religious Disputation of Poissy was decided on. In the King's presence, the hostile parties met in open debate. Against the assembled prelates the government put up the best preachers of the Reformed Church. On the Catholic side appeared the Cardinals of Tournon, Lorraine, Bourbon, Armagnac; the most renowned bishops, and the doctors of the Sorbonne and other universities. For the Huguenots appeared Theodore Beza, and supporting him were Peter Martyr, Francis de St. Paul, John Raimund, and other preachers from Geneva and Germany.

Beza was the head of the assemblage: an earthy, humorous peasant, unafraid, a sly grin on his broad face, who as a student had penned wanton poems in the manner of Ovid and Catullus, mention of which still made him blush, the great thinker, Calvin's dauntless apostle and intimate friend. He spoke first. He strode to the center of the hall, knelt, and prayed fervently for Divine assistance. Then he explained his creed, violently assailed the Sorbonne as responsible for the persecutions, and closed with a defense of all the points contested by the Roman Church. At first he was heard quietly. But when he came to talk about the presence of the body of Christ in the sacrament, the audience became restless: not on account of the subject but because his realistic treatment of it, so different from conventional piety, shocked the Catholics.

The Cardinal of Lorraine rose to reply—and with him rose the hopes of the orthodox among those present. Excelling in rhetoric, armed with complete knowledge of classic and modern theology, a diplomat both brilliant and solid, as factual as Augustine and as imaginative as his protégés, the poets Rabelais and Ronsard, cold, cruel, biting —proudly assuming responsibility for the bloodbath of Amboise—thus he appeared. His arguments struck like blows. And when he concluded, the Cardinals and bishops surrounded the King and cried: "Sire—this is the true faith; this is the pure doctrine of the Church; we are all ready to subscribe to this and, if need be, to seal it with our blood!"

Beza wanted to reply but it was too late, the session too tumultuous. It was adjourned. But those that followed were no less tumultuous. The King's Council advised him henceforth to stay away, lest his youthful brain, not yet able to know truth from falsehood, absorb erroneous, non-Catholic ideas. The Disputation gradually turned from a public event into a private affair. By the Cardinal's deft strategy, Holy Communion became the main point at issue; and now he drew German Lutherans into the debate, who bitterly opposed the Calvinists on that question. His Eminence's intention was plain: not only should the opposition be discredited by this show of internal wrangling, but the Huguenots' friendship with the German Protestants should be disrupted, and their hopes for German succor dashed.

It is uncertain whether Cardinal de Guise accomplished this purpose. But he did accomplish something else: he made the King of Navarre waver. Anthony's simple mind, comprehending only unequivocal formulae, was greatly upset by the discord among the Reformed preachers. He could not hide his dismay and uncertainty—how could a man be certain if any misstep was treason?—and soon the Catholics, with a knowledge of human nature born of a thousand-year-old tradition, discreetly started wooing him. When the Disputation of Poissy ended, it was without result, and with each party proclaiming itself the winner.

Then the deputies met again, this time in Pontoise. They demanded a complete reform of Church, judiciary, and officialdom; that public offices should no longer serve private interests. The incumbents should have a tenure of three years, not be appointed by the King but elected by the people, and be paid so little that no one would seek an office out of mere greed. At regular intervals, the *States-General* should vote on new laws, taxes, constitutional changes, war and peace—in short, on all matters of foreign and domestic policy. And a sensational demand: the nation's budget should be balanced by the secularization of almost all Church property. No ecclesiastic benefice should yield more than five thousand livres to its owner; the rest should flow into the royal exchequer. The first portent of a still remote future—of the Great Revolution!

Even though few—very few—of these plans were realized, a wealth of new ideas had begun to spring up. Hope stirred again—everything seemed new. Had not the floodgates been opened? Had not the break-through of great reforms come nearer? Conference still followed conference, but in January, 1562, an edict was issued granting Protestants the rights of sermon, prayer, and worship.

The Guises and their fanatic adherents breathed fire. The clerical fury knew no bounds. What an edict! The Duke vowed to pierce it with his sword, pledged his word. If the edict—a political as well as an ecclesiastic innovation—was allowed to stand, the motions for social reform made by the pro-plebeian bishops might be carried any day.

Secularization of Church property! Restriction of expenditures for the high nobility! Support of commerce and trade! What did it mean but a weakening of the feudal lords in favor of the bourgeoisie? An even more conscious elevation of the wealthy urban patriarchate over the titled landowners? It must not be—but the counterblow would have to fall suddenly and effectively, if the poison of the changes, already noticeable, were not to infect all groups of the population.

Moreover the political faction of the Huguenots raised their head. How they paraded and boasted! Their leader, Condé, went to church, right in the capital, surrounded by gangs of armed co-religionists in military formation. It was believed that twenty thousand Huguenots were in Paris. Their plans were unknown, but if a *coup d'état* was on their program, it was bound to succeed.

The Duke of Guise had already proved in Italy that he could act. At first, however, he retired from the Court. He went to Joinville, a village on his ancestral domain on the border of Champagne and Lorraine. He apparently intended to lead a wholly private life. But the Constable called him back to Paris, whether in the hope of keeping an eye on him, or because for some time they and Saint-André had conspired together. The Duke set out accompanied by his brother, the Cardinal, many noblemen of his following, and two companies of lancers.

On March 1, they rode through Vassy, a little town in Champagne, and heard the ringing of bells. When they inquired they were told that the Huguenots had met for divine service. The ducal soldiers laughed broadly, on their chargers: let's have some fun with these pietists! They were tough fellows, bored by the ride and impatient for adventure; the crisp Spring wind was chilling and it seemed a good idea to warm up. Howling and rattling their arms, they trotted to the meeting-house. The Protestants shut the gates, but when the wild crew clattered around the house, roaring threats, they ran out, unarmed, and defended themselves with stones picked up from the road. A moment, and the battle was on. The Duke came up, rode down what got into his way, shouted and laughed until a sharp rock hit his side. He was only lightly wounded, but blood oozed through his vest. It maddened the Catholics. Intoxicated with hatred, they charged without pity. Some of the Protestants were slain in the street, the rest were chased back into the meeting-house and murdered there; the preacher, badly wounded, fled over the adjoining roofs and bled to death.

Sixty peaceful people had wanted to worship God, and none of them survived. The Duke of Guise summoned the mayor of the town for a tongue-lashing: how could he have the audacity to let heretics worship? The mayor excused himself: under the edict, the Huguenots have that right. "Then I'll smash it with my sword!" the Duke shouted into his face, blind with fury.

The massacre of Vassy served as a signal. Soon after, at Cahors, a Reformed meeting-house was surrounded and set afire. None of those gathered there saved themselves; if they escaped the fire, they were cut down outside. In Toulouse, the harried Protestants and their women and children, four thousand altogether, were promised safe conduct; and then, because a promise to heretics need not be kept, all were butchered. The edict of January, intended to avoid civil war, brought it about.

After his exploit of Vassy, Guise rode into Paris, the most Catholic city in France, and was received as if he were the King, with flowers thrown in his path. Foretasting the impending triumph, people strolled on Sundays and voiced their feelings without first looking about whether it was safe. Secret stores of arms were distributed quietly among the citizens.

The Prince of Condé collected the most faithful, to whom his brother, Navarre, no longer belonged. He told them that no choice remained, that they had to yield; but all raised their hands, vowing to avenge the dead of Vassy and Toulouse, as they left the city with him.

The wheel made a full turn. Sharp measures were taken in Paris. Anyone suspected of sympathizing with the new religion had to leave town without trial. Cardinal de Guise himself preached a series of sermons in which his oratorical talents shone in full splendor. Men who had yesterday damned him to death acclaimed him today. A continuous, ornate festival went on around him. The houses were decked out with flags; unceasingly, troops of citizens marched through the streets, muskets shouldered, flowers fixed to their helmets. The bells rang from the church spires. The militia, twenty-four thousand strong, had been quickly mobilized and showed off at daily drill. The recent wails over the Cardinal's corrupt administration were forgotten. And the Constable, not to be outdone by the Cardinal, gave the Parisians a special treat: he ordered the public burning of the Reformed preachers' pulpits and the pews of their flocks, as well as of all suspicious books. Daily, processions moved through the city.

Although much had been gained by this peaceful conquest of Paris, so long as the Guises did not have full control of the government a majority might still try again to untie the Gordian knot. The point now was to cut it, with one swift stroke. It would have been easy to reach an agreement with the Queen Mother, in spite of her relations with the Huguenots which had of late become dangerously intimate; a much more serious problem was still the King of Navarre. Overnight he had risen from traitor to regent of France and, as a Bourbon prince, he was impervious to direct methods.

Granvella, the Minister of the Spanish King who was in close contact with the Guises, worked out a promising plan. Was not Anthony of Navarre a simple, rather vain man, who knew no lovelier dream than to get back the kingdom of Navarre of which the Spaniards had robbed his father-in-law? Well, why not enter into negotiations with him, not really compensating him for the loss but arousing certain faint hopes? If he later referred to any vague promises, they could all be proved to have been tentative. The point was to offer the bait long enough to pry him loose from his party. Afterwards, he could be dropped at will.

And so we find Navarre in talks with the Papal Legate and with the Spanish Ambassador, about recompense for the lost little domain. It was a naked, unashamed business deal. He asked quite frankly: "What do I get out of it?" The question was expected, of course; and Sardinia was held out to him, or a piece of North Africa. The Ambassadors of nearly all the Catholic Courts joined in the negotiations. At last they got him to seal his desertion with a promise to repeal the peace edict issued by himself.

The Queen Mother, through all this, had not been lost sight of. Her correspondence with the Prince of Condé was carefully weighed. One could feel her wriggle and twist in it, trying to escape the Guises' growing influence; one had to be on guard hourly against her animal shrewdness. To be free again, she had gone to Fontainebleau with her son and the Court. From there she tenderly wrote Condé, imploring him to protect her and the innocent child against those who would ruin the realm. Condé still felt he was too weak, and hesitated. But the Catholic nobles were quick in making decisions; while he reflected, they appeared before Catherine. What did they wish? Nothing of importance: merely to lead her back to Paris.

She resisted for a time, complained, cried, correctly prophesied that civil war would result if the King were made a Catholic symbol exclusively and the edict repealed. The Guises were unimpressed. She finally agreed to follow them, at the same time sending letters to Condé, expressing regret at not being able to join him because the others had struck first. On the trip the young King wept incessantly, for two days and two nights. He did not understand what was going on; comprehended only the sinister rush of preparations, the disrespectful tone of the gentlemen toward his mother, the silence in which she sat beside him with angrily clenched teeth.

When Condé received the news on the road, he sat frozen on his horse. So the others had been too quick—or had the Queen Mother betrayed him? He and the Admiral held a hurried conference. The Prince sighed: "We have gone so far that now we have to swallow or choke."

They rode on in silence. They knew that the abduction of the royal child, who now had to sign whatever was laid in front of him, would mean the repeal of the edict—and with the repeal, war.

Condé aged in a few weeks. His volatile *joie de vivre*, his ever-genial humor, his lust for adventure yielded to depression. Many attempts were made to bribe him, not by means of vain images, as with his mediocre brother, but with binding offers of sovereign principalities. The bribers had misjudged him, for the creed he confessed set him a task in life from which he would not swerve for the slightest compromise. As if striking the offers in the face, he declared in a series of angry manifestoes that the Queen Mother and the young King were captives of the Guises, and that the good of France required him to take up arms for their liberation.

The army he gathered around him was bold and aggressive. Its leaders, under him, were the three Châtillons, the Counts of Porcien, Rochefoucauld, Rohan, Gramont, and Montgomery—members of the first families of France, who as individuals had embraced the Reformation. Three thousand nobles served with Condé's troops. Many towns opened their gates to him. While in Paris the January edict was repealed, the Prince proclaimed it the length and breadth of the land. Soon France resounded with arms. Every province was split in two. Even within families enmity and hatred rose. There was no place—in Gascony or Normandy or Languedoc or Touraine—which was not the scene of tragic murder, arson, betrayal, and rapine.

10

WAR BEGINS

UNDER Francis I, even under Henry II, the unrest throughout France could still be attributed to different views on sacrament or predestination, or to abuses in the Church and demands for their adjustment. Now, the assemblies of Fontainebleau, Orléans, and Pontoise had shown that the struggle raged with equal ferocity over economic and constitutional issues, and that the classes were no less than the creeds at swords' points. Political factions had banded together with religious ones, and it was an open question whether the former were not using the latter for their own ends. That the opposition groups —the lower nobility and clergy, and the bourgeoisie— rallied behind the abused Princes of the Blood, or that certain archbishops and the Admiral made themselves the advocates of the oppressed, did not alter the clearly evident class division. At the start of every revolutionary action in history some members of the ruling class have sided with the rising masses. This is a phenomenon of no greater import than the subservience shown to the mighty by many of the oppressed.

The wars of the past decades had increased the taxes exorbitantly. The *taille*—a tax imposed on the Third Estate while nobility, clergy, and higher bureaucracy were exempt from it—threw its burden almost exclusively on the working peasant. In sixty years, its nominal annual yield had increased from two to six million livres. Besides, there was an astonishing number of other taxes, war levies, and public collections taken up at every opportunity. And, in addition, there were indirect taxes, chiefly on salt and liquor, and duties on both imports and exports.

The peasant was the worse off the fact that, before Francis I had incurred his war debts, agriculture had flourished. Many historians try to paint the French peasantry as having always lived like starving cattle. This is not a true picture. Only three or four decades before this era, agriculture was such a remunerative pursuit that a law had to be passed against the cutting down of forests. And the peasants had gradually won rights assuring them a measure of self-government; each rural community having a village council to run its affairs, and electing its own bailiffs and a delegate to the district assembly which in turn chose the Third Estate deputy to the *States-General*. But this had lasted for only about a generation. Under the weak successors of Francis I, the peasant's rights dwindled fast; he was soon so impoverished that he often had to leave his soil because it no longer afforded him a minimal subsistence.

The lower nobility were beset by similar adversities. The produce of their small estates did not suffice for the household, family, and servants, and they had to buy in the face of rising prices. It is little wonder, with the incessant requisitions of horses, cattle, and fodder for war, with military service keeping the younger noblemen from productive work, and with the expense involved in seeking a career at Court, that, not to be completely *déclassé*, the little aristocrat had to play up to the great aristocrat and let himself be kept, as page and later as an officer or petty official.

Opposed to the pauperized classes were the high nobility. They were more firmly in the saddle than ever, due to the farming-out of their lands, and the benefices which the Crown handed out liberally to insure fidelity and war service. The Guise estates were scattered over half a dozen provinces; Constable Montmorency, the richest man in the country, owned no less than 130 manors and over 400 secondary fiefs. It was the same among the ecclesiastics. The episcopate and the propertied orders rolled in wealth, while the village parson could not make ends meet. The three ancient powers—monarch, high nobility, high clergy—were dependent upon each other; none could maintain itself alone.

Between the classes, at least originally, stood the *bourgeois*. They stood apart, industrious, reliable, working hard to strengthen themselves. They inhabited towns, haughtily shut off from the country by means of walls and towers and the latest armament. They clung tenaciously to constitutions they had given themselves, which differed from town to town. Heading their communities was an aristocracy, originally elected but gradually grown hereditary. High politics, especially the foreign kind, did not interest the *bourgeois*. They worked only for the common good of their towns, and since they alone carried on trade, the bulk of the ready money remained in their hands, including the revenue from the new trans-oceanic colonies.

But more and more, the Court found that it needed money. To get its hands in the well-filled urban cash drawers, it had to ride roughshod over the privileges of the towns. It was a vicious circle: hounded by the cupidity of the great lords, the monarch robbed the bourgeoisie, driving it into a union with the rural disinherited, who in their turn were after the wealth of the great lords.

The Prince of Condé's army was increasing hourly, but he impatiently sought allies even outside France. Landgrave Philip of Hesse, realizing that the Prince's cause was also that of the German Protestants, sent Marshal Rollshausen with a few thousand horsemen to free the King and the Queen Mother from the bonds of the Catholic party. And Elizabeth of England, seeing danger in the possibility of the Norman ports getting into the hands of the Guises who had caused enough trouble in Scotland, concluded a pact with the Huguenots, pledging money and men in exchange for the promise of Havre de Grâce.

This surrender of French soil was an action of ominous import. It looked very much like treason, and swelled the ranks of Condé's enemies. Quite possibly, Elizabeth's aid was more than offset by the impairment of the party's strength at home; above all, Condé had lost by it the sympathy of the Queen Mother. Until the last she had been conspiring with him; now she was enraged. It was her late husband who had victoriously driven the English from French soil. Were they now to regain a foothold under her regency? Condé could have rendered the Guises no better service. Catherine moved decisively into their camp.

The prelude to her new course was the young King's formal appearance in the *parlement* of Paris. In his presence, the Chancellor read a fanatic diatribe against the Huguenots, stating that their blind partisanship had killed all their patriotic feeling and that they were not above handing the country over to Germans and Englishmen. He charged them with looting and murder and with the intention to usurp the royal power itself. His address was extraordinarily effective. Coligny, his brothers, and all outstanding party leaders were outlawed, stripped of their honors and offices, including titles of nobility; their estates and possessions were declared forfeit to the Crown, and the people were allowed to kill or capture them when and wherever they found them.

It was the declaration of war. The Huguenots fought with desperate courage, but on the whole their hurriedly raised, ill-disciplined, and badly trained troops were no match for the King's veterans. Catherine joined the army with her son, and as a lone woman among soldiers proved her forceful nature. She rode through the camp like a man, disregarding cannon balls that struck near her. She conferred with generals and stood beside the firing musketeers. Her energy was responsible for the quick capture of Bourges; and it was she who defeated the plan to besiege the arch-heretical Orléans, by pointing out the supreme importance of keeping the English out of the realm.

"What is Orléans?" she exclaimed. "There are Huguenots there, nothing else. But Rouen—that is the door to the heart of France! Once the English hold it, they will hold Paris. And if we give them time to fortify it, it will be impregnable."

Rouen was well provisioned and well armed, and its siege presented more difficulties than had been expected. On one side it was protected by the Seine, on the other by a hill ironically named Mount Catherine, on the summit of which lay a modern, all but inaccessible fortress. Furthermore, the weather was bad. It was a rainy, dreary autumn. Water streamed down the hillsides onto the plain where the royal army was encamped. With the trenches flooded, the soldiers lived in a morass. Epidemics broke out. Spirits sank. Meanwhile, week after week passed, month after month.

Perhaps Rouen would never have been taken if the Huguenots, then in the infancy of their discipline, had not been guilty of continuous negligence. Their sorties were full of youthful fire, kindled in hot zeal by the preachers, but in their enthusiastic charges they were insensible to losses which in the long run were bound to cripple their army. Their commander, Montgomery, could not prevent his subordinates' irremediable stupidities.

The rains kept falling, as if Heaven wanted to drown the besiegers; of them, only Anthony of Navarre, now with the Queen Mother leading the fight against his former friends, was tireless. One day, when he was reconnoitering the battlements, he met his fate. A musket ball hit him in the left shoulder, so hard that the bone of his arm was splintered. He was carried to his tent unconscious, and the assault which had been set for that date was called off.

Around his bed stood the King, the Queen, the generals and surgeons. The army was so depressed by the blight of ceaseless rain, and further by news that the King of Navarre was dying, that the Duke of Guise and the Constable had trouble getting the men into action. Again it was Catherine who saved the day, with a great oration. Her son, she asked, the innocent, persecuted, royal child, did they want to leave him to the mercy of the English? It was a matchless slogan.

Amid jubilation, she ordered two thousand cannon shots

to be fired at the walls of Rouen, to be followed by an immediate assault. The masonry could not withstand such a cannonade and the walls tumbled, opening a wide breach. The advancing soldiers of the King were met by the Huguenots with the fury of the damned. The slaughter lasted a full day and, in the evening, the Catholics were forced to withdraw.

Not until the next day, October 26, at the break of dawn before the mists had lifted, were the exhausted, hungry defenders overwhelmed by a renewed onslaught. The entering royal army, drunk with blood, massacred defenders and non-combatants alike. The Count of Montgomery and his staff escaped in a small galley to Havre de Grâce, and thence to England. Huguenot leaders who were captured were quartered. The town was sacked for two days, then set afire. On the third day the King made his entry, with the Queen Mother and the entire *parlement*.

The affable King of Navarre, whose life the surgeons had been unable to save, had long been a prey of his vacillation. Perhaps he had never been a true Huguenot; perhaps he had always only thought he believed what his wife's fanaticism and Beza's preaching would have him believe. First the Cardinal's oratory had made him waver, then the image of a Sardinian kingdom, conjured up by the clever Spaniards, had sealed his defection. The Guises and the Papal Legate had even suggested an annulment of his marriage to Jeanne d'Albret, so that he might wed Francis II's widow, Mary Stuart; they had also offered him the hand of Margaret, Charles IX's sister. But he had rejected these importunities.

Jeanne d'Albret had been estranged from her husband

for years. She now retired to Béarn, to live solely for the education of her children, whom she had brought up chiefly by Calvinist preachers in the classic-humanist tradition. What plans and dreams she must have harbored! Under the Salic Law, if the Valois should die out—and not a few signs indicated that this might happen—her son, the nine-year-old Prince Henry, would become King of France.

After his brother's death, it was the Prince of Condé alone who personified the Bourbon spirit and prestige. Lacking Anthony's flexibility, he glowed with eruptive passion, always wanting everything or nothing and as extravagant in his ambitions as he was in his sensuality. He plunged into voluptuous affairs, only to tear himself from the arms of his paramours in pursuit of new and exciting plans. Nothing could discourage him for long. Rouen was lost. But there was Paris—Paris, the heart of France; he would strike a death blow at the enemy's heart. With a single stroke he would decide the campaign!

Daily there was bitter wrangling between him and the Admiral, who grew ever more cautious, paler, sicklier. "We have only a few towns left?" Condé exclaimed. "There'll soon be many again. We've suffered a set-back, but no more. Andelot has joined forces with the Germans, that is all that matters."

"And the others have joined forces with the Swiss. And with three thousand Spanish infantrymen," Coligny said.

The Prince would not listen. He set out to take Paris. When he realized, much too late and after very painful losses, that this was an absurd undertaking, he decided to strike at rich Normandy. Plans had been made for seven thousand Englishmen to join him at Havre de Grâce, with twenty cannon and 120,000 ducats. The ducats were the most important item; for he was no longer able to pay his troops, and knew that many of the mercenaries would desert unless he could soon make connection with the English.

Overnight, noiselessly, leaving all unnecessary baggage behind, his army broke camp before Paris and, in forced marches, headed for Normandy. The Catholics did not learn of his departure until the next day, and then rested for two more days before following after him. Despite his three days' start they quickly gained on him; the rains and the dense net of rivers in the region slowing him down, while the Catholics used the bridges in the towns which belonged to them.

Condé led the main body of his troops, made up of infantry. The vanguard, under the Admiral, consisted of the German mercenaries who were sent far ahead so that they could take their pick of quarters and booty before the other troops arrived. The rear guard were French cavalry, led by the Count of Porcien. Near the town of Dreux, Condé changed the order of march. Without informing Coligny, he advanced so fast that his troop was soon in the van. The whole army became disorganized and Coligny, outraged by such carelessness, ordered the march halted for a day to restore the original formation. This, the Prince's second mistake, was to prove more grave than the first, for it enabled the enemy to catch up with the Huguenots.

The town of Dreux lies on the border of old Normandy, on the shallow little Eure river. The Huguenots crossed this on December 18, moved into quarters in the surrounding villages, and sank into deep slumber after the strenuous march. The royal army reached the opposite bank at night, in thinly veiled, snow-scented, uncertain darkness. It encamped noiselessly. Condé, believing it to be much farther away, had not bothered to post sentries. But the enemy commander was the widely experienced Constable, who had issued precise orders to every detachment, and when the moon unexpectedly broke through the veil of mist he led his whole army across the stream without meeting an obstacle. Marching on a little, he occupied a road ahead which the Huguenots had to use. His corps, with the Swiss in the center, held one side; that of the Duke of Guise—Spaniards, Gascons, and German auxiliaries—the other. And this latter wing was so well screened by trees, shrubbery, and houses that it could not be seen by the Huguenots.

Dawn broke; the sun rose, late and cloud-enveloped; thick hoarfrost covered everything. Coligny, one of the first to awaken, suddenly saw the Constable's cavalry close by. Dismayed, he investigated and found that once again Condé's thoughtlessness had led the army into a trap. Composing himself with difficulty, he turned to the Huguenot leaders: "Gentlemen, we can no longer seek salvation in the speed of our legs. But are we not soldiers? Let us seek it in our swords."

The Prince, wanting to make up for his mistake, advanced impetuously against the Constable's battle line. He failed wholly to notice Guise's corps at his back, an amateurishness at which Montmorency laughed aloud. He opened fire with fourteen cannon. Now Condé had the trumpets blow the charge and his cavalry swept over the frozen earth until "the air boiled from the breath of the horses," as one chronicler tells us. With full force they smashed into the Swiss, who stood like a wall. Even after they were run down by the horses they fought lying on the ground; more stubbornly, the fewer of them that remained. By then, the Admiral was attacking the Constable's cavalry, and the best of the Catholic nobles went down under the onslaught. The battle swayed back and forth. Montmorency, fighting strongly despite his age, was surrounded, wounded in the left arm, pinned under his horse, and made prisoner. Eventually, his force was driven to flight by the Germans with such vehemence that they trampled each other down and the horses rolled over them. And still the Swiss stood fast, fighting with rocks when sword and lance gave out.

And what had the Duke of Guise been doing meanwhile? Why had he remained idle in his hiding place? Why had he not acted before the Constable was unquestionably routed? Why had he not ordered an attack when he saw the Catholics giving ground? His enemies later charged that he gleefully contemplated his rival's ignominious defeat; while his adherents praised him as a great tactician who, regardless of sacrifices, always keeps the final goal in view. Whichever it was, when the report of Montmorency's capture reached him, when he could be sure that the Huguenots had broken ranks in wild pursuit and pillage, he gave the order to attack. In a few terse words to his officers he outlined their chances, now that the enemy had carelessly split and exhausted themselves, and, at the head of his cavalry, stormed over the field.

Coligny saw this new host appear just when he thought he had won a complete victory. With the utmost rigor he brought his troops back to order. But Guise's Spaniards, fresh and riding with full élan against soldiers barely able to lift their arms any longer, carried death and confusion before them. Condé's squadron fled; he himself was cut off and captured despite desperate resistance. The Admiral saw that the battle which had seemed won, was lost. And, as always in misfortune, he displayed his gift for leadership, apparent in retreat as much as in attack. Slowly, in little feints, he broke up his army into small units which took to the woods, and did not re-form it until after dark, at Neuville, some miles away.

There he met his brother Andelot, the Count of Porcien, the Count of Rochefoucauld, and the Germans who brought the captured Constable with them. A war council was held that night, and since Condé had been taken prisoner, Coligny was chosen commander of the Huguenot army.

The Duke of Guise, however, had won the field. At dusk he led his troops into the village of Blainville. He himself took up quarters in a low mud hut, furnished with a wobbly table and a damp, narrow bed, had dinner served for two, and asked his prisoner, the Prince of Condé, to be his guest. So the two princes, the most embittered and implacable foes, sat face to face, ate and drank and discussed the fickleness of fortune. Then, exhausted after the hard day, they slept in the one bed, under the one blanket.

The battle of Dreux plunged all France into deep mourning. The flower of the aristocracy, and eight thousand soldiers, had died. There was only one person who was pleased with the outcome of the tragedy: this was Catherine de' Medici. The prospects of peace growing out of the dreadful weakening of the parties seemed brighter to her. Condé, her most violent opponent, was a prisoner, and so was her adviser Montmorency, the know-it-all who had got so much on her nerves of late. The Admiral had lost prestige, too. And the Duke of Guise, although Commander-in-Chief now, met with such universal suspicion and reproach, for his belated action, that she expected him to mind his manners with her for a while.

In any event, she was determined to exploit the situation and greatly increase her influence.

11

DEATH STRIKES THREE TIMES

BUT Catherine was wrong about her new Commander-in-Chief. Guise behaved like a dictator. None of the pamphlets attacking him on all sides seemed to touch him. His manner of speech grew even more overbearing, his ambition more overt. Fully aware of his strong Catholic backing, he ruthlessly pushed his friends into every influential position in the army and at Court.

The first big enterprise he launched was a siege of Orléans. It was intolerable that the Protestants possessed a fortress in the center of France, on the Loire, where the most important roads crossed. Not only were the adherents of the new religion in the majority among the townspeople, but throughout the region powerful nobles were turning more and more toward it, and the university, whose student body was largely German, was a focal point of oppositionist education. Contemporaries called Orléans another Geneva. Morning and evening, psalms resounded in the streets; dissipation was punished severely; neither dice nor card games were played; and the soldiers were forbidden to consort with women. Far from showing tolerance, the Protestants claimed to have the only true faith; and whoever opposed it was obliged to leave Orléans.

In the middle of the hard winter of 1563, heavy artillery appeared before the town walls. The black barrels of the guns stood out menacingly against the snow. The army that had brought them from Paris was accompanied by the Queen Mother, who did not want to let Guise out of her sight. She moved into poor quarters and for hours on end sat huddled before the hearth, staring at the fire. Orléans was defended by Andelot, who, though ill with fever, could not be dissuaded from personally inspecting the battlements. The Admiral, his brother, was on his way to Normandy to meet the English, without whose money the Germans would not continue to fight.

The Loire divided the defiant town into two unequal parts, which were connected by a bridge. On one side was Orléans proper, on the other the sprawling suburb of Porteret. Two fortresses, the *Tourelles*, dominated the river; and a high, square tower of medieval construction defended the main gate. The Duke of Guise glowered at the town. "This cave," he told the young King, "is inhabited only by foxes. But I'll smoke them out."

Charles IX was apprehensive. He felt uneasy about the defenders, who were his subjects even though their prayers differed from his. But the Duke remarked, offhand, that His Majesty should graciously withhold objections if he, Guise, had every living thing there killed.

"Everything?" the King inquired.

"Including cats and dogs," replied the Duke.

But once again the God of the Calvinists proved mightier than the mighty House of Guise. He acted, as

Who could stand up to her now? Those who had thought themselves wiser and stronger than she were in their graves. The grave had served her well; from the day her husband had died, always it had enriched her life. The Duke of Guise was gone; Marshal de Saint-André; the King of Navarre. And knowing full well that the country was bleeding from deep wounds, that it was more bitterly divided than her courtiers would admit to her, she hit upon an excellent idea. She and her son would travel through France for a few years. She would present him to the people and to the various *parlements*. He would win the hearts of all parties; and she would have personal talks with neighboring princes in order to strengthen the international position of the French throne.

Such a journey of the Court was a huge undertaking. For the whole entourage, from the highest officials to the stable hands, went along, several thousand persons in all. Catherine herself took all her ladies and maids, at least two hundred young women, mostly between fourteen and eighteen years of age, in beautiful attire. They rode on thoroughbreds, heavily made up, with their eyebrows blackened and with white and red paint deftly used to make their eyes seem almond-shaped and their mouths as small as possible. Considering that each damsel had a retinue of her own—hairdressers, cooks, pastry-cooks, tailors, and physicians—and adding to these the armed guards, government clerks, and servants of various kinds, one can imagine the sums spent on such a trip. But when the cavalcade moved across country, with gaudy plumes fluttering from wide hats and music mingling with laughter, it made a picture that deeply impressed the people.

Life was gay and undisciplined at this itinerant Court.

Morals and modesty were unknown; license was in style. Catherine's lovely daughter, Margaret Valois, who was to become the famous Reine Margot, led in these matters. Still half a child, she made it the fashion for breasts to be uncovered—a coquetry which was heightened by constant motion. At overnight stops only the Queen Mother sat on a chair; the rest of the company relaxed on hassocks, and not infrequently, "for reasons of more pleasing conversation," the ladies perched on the knees of the young gentlemen or the young gentlemen sat in the laps of their ladies.

Catherine's chief aim was to meet in conference with her son-in-law, Philip of Spain. Thus she hoped to soothe the French Catholics' feelings and at the same time to exert pressure on the Huguenots. Lastly, she wanted to arrange marriages between her children and the Spanish Court. Philip was evasive, however. He would go no further than to send his wife, Catherine's daughter, and the Duke of Alva to Bayonne on the frontier for discussions.

These took place in June, 1565. The Queen Mother was not sparing with receptions, stage shows, ballets, and balls, and her diplomacy was flawless. But the Duke remained unmoved. "If there is to be talk of marrying," he said, "I must first have a guarantee that the heretics will be chastised."

His demand was seconded by a great many of the French. The Duke of Montpensier, the daredevil Montluc, and last but not least, of course, Cardinal de Guise, agreed with him. The Cardinal urged that all Reformed preachers be banished.

"Banished?" Alva flared up. "And where to, please?

them had been broken. Any kind of toleration had been rejected. And so they, themselves, veered from the path of patient suffering which Calvin, who had died in 1564, had exhorted them to follow. The chaos of the war-filled years had brutalized the battlers.

Wherever troops had passed, nothing remained but burned-out homes, devastated fields, and corpses dangling from trees. The dark savagery was boundless. Vengeance for the persecutions was wrought on churches and convents: altars were upset in blind wrath, holy vessels desecrated with filth, images and statues burned, monks tortured and nuns raped. The bestial lust did not halt before dead bodies. One fellow made a necklace for himself out of monks' ears; another beat a drum with the bones of a dismembered nun. Children were impaled. Hell returned to earth, in the name of Heaven.

Condé fell back upon his original plan to end the war with one blow: the capture of Paris. He encamped at St. Denis and cut the city off from all supplies by land and water. The royal garrison was commanded by the Constable, and when famine spread and there was still no military action, the Parisians began to grumble: his army was far superior to the enemy's, so why did he let himself be cooped up and starved out? Finally, on November 10, he marched out to force an issue, and a brief but violent engagement ensued.

The Constable fought as though still in the prime of his life. He received four slight wounds in the face and a blow on the head with a bludgeon, but fought on. When Robert Stuart, a Scot, aimed a pistol at him, Montmorency roared: "Don't you know me? I am the Constable!"

"That's why I'm killing you," Stuart said, and fired.

Montmorency fell. But he still had the strength to strike the other in the face with the hilt of his sword and break his jaw. Then he lost consciousness, and some of his men dragged him away like a felled ox, with blood gushing through his armor. He was seventy-four when he died, and the victory in his last battle remained with his King.

At that time the Queen Mother might have had a chance to win the war outright. The Duke of Alva offered to come to her aid with an army of twenty-thousand. To Catherine, however, his assistance seemed dangerous. "Nothing easier than to get the Spaniards into France," she told the Council, "but how are we to get them out again?"

She preferred to aid herself, with little ruses, short truces, clever negotiations during which she armed at full speed. She insisted that the chief command be given to the King's brother, Henry, Duke of Anjou, her favorite among her sons. By now she herself dreamed no longer of an understanding with the Huguenots. She was entirely under the Cardinal's influence. Besides, the widow of the murdered Duke of Guise and his young, hot-headed son were clamoring for vengeance. They even forced Catherine to drop the pacific Chancellor L'Hospital.

And there was always Alva, stirring them up, spurring them on, from Flanders. A prince, he wrote, who makes a pact with his subjects can never again rely on their obedience; and the granting of spiritual concessions is *a priori* forbidden to him, for that would mean encroachment on the rights of God. Whatever Alva did in Flanders to their co-religionists served as a dreadful warning to the Huguenots. They knew that theirs would be no better fate if once they were to let him set foot on French soil. A few months earlier Count Egmont, the great Flemish leader, had died on the scaffold in Brussels. Would the Queen Mother profit by the example? Had she perhaps made an agreement at Bayonne, after all?

Condé had reorganized his forces, with funds obtained from sales of Church property, taxes from the provinces, subsidies from the rich Reformed town of La Rochelle, English money and cannon, German auxiliaries. All this aid—miraculous after so many set-backs—was due to the Admiral's tireless diplomatic activity. At the beginning of the year 1569, the Huguenot army was ready once again for large-scale campaigning.

The enemy's titular leader was the Duke of Anjou, the future Henry III. The bitterest foe of the Reformation, he had pledged his word not to return to Paris until the adversaries were exterminated. The fame he gained in the months to follow lasted throughout his life; but in reality it was Sieur de Tavannes who was in command.

The tragic battle was that at Jarnac. For there, fighting bravely, the thirty-nine-year-old Prince of Condé lost his life.

His troops suddenly came face to face with the enemy. Though heavily outnumbered, he attacked. In the first onrush his forces broke against Anjou's iron squadron; he rallied the remainder, led them forward again, was thrown back a second time; undaunted, he charged once more—in vain. His vanguard gave way, carrying the rear with it. In the frenzy of swordplay, Condé took no heed and was quickly surrounded, still slashing at everything in reach. He could no longer command, no longer shout; his mouth was full of blood. His horse was shot from under him and

Drawing by Janet

CATHERINE DE' MEDICI
1570

CHARLES IX
King of France

a bullet hit his leg, but he kept on fighting, kneeling on the leg that was unhurt.

In the end, weakened from loss of blood, he had to surrender to two noblemen, who swore to protect his life. The captain of Anjou's guards, Montesquiou, came up. "I am lost if you do not save me," Condé told his captors, but already Montesquiou had raised his pistol. Condé hid his face, like Julius Caesar centuries before, and the shot shattered his head.

The best of the Huguenots went to their deaths with him. The battlefield was strewn with corpses: boys of the families of Saintonge and Poitou, veterans who had fought under Francis I, and many horses. Night fell fast, a bloody, torn sky rapidly bringing impenetrable blackness. Those still alive scattered in all directions; Coligny and Andelot withdrew to St. Jean d'Angély, and Montgomery to Angoulême.

The Duke of Anjou, however, entered Jarnac by torchlight. A drunken, howling band of soldiers led a she-ass with the dead Condé on its back. When the Duke heard of it, he had the body brought to his house and ordered heavy punishment of any further outrage; and a few days later he sent the remains to young Henry of Navarre, the Prince's nephew, for burial at Vendôme in the crypt of his ancestors.

But in Paris, the mob chanted a vile rhyme:

From the fray at Jarnac
The great foe of the Mass
Rode away on the back
Of a little she-ass.

12

THE GREAT RECONCILIATION

A COMRADE-IN-ARMS, faithful to the last breath; a good ship carrying those who trust her until she goes down—such, to the Huguenots, was the town of La Rochelle. France's outstanding port of trade, it lay on rocks which gleamed proudly in the sunlight and for them it was called "the white town." The land around it was fertile; the islands off-shore provided bases for German, English, Flemish, and Breton auxiliaries; its fortifications were impregnable with the siege implements of the time.

Unaided, during the reign of Henry II, La Rochelle had thrown off the English. The feat remained unforgotten: by way of reward, the town received many privileges which it would never yield afterwards. It did not even permit a royal citadel to be constructed within its walls. The townsmen, raised on Atlantic storms, could not understand the vivacious, Catholic-gay Parisians. Most of them early turned to the Reformation. When the Protestant center at Orléans finally fell, and the King had its powerful ramparts leveled, La Rochelle became the new capital of the movement. Less modern, sumptuous, and civilized than Orléans, it was more rugged and war-like. And it was the gateway to England.

Many times in past years the Huguenots had fled to La Rochelle. Now Jeanne d'Albret, herself, arrived there, feeling no longer safe in her modest Béarn on the Spanish border, for an attempt to arrest her had been made. From this new stronghold, new campaigns were launched, St. Jean d'Angély and Niort occupied; from here negotiators, headed by Odet de Châtillon, took ship for England, protected by a small but battle-tried fleet.

After Jarnac, the Huguenots faced a crisis and, when the question arose of who should succeed their beloved Prince, it was in La Rochelle that consultations centered. Would the masses accept Coligny, a petty nobleman, as leader? Condé had been jovial, unrestrained, a soldiers' idol; the Admiral was taciturn and unfathomable, always distant, soft and slow of speech. On the other hand, he was one of the world's most admired men, more famed than the King, in daemonic depth comparable only to Alva. His disciplining of the army was a feat far beyond his time. And he was truly religious, more so than all the rest. He had a direct relation to God; knew more about Him than any of them. He was indispensable—the cement that held the group together and saved them from final collapse.

If he had not been a consistent political realist, Coligny might have aspired at that time to full and exclusive command of the Huguenot forces. But he knew that in war symbols mean more than they do even in peacetime; and so he himself summoned Jeanne d'Albret before the army, that she might give her son, the fifteen-year-old Henry, the place which was his due by birth.

Jeanne arrived in camp with two young princes: her son and that of the murdered Condé, who was a year younger. At Cognac, she mustered and addressed the troops; spoke like a man, tersely, without gestures, pale and gaunt of face, urging them never to desist from battle for the creed. "Friends," she said, "you see that God has not forsaken us. He gave the Prince of Condé valiant fellow-fighters, heroic officers who will take his place and help us surmount his loss." She pointed to the two boys at her side. "I give you two sons to guard, two orphans. Stay with them."

The old warriors were moved. Loss, dejection, discord, all were forgotten. Henry of Navarre—still a child, impatient, and eager to see battle—also made a speech, which rang a little too belligerent and boastful: to the end he would protect the faith, and persist in the defense of the common cause until victory or death decided it. The younger Henry of Condé was much too shy to express himself other than with a helpless gesture.

Thus Henry of Navarre became the head of the Huguenot party. And Queen Jeanne had gold coins struck in memory of the day, with her picture on one side, her son's on the other, and this inscription:

Pax certa, Victoria integra, Mors honesta.

Young Henry's childhood had been spent chiefly at Coarasse Castle, five miles from Pau. He was a country boy, almost a peasant, naïve and provincial, accustomed to climbing the mountainsides bare-foot and bare-headed, and living on hard bread, beef, and cheese. Only once, after the death of his grandfather, had he been to Paris. Then his rough mountain speech and precocity had so amused Henry II that he wanted to have the child continually with him.

"Would you like to be my son?" the King asked.

"Thanks," replied the tot in genuine Béarnais; "I've got a father."

"Well, then, would you like to be my son-in-law?" The marriage thus mentioned in jest was later to be consummated in earnest.

Under the Admiral's guidance, the two princes learned about war. They met danger. In the battle of Moncontour they experienced crushing defeat and fearful slaughter. However, the beaten army recovered quickly, reorganized, seized the Loire regions, and began to threaten Paris itself.

In Paris the Court was deep in deliberations. Things could not go on as they were. Factionalism was ruining the state; even governors were beginning to feel independent. It was an era of incurable political confusion, and the Queen Mother had spun so many webs that she was unable to disentangle them herself. Besides, her son had gradually outgrown her tutelage and was asking—though not often—to be heard and heeded.

Charles IX had slept in his mother's room until he was ten years old. Even as an adult he could bring himself only with difficulty to contradict her. He had learned from her what she could teach: cunning, intrigue, and vindictiveness; and from his environment, all vices and a deep contempt for men.

He was thin and pale, had bloodshot eyes, and was incapable of walking erect—an omen of his chest illness. He had hardly escaped from the prison of his mother's bedroom when he felt the need to convince the world of his power and, lacking real energy, plunged into physical exertions. He became a rabid hunter. He dictated to his secretary, Nicholas de Neufrylle, a treatise on stag-hunting which was republished several times after his death, and he carried on a vast correspondence with all the famous hunters of his time. Catherine gladly left him to this passion. The more he roamed about the woods, the less he could be in her way at Court.

His "sport" was sadistic butchery. Armed only with a hunting-knife, he went after any wild beast. He had to see blood spurting. When he came upon donkeys on the road they were decapitated with one stroke, for the fun of it, and he competed with the royal butchers in pig-sticking. One day he saw his favorite, Sieur de Lanssac, riding a mule, and immediately desired to kill the animal. "But, Most Christian Majesty," Lanssac inquired, "what difference of opinion can exist between you and my mule?" The King blushed and spared the beast.

Strangely mixed with this cruelty was an odd love of music, an almost feminine tenderness toward the lute. Charles had an excellent voice and liked to sing in the choir. He wrote sonnets, composed airs, would argue about ancient civilization and the evolution of the French language; in the evening he enjoyed the company of scholars and poets. He was even capable of feelings that resembled love. Their object was Marie Touchet, daughter of a royal councilor at Orléans, a beautiful, soft-skinned girl with very fair hair—not a French type, rather like a maid of Flanders. He got along, too, with his wife, the Emperor Maximilian's daughter, Elizabeth, but Marie, and the pleasant sojourns at her estate of Belleville, became too much of a habit for him ever to leave her.

It was inevitable that a problem as complex as that posed by the Huguenots would get on the nerves of so primitive and irresponsible a King. He had hoped that his ambitious brother, Anjou, would quickly redeem his pledge and destroy the Protestants. But neither the overwhelming victory at Jarnac nor Condé's welcome death, not even the defeat administered to Coligny at Moncontour, increased the prospect of quiescence. In June of that year, the successes might as well not have been gained. The Admiral was not to be discouraged. Though he had recently lost his faithful brother Andelot and though a price of fifty thousand gold pieces was on his head, he appeared more of a menace than ever.

The Queen Mother's ultra-Catholic policy of the past years had been unlucky. The plans for a Spanish marriage had miscarried, in the face of the Madrid Court's arrogance; she had not even managed to catch the unimportant Portuguese King for her pretty daughter's husband. Letter upon letter had been written, immense bribes had been paid, but she was no nearer her goal. Her maternal vanity was stung; rancor against Spain ate deeply into her heart. A great coup suggested itself to her: an alliance with the Huguenots, a common front against the hated Philip and the Pope! She negotiated even with Elizabeth of England, the arch-Protestant, trying in a most unqueenly manner to talk her into marrying one of her three sons, offering each in turn.

Only then did Madrid become seriously worried. Philip II, aware that he had gone too far in his contempt of the Valois, ordered his Ambassador to France, Francis de Alava, to leave no stone unturned to foil Catherine's plans. Alava chose to be blunt. He told truths to the French Majesties that they had never heard before, and slammed the door behind him when he was finished. King

Charles vowed that he would never, under any circumstances, deign even to converse with heretics; but by an unfortunate coincidence, he had on the day before handed the draft of a treaty to some Protestant delegates, in which the Huguenots were promised freedom of conscience, full amnesty, and cession of two fortified strongholds. The draft, of course, had reached Alava's hands within the hour. He sent it to Philip, along with the report on his interview with the King.

The Ambassador had no better luck with the Queen Mother. She also swore false by her entire Godless heaven. "What can I do, a poor, weak woman?" she cried, tearing her hair, "Who will listen to me? That treaty was submitted to the Council and approved before I even knew of it!"

"I am not surprised," said the Spaniard. "After all, Your Majesty has placed men on the Council who are working hand in glove with the heretics."

Catherine moved close to him and whispered into his ear: "I will tell you the whole truth. I am being thrust aside." She shrugged, sadly. "It is the fate of every mother, when her children grow up."

It was a fact, of course, that there was no country in Europe then which pursued a straight policy. Spain—the same Spain which never stopped urging the Valois to chastise the heretics—tried to get on good terms with heretical England and granted the Moslems a very favorable peace. The same England which on ideological grounds wished to see the Netherlands free withheld aid from them on commercial grounds, dreading Dutch competition as much as the rule of the seas by the Spanish Armada. The German Protestant princes, terrified by the French campaign of annihilation against the Huguenots, kept aloof nevertheless, because at bottom they hated Calvinism more than Catholicism. And Catherine, when the plan of a Portuguese marriage for her daughter had definitely failed, wondered whether to marry the girl to the young Duke of Guise—so as to strengthen the Catholic party—or to young Henry of Navarre, in order to destroy it. Behind the different policies, programs, and slogans of all the European Courts was a single fear: that the monarchies might not be able to maintain themselves against the reactionary power of feudalism and the revolutionary one of the Third Estate.

The idea of a union between Margaret Valois and Henry of Navarre gradually assumed more definite form. Margaret, to be sure, found her intended groom disgusting and did not want even to see him. She was in love with Guise, but now her mother would no longer hear of this infatuation. There were terrible scenes. Once, Catherine so lost control of herself that with the King's help she spanked the stubborn girl. A complete estrangement took place between the Court and the Guises. The Cardinal, abandoning the remainder of his influence, went into seemingly voluntary retirement in his diocese. On July 3, Alava reported to King Philip: "It is certain that a marriage between Princess Margaret and the Prince of Béarn is being negotiated." And he added that this was held out to the Huguenots as a strong inducement for making peace.

Alava's information was correct. The Queen Mother sincerely wanted to conclude the match. For centuries she has been accused of staging a gigantic act of reconciliation to lure the heretics to Paris into a death trap, but her accusers have never offered a shred of evidence. On the other hand, many documents attest to her deep longing for peace, her vindictiveness against Spain, and her constant fear of being overthrown by the Cardinal. She sought to avenge herself on all of them at once by making the impecunious, outlawed Béarnais her son-in-law, over all protests of the powers and regardless of her daughter's dreams.

She did have a scheme in mind, but one quite different from that attributed to her: once young Henry was softened by Court life, she hoped to succeed in weaning him away from Protestantism. This would be a blow from which the Huguenots could not recover. There was another reason, too, why she thought it advisable then to keep them in a friendly mood: Elizabeth of England, having spurned Charles IX, was now to be prevailed upon to marry Catherine's favorite son, the victorious Henry of Anjou. This dream filled her mother's heart with a genuine passion. She used every trick in her bag, and forgot all dignity in her persistent efforts. And Elizabeth, without the slightest intention of tying herself to this much younger man, was skillful enough not to let the glittering bubble burst for quite a long time.

The lonely Coligny, a better statesman than general, saw a great opportunity in the confusion. If the Court could be turned against Spain, might it not also be brought into full alignment with the Huguenots and English, for the liberation of the Spanish Netherlands? The Dutch Protestants under William and Louis of Nassau-Orange were still fighting, undaunted by their defeats at Alva's hands; French and German troops, English money and ships, would enable them to drive the "Bloody Duke" and his inquisitors out of their country. It was not the religious vision alone which obsessed the Admiral's mind. It was also that of finally turning France as well as the Netherlands into free, representatively governed countries.

Courier after courier left Coligny's study in La Rochelle. They went to the Germans, to the Flemish rebels, to spies in Alva's army, to the Counts of Orange, to Geneva. Coligny's truly statesman-like wisdom had raised his party to the level of an independent power, standing beside the Crown and extending far beyond the boundaries of France. This independent power could not tolerate Alva's regime in the Low Countries, entirely aside from its feature of religious persecution. All constitutional privileges had been suspended. Royal Spanish tax-collectors were squeezing the last coins from the poor. Thousands of hard-working citizens, tradesmen, artisans, were being forced to leave the country, those very groups which in France had joined the Huguenot movement. *Vivre en travaillant ou mourir en combattant*—this slogan of future revolutions first appeared here, though still in nebulous form. This, nothing else, was the war aim of the outlawed but untiring Orange. He needed aid; and Coligny grasped the extended hand.

By allying itself officially with the revolt of the Dutch and Flemish towns, the Huguenot movement finally came into the open as the first great prelude to *bourgeois* revolution.

Now the Queen Mother decided to invite the Admiral to Paris, to be her and her son's guest at Court. Coligny hesitated. His friends warned him. His second wife, Jacqueline d'Entremonts, burst into tears and would not let him go. But if his plan was to be carried out, if all

Frenchmen were to be united against Spain, if civil war was to be definitely ended, there seemed to be no choice. Still, he first sent his son-in-law, Téligny, to the capital.

The Court not only received Téligny with full honors but immediately entered into serious discussions with him. Coligny heard, too, that Count Louis of Orange had been cordially received and was daily closeted with the King. He learned with satisfaction that Marshal Francis Montmorency, the Constable's son who favored conciliation, was gaining in influence. And Catherine requested Papal dispensation for the proposed political marriage: "For We set great store by this marriage, for the peace of Our Kingdom, hoping also to win the aforesaid Prince for Our religion." Téligny, for his part, assured the King that his father-in-law, if called to administer the government, would restore the national credit: he had drawn up a detailed plan for paying off all debts in three years, without touching Church property or robbing the population.

On August 12, the King and his mother traveled to Blois, to meet Coligny. In La Rochelle, the Admiral's friends still advised against the trip; letters of warning, from people stating they had authoritative information of plots against him, piled up on his desk. But he said he had often deferred to the views of others; this time he asked them to trust his own decision.

And indeed, his reception at Court was beyond expectations. He wanted to kneel before the monarch, but Charles forestalled the gesture and took him in his arms. "At last I've got you!" the King exclaimed. "I've got you, and I'll not let you leave me again! This is the happiest day of my life."

Coligny met the same gracious treatment at the hands of

the Queen Mother and all the dignitaries present. For days the event occasioned brilliant celebrations. But not all hearts were glad. To many, the triumph seemed unreal, a phantom against a background of evil premonitions. The Duke of Montpensier, a great Huguenot-hater himself, met Coligny one night in the palace yard at Blois and could not hold back a word of warning. "How little you care about your life," he said, "going about here without a guard. You don't seem to know what kind of people you are dealing with."

The Admiral thanked him, smilingly. "After all, I am in the house of my King and master."

"Quite so, but how much longer will the King be master in his house?"

13

ST. BARTHOLOMEW'S DAY

COLIGNY was at the peak of his career. In May of the year everything seemed already won for him. Elizabeth, having broken completely with Philip, concluded a protective treaty. The Prince of Orange, with English and Huguenot support, fanned the flames of revolt in the Netherlands and took Valenciennes and Mons; the conflagration spread through Holland, Zeeland, Utrecht, and Upper Yssel; a French fleet rallied against Spain. The twenty-two-year-old, sallow, coughing King Charles had eyes and ears for the Admiral alone, sat talking with him far into the night, and waxed enthusiastic about his plans. Since the time of Constable Montmorency under Henry II, no man had wielded such influence at Court. And there followed even greater favors: the King ordered 200,000 livres to be paid the Admiral out of the treasury, to reimburse him for his losses during the civil war, and assigned to him for one year the income of his late brother—Cardinal de Châtillon, recently deceased in exile—which had been confiscated as rebel property.

And Catherine? So far, she alone had managed her son. It was her boast that while she had not always borne the crown she had always borne the burden of the government. And here a man who had been outlawed, sentenced to death *in contumaciam*, was in a position of complete authority and setting France against the Catholic powers. Catherine, who had become Queen over Spanish objections, did not love the Spaniards; but their principles were hers. To break with Spain would mean to break with the Pope; and although lately, in a vengeful mood, she had played with such dangerous ideas, she would never dare approach them seriously.

Meanwhile an eighteen-year-old prince was traveling through France, carefree as a bird, at the head of a long procession of cavaliers, coaches and pedestrians: Henry of Navarre, the son of Jeanne d'Albret. His goal was Paris, where he was to marry the sister of the King of France. It was like a fairy-tale. The country folk who saw the glittering train greeted the Béarnais jubilantly. For these people of Poitou had gone through so much, suffered so horribly under royal lansquenets, Protestant rebels, and adventurers from the world over, that they knew what peace would mean for them. And the young prince, who so far had known only danger and distress, was happy.

His bride-to-be, Margaret or Marguerite—she liked to be called Margot—was eighteen too, beautiful, chic, witty, educated, admired. She would probably be anything but tyrannical, for she loved her freedom; she would prize the right to her own little affairs too much to object to his. Love would be no different from war; one must wait and see how it would turn out. Never mind those worried, excited letters from his mother, who had been most unfavorably impressed by the negotiations with Catherine and the King. How besmirched she felt by all the malice and the dirt! How she exaggerated everything! He would not let her spoil his mood now. He would take what came his way on his parade to Paris; country girls are no prudes, at least not with a prince.

But in Chauny a runner brought sad news; his mother had died. It was June 9.

Jeanne had been carried off by a sudden illness in Paris, where she had gone for the wedding preparations. Immediately a rumor spread that she had been poisoned—a rumor which has persisted though it was never proved and altogether is not very probable. Whatever the truth, from this day on the political changes, noticeable during the preceding weeks, were apparent. The Queen Mother launched a determined drive to make war with Spain impossible. Circumstances played into her hands. A Spanish sea victory off Lepanto had increased Philip's military prestige; it seemed dangerous to cross him. In July the Huguenot leader, Genlis, had suffered a fearful defeat at the hands of Alva; more than 3,000 men had died on the field and the rest, in flight, were beaten to death by peasants. England withdrew from the alliance, while the Germans kept discreetly aloof. And the Parisians were murmuring that they would no longer put up with a heretic as the King's most influential adviser.

The height attained by the Admiral for so short a time lay behind him. Catherine sensed it. She turned each reversal into a point for argument. But the King was still so greatly under Coligny's influence that he would rather have parted with her than with him. It was a stubborn struggle for the consumptive Charles, who could neither free himself from his mother nor from the Admiral, who would debate all night, fly into rages, and then cry like a child at Marie Touchet's. Coligny was bursting with impatience; daily he heard of new executions and sadistic oppression of his co-religionists by Alva, the great enemy. If help was not rushed to them immediately, they were lost. The aid promised by the pious Palatine Elector, Frederick, was checkmated by the desertion of the Elector of Saxony, who had lined up with the Emperor. God! with their little politics they were forgetting the true, the great politics. If Spain were to subdue the Netherlands for good, there would be an end to freedom in the rest of Europe.

Naturally the Catholics were marshaling all their strength. The ambassadors of the Italian states—Venice, Savoy, and Florence—displayed a violent activity; Emperor Maximilian wrote his son-in-law letters of protest; the German Catholics of Trier, Cologne, and Bavaria supported Alva. The Guises returned to Court, where the widow of Francis de Guise, now married to the Duke of Nemours, renewed her demands for vengeance. It was Catherine who was the will, brain, and spirit of the party. She loathed Coligny for having wormed his way so deeply into the royal confidence that even after an adverse decision of the Council he dared to work for the liberation of the Dutch. She hated him for still another reason: as long as he lived, she would never be able to turn young Henry of Navarre away from Protestantism. She consulted the Duchess of Nemours, who had a ready answer: kill the Admiral. The two were agreed and informed the young Duke of Guise, and he again thought they could safely ask Anjou, Catherine's favorite son, to join them.

"Who shall do it?" the Duchess asked.

"You," replied her son.

The very thought shows how this woman, Italian like

Catherine, must have hated the Admiral. She would never believe that it was not he who had had her husband murdered before Orléans. Of course she declined to strike the blow herself, but she promised to find the right person.

Margaret Valois was married without Papal dispensation in Notre-Dame on August 18, 1572.

The King of Navarre and his retinue doffed their mourning and donned gorgeous raiment. Margaret, with the crown on her head, was covered from top to toe with precious stones. She wore a sky-blue cloak and a train, four ells long, borne by three princesses. But she was in bad humor, this little *mondaine*, said to be the most charming of French women. This marriage had been forced on her by her brothers, who would otherwise have poisoned her, and she, the greatest voluptuary of her age, loved life too dearly for that. The clumsy provincial was not in the least to her liking, and during the entire ceremony she said not a word to him, but threw loving glances at her latest favorite, La Molle. She did not even find it worth while to make her responses. The bride's mood may have been infectious. There were balls, theatrical performances, fireworks; but, strangely, the whole atmosphere in Paris was depressed. When the wedding guests returned to the Louvre, the crowd burst into cheers—for the House of Guise. Coligny's friends urged him to go away, but the Admiral replied that the Protestant quarters in Paris had asked him to stay and he could not leave them unprotected.

The festivities were hardly over when Catherine deemed the moment ripe to strike.

On the evening of August 21 a certain Maurevel, a well-tested tool in the hands of criminals, was brought to the house of Canon Villemur, a former teacher of the Duke of Guise; Coligny passed this house every day on his way to services. The Canon's maid-servant hid Maurevel in her chamber for the night, and in the morning, as Coligny turned the corner, a shot rang out. From behind a curtain draped over the window, Maurevel threw his weapon on a table and leaped on a horse that was held in the garden for him. It turned out that he had not killed Coligny, the bullet having lodged in the Admiral's arm. Several of his retinue rushed into the house but found only the smoking gun. Coligny was taken home, and the King of Navarre came there at once. Everywhere, in chambers and ante-chambers, excited, horrified Huguenots stood about, unanimously accusing the Dukes of Guise and Anjou. Their indignation grew as they talked; some even wanted to storm the Louvre and kill Guise. Others held them back, lest a still greater calamity befall the Protestants.

The King, as a historian has noted, looked like a corpse, himself, when he heard the news. "My friend," he said to the Admiral at his bedside, "you have the wound and I the pain."

Charles was in unwelcome company, with Catherine, his two brothers, and a few rascally devotees of the Queen Mother. Coligny asked to be left alone with the King. He had some counsel to give him before his death. Weakened by loss of blood and beset by a raging fever, he struggled to remain conscious. Hastily, in a broken voice, he begged the King to rule alone and never again to trust his mother or any of her friends.

Since her plan had failed, the Queen Mother knew what to expect: the avenging revolt of the Huguenots. She knew, too, that it would have to be forestalled, at a single blow. At noon that same day she summoned her friends to a conference in the King's chamber. She instructed her confidants well; a second failure was out of the question. Gondy, a favorite who went through thick and thin, a henchman on principle, undertook to persuade the King of the existence of a Huguenot plot from which the would-be assassins had tried to save him. The King found the company in well-simulated excitement, but it took two hours and some forged evidence to convince him. When even then he would not consent to the use of force, Catherine put on a magnificent display of sustained weeping. She would go back to Italy, to spend the rest of her days in exile, in a convent, if the plotters were not finally punished for the misery they had brought on France. She kept this up until the exhausted and tortured King cried: "All right—but then kill them all, every one of them!" and ran from the room.

Late in the evening of August 23, the Provost of Merchants, Charron, and his predecessor, Marcel, were called to the Louvre. The King asked how many citizens in Paris could be counted on for blind obedience. Marcel explained that this depended on how much time he had; in a month's time he could guarantee 100,000 men.

"How many if I need them today?"

"Today? Twenty thousand."

Charron was ordered to arm them at their quarters and to close the gates of the city. It was decided to spare the two Princes of the Blood, Navarre and Condé. The other victims were put on lists distributed to all officers who were reliable. For himself and his friends, the Duke of Guise demanded the distinction of being allowed to kill the Admiral.

Deep quiet reigned in Paris for several hours.

Catherine could not sleep. She made those who had not been let into the secret stay in their rooms, out of contact with the others. She had a long talk with her daughters. Margaret knew nothing, but her sister, the Duchess of Lorraine, clung to her, whimpering and afraid to let her go to sleep. Catherine also visited her son again, probably to make sure he had not changed his mind. Ever at her heels was the Duke of Anjou, who, with Henry de Guise, had undertaken the organization of the crime. It was an eerie, oppressively hot August night.

At three in the morning the great bell rang from the tower of St. Germain-l'Auxerrois, and the killing began.

The mob poured into the streets, howling: "The King wishes it! The King commands it!" Doors were forced, windows smashed, people were slain with swords, daggers, rifle butts, bare hands. Trust in the King's hospitality had brought the Huguenots to Paris; now they were set upon in bed, at table, in the street, and cut down without distinction—master and servant and woman and child. Inhuman noises filled the air: shouting, screaming, yelling and, in between, again and again, the bells—the sacred bells that gave the treacherous sign.

Before the Admiral's house, the Duke of Guise was already waiting with his band of killers. They tore at the bell, the gatekeeper stepped out, and collapsed, stabbed. Of the five Swiss guards whom the King of Navarre had left for the Admiral's protection, one was shot down; the others retreated and barricaded the door leading to the stairs. The servants woke up and came running in terror, but Coligny, rising and dressing quickly, told them to save themselves: "I know what is in store for me. I commend my soul to God." They fled, all except his faithful valet. The door gave way, and the first to enter the room was a young fellow named Besme.

"Are you the Admiral?"

"Do as you were told."

The assassin ran a sword through the Admiral. The others finished the task, each plunging his dagger into the body.

"Done?" Guise called from the street.

"Yes," answered Besme.

"Throw him down, then."

The murdering louts opened the window and tossed the corpse into the street, where Guise had the Admiral's head cut off. They did a complete job in the house, killing Téligny, the son-in-law, Guerchy, his lieutenant, Colonels Montaumar and Rouvray, and every servant they could find.

Meanwhile the executioners, wearing white armbands and white crosses on their hats, ran wild through the streets, killing every one found without similar badges, breaking into every house not marked with chalk. On the right bank of the Seine, near the Louvre, where the streets ran sharply downhill, blood flowed in streams. Windows shone eerily, shadows flitted from one to the next as if ghosts were chasing one another; and still the bells tolled on, from every spire now.

In the beginning the leaders kept to their lists, but soon they were unable to prevent people from massacring any one they wished to kill. There were Catholics who perished too. Private grudges were satisfied. Ramus, the most famous scholar of the Sorbonne, who had rendered immortal service to that institution, was murdered by a colleague with whom he had a scientific feud. Tavannes, the victor of Jarnac, rushed through the streets with his sword unsheathed, screaming: "Bleed them! Bleeding is as healthy in August as in May." The Commander of the Guards drew his men up in the Louvre courtyard, had the Huguenots called from their bedrooms, and had them struck down with lances as they appeared. In this manner the Count of Rochefoucauld died, as did the Chancellor of the King of Navarre, the Marquis of Renel, and two hundred others.

Only a few Huguenots escaped. Some, who lived in the suburb of St. Germain, managed to flee before the mob there had been instructed. Among them were Montgomery and the Prior of Chartres. Montgomery, considered as second to Coligny and the latter's successor, was awakened by the sound of bells and shots, and immediately grasped the situation. He leaped on his horse just as Guise and the Duke of Aumale came rushing up. Luckily, he had a better mount than either of them, and they had to pursue him in the gory dawn to the village of Mont-l'Amaury, where their horses collapsed. Another Huguenot, a youth named La Force, managed to save himself only by lying beneath the corpses of his father and brother for a whole day.

Only rarely was it pity that saved a man. In the Louvre a young fellow, already wounded, fled from room to room before the killers, opening one door after another, until he stood before Margaret of Navarre, trembling in her nightgown, with her hair undone. He threw himself into her arms and they fell on the bed together. Margaret had never seen the man. And the soldiers would not have yielded even to her pleas had not the captain of the Royal

Guard arrived and burst out laughing at the tragi-comic spectacle. He spared the knight's life, and Margaret, her nightgown soaked with blood, hid him in her closet. She still did not know what was happening and, hastily putting on a cloak, ran to her sister. There, three steps away, soldiers were thrusting their halberds into a nobleman named Bourse.

Some contemporary writers—even Brantôme, who was so abjectly tied to the Court—report that Charles IX stood at a window of the Louvre and shot at the fleeing Huguenots, screaming incessantly like a madman: "Kill! Kill!" It is not improbable. For, after all, this man who had sat admiringly at Coligny's feet was the same who beheaded mules for the pleasure of it and had acquired mastery in pig-sticking.

The next day the Louvre remained closed. A strange silence reigned, and the black gates looked as if they had not been opened for years.

The King did not leave his room until shortly before noon, looking green and unwashed. He and his mother summoned Henry of Navarre and the Prince of Condé; neither, at first, was able to say a word. Catherine attempted to justify the bloody night. She had acted only in self-defense. Far be it from her and her sons to blame the Princes for the evil plans of the Huguenots; their youth deserved indulgence and one could promise them their lives. More, even: if they embraced the Catholic faith they would be loved and honored. Navarre feigned abject submission. He would obey the King's command, if his last wish were granted and the few of his men who had not died were pardoned. The King consented. The Prince of Condé, wilder, more rash, less diplomatic than his cousin, resisted strongly. He shrieked into the King's face that this murderous deed was a disgrace for a monarch. "It will not go unpunished, Sire," he blurted out, "I shall see to that!" The King shouted him down, shouted louder and louder; finally, no longer knowing what he was shouting, he drew a dagger to stab the Prince. His mother held him back. In the end, he presented Condé with an ultimatum: become a Catholic within three days, or die.

On his mother's advice, the King appeared before the *parlement* on August 26 and assumed sole responsibility for the dreadful night. At the same time new orders to kill were carried swiftly from town to town to the provincial governors. Thus began the massacres of Meaux, La Charité, Orléans, Saumur, Lyon, Bourges, Toulouse, Bordeaux. Some governors, to be sure, declined to obey the orders, among them Montmorency, the lord of the Ile de France. The King's command was most sharply rejected by the hangman of Troyes, who refused to undertake the executions because "it was not his profession to kill without a sentence." According to conservative estimates, 2,000 people died in Paris and 20,000 in France. Some guesses go as high as 70,000. Even after formal orders had been issued to desist, the unleashed fury blazed forth again and again. The blood that had been spilled had not quenched the thirst but awakened it. Stories, rumors, superstitions, ghost-mongering, and a general dread of revenge filled the heated minds.

In Rome, however, Pope Gregory XIII had the bloodbath celebrated jubilantly. The messenger who first brought the good news received a thousand talers, and a *Te Deum* was sung before the whole College of Cardinals. Gregory requested the French Ambassador to inform his

King that the events in Paris had delighted him more than fifty victories like that of Lepanto. The city was illuminated, a great procession arranged, and a medal struck in commemoration of the event.

Philip II was pleased too. But his pleasure was more plainly of a political kind, and his extravagant congratulations had an undertone of irony. What greater stupidity could the French King have committed? He had deprived himself of his warriors most fanatically opposed to Spain, forfeited the favor of every Protestant in the world, and lost his German, Dutch, and English alliances. He stood alone against the might of Spain. Philip, who had never laughed, now smiled.

And Charles IX himself? He was sick, spat blood, sobbed suddenly during conversations or at games, and had to be comforted by his nurse. He aged alarmingly, according to the Venetian Ambassador. He no longer enjoyed the hunt or music and, when addressed, lowered his head, never raising his eyes. About a week after the massacre, in the middle of the night, he called for his brother-in-law, young Henry of Navarre, who found him standing barefoot beside his bed, pointing with outstretched arm to the dark corners of the room and asking: "Do you hear? Do you hear?" To Henry, too, it seemed as if he heard crying, howling, sighing voices in the distance. They both thought new riots had broken out, and sent for news. But nowhere had anything been heard. The city lay in deepest silence.

The sun rises, Paris opens its gates, the night watchman snuffs out his lantern, market carts rumble along the streets, soldiers drill, workmen tie their aprons on, and the Queen

Mother, incredible as it may sound, still wonders how to play Catholics and Protestants against each other and stay on good terms with both. Her letters to her ambassadors go on as usual. She continues with the old plan of placing Anjou, spurned by Elizabeth of England, on the Polish throne, which the impending extinction of the Jagello dynasty would leave vacant. The same negotiations go forward to further a match between her youngest, Alençon, and Elizabeth. Hopes had long been cherished to fool the Protestants with some threadbare edict, and Catherine issues one. While it prohibits sermons and meetings, it seems to grant individual freedom of conscience. With all her cunning, Catherine is incorrigibly naïve, thinking it possible that people might still trust her.

The fact that the Huguenots, even before St. Bartholomew's, were weary of war and insecurity had been shown by their increasing readiness to compromise. The generation whose glowing élan was represented by the late Prince of Condé, which stormed, psalm-singing, against the walls of Paris and wanted all or nothing, had aged, and the new one had other ideas already. It sought to water down the revolutionary firmness of its elders; the hard, thin-lipped, joyless combativeness of Jeanne d'Albret was never wholly understood by her son. It is always like that: a generation is effective for about thirty years, but as its second half comes under the influence of the next one, no revolution lasts in its initial vigor for more than fifteen.

Against their will, the Huguenots were forced to recognize that their longing for quiet and work had been premature. Their host of martyrs proved that the government was aiming at their destruction. The Queen Mother's edict was a farce. No, it was better to die in battle than to be stabbed or strangled in bed. The adversaries were still raging. Long after the bloodbath, the prisoners in the Louvre were arraigned before a corrupt tribunal and sentenced to be quartered. After his headless corpse was strung up on a gallows, the Admiral was branded as a heretic and rebel, his castle of Châtillon razed, and his wife and children were about to be seized when they made a quick flight to Geneva. If one did not want to perish altogether, one had to fight more implacably than before. So it was that the Protestant towns of La Rochelle, Nîmes, and Sancerre, as well as a number of smaller places, refused to admit royal troops; and that Charles IX raised four armies against La Rochelle, with Anjou in command.

During all this time the efforts to convert the King of Navarre and the Prince of Condé continued. They were belabored from dawn till dusk by their uncle, pious Cardinal de Bourbon, and instructed by the Jesuit Maldonat. The King of Navarre did not resist long, whether out of diplomacy or out of the wish to avoid more bloodshed among his followers; but the Prince of Condé proved himself a true son of his father. He was intractable, disregarded each time limit set for submission, cocked his head in boyish arrogance at Charles, and did not trouble to answer him. At last he was sternly told: "You'll go to Mass or to the gallows. Which shall it be?"

The Princes were led to Mass. They were forced to write letters to the Pope asking for absolution, and also to their former co-religionists explaining how deeply they were now convinced of the fallacy of Calvin's doctrine. There was no Protestant in France who did not know what to think of their "voluntary" confession, or of the

King's particular piece of malice which required the Princes to join the army besieging La Rochelle.

And what an army it was! All the leaders disagreed with one another. Even the Catholic generals were disgusted at having to serve under Coligny's assassin. The memory of the blood that had been shed disturbed their social pleasures. They thought they saw drops of it on the gambling-table, on young Guise's rolling dice, and the game broke up amid general horror

How different it was in the beleaguered town! Every one in La Rochelle knew there was more at stake than life or death. By orders of the Burgomaster, Jacob Heinrichs, the citizens were divided into eight companies of 200 men each. The town council formed a company of its own, 150 strong; 1,500 veteran volunteers and numbers of noblemen hurried in from the neighboring districts. As drill and work on the fortifications went on, more than fifty priests went about, preaching and exhorting the people to stand fast. Prudently, munitions and artillery had been hoarded, powder-mills built, and provisions stored. La Rochelle was ready for a long siege. And, as though Fate itself had lent its aid, the King committed a surprising blunder.

One of the bravest Huguenots under Coligny had been La Noue. At the time of the massacre he had been fighting in Hainaut and thus escaped death. When he had been forced to retreat before Alva he sought the protection of his old friend, the Duke of Longueville. La Noue was so highly thought of by both parties for bravery and integrity, and for his earnest love of peace that Longueville ventured to introduce him to the King, for the purpose of frankly discussing the possibilities of reaching some agreement. The King suggested to La Noue that he go to La Rochelle and, by promising the townsmen the maintenance of their privileges, persuade them to submit. La Noue consented.

He met the delegates of La Rochelle in a nearby village. They ignored his greeting. "We were invited to negotiate with La Noue," they said, "but you are not La Noue." He tried to re-establish their former friendly footing but in vain. "It doesn't matter that the person here looks like La Noue if he is a man of quite a different character." La Noue pointed to his artificial arm, reminding them that he had lost his own in battle for the common cause. They replied coldly: "We gratefully remember the services of La Noue, and that is why we cannot believe that you and he are one and the same."

His request to be allowed to enter the town and speak to the people themselves was granted. La Rochelle received him joyfully but would not hear of peace proposals. When he was given a choice between boarding a ship bound for England and living in the town as a private individual he cried, with tears in his voice: "There is a third way: let me lead you! Trust me! Put me in command and you will see that I am the old La Noue!" From that day La Rochelle defended itself with a ferocious strength. Women, too, took part in the fighting. The sallies of the militia went so far into the royal encampment that several positions, already taken by Anjou, had to be yielded.

A single town withstood the power of the realm, but naturally its situation grew worse every day. The doom of the Huguenots would have been but a question of time had not—once again!—the unexpected happened to avert it: in this case, the choice by the Poles of Anjou for their King, on May 9, 1573. Immediately, the Duke lost all interest in La Rochelle, Catholicism, or military fame. It was a splendid excuse to end the boring siege, and he hurriedly opened negotiations and signed, without closely reading it, an edict granting religious freedom to the leading Protestant towns. Then he set off with his army for Paris and presented to the Court the accomplished fact.

At that time Henry of Anjou—of whom French history still unfortunately has much to tell—was twenty years old. He is said to have had a noble bearing, attractive features, and the most beautiful hands in France. But he was no more than a young fop, vain and perfumed, ill-mannered and effeminate, cunning and slothful. He spoke in an affected manner, moved softly, dressed with a woman's finesse. His coats and cloaks were embroidered with emeralds and pearls; his hair was delicately curled and powdered, and almost daily he set new styles for underclothing. Both his ear lobes were pierced, and hanging from them were pendants of pearls. He had a passion for lap-dogs and yearly spent more than 100,000 gold ducats on them.

When he started for Poland, on September 28, Charles IX accompanied him to the frontier—not out of affection, but to be quite sure that he was really rid of his brother. At Villers-Cotterets the King was met by a delegation of Protestants. They brought a petition begging him in impassioned words to give some effect, at last, to the freedom of conscience now granted only on paper. Catherine, who was with her sons, was beside herself. "If Condé were alive and had 70,000 men and the strongest towns, he would ask half of what these rogues have the insolence to demand." There was no quieting her and the Huguenots preferred to beat a retreat. A sudden illness prevented the King from traveling further, but the Queen Mother continued as far as Lorraine. She found it hard to part from her favorite son. She embraced him tenderly: "Go, my son. I take comfort in the knowledge that you will not stay long."

Henry's retinue numbered 1,200 persons. The further he got into Germany, the colder his reception was; in Speyer, where the people were waiting with arms, streets had to be closed by means of chains to assure his safety. The most distressing experience was his arrival in Heidelberg. When he rode into Count Frederick's courtyard, the place was dark and no one came to greet him. The old Count excused himself as being ill. In the room assigned to the guest, a painting hung opposite the bed: the murder of Coligny. Henry turned away, and saw himself suddenly surrounded by German Protestant nobles who stared at him in silent reproach. In the morning the Palatine Elector himself led him before the picture, and pointed to the portrait of the Admiral: "You have murdered the greatest general in Christendom, a man who rendered you and the King great services." Henry offered the alleged plot as explanation, but the old man interrupted him with: "Thank you. We know better," and left the room.

It soon turned out that the Queen Mother had been right. The events of the past years had undermined Charles's health. He grew emaciated; soon, he was so weak that he could no longer stand on his feet. He suffered a hemorrhage. In a testament, he implored his mother to attend conscientiously to the affairs of the realm until his successor, the King of Poland, returned. In the last days of May his condition took a turn for the worse, and the physician forbade the sick-room to every one but the patient's former nurse, of whom, though she was a Huguenot, Charles was fonder than of his whole family.

On the anniversary of St. Bartholomew's, when she tried to leave his room, the King screamed like a child: "Don't go away! They want to kill me!" He buried his head in the pillows and sobbed, racked by remorse. When she leaned over him to ask if there was anything he wanted, he groaned: "How much blood, how much blood!"

"Sire," the woman consoled him, "the deeds will be visited upon those who made you commit them. God will forgive you."

He died the next day.

14

THE THIRD PARTY

JUDGING French history in these decades by events alone, one cannot fail to get the impression that the whole nation was actuated by blind hate. It was almost like that, but not quite.

The Venetian Ambassador to the French Court reported that all intelligent men, no matter of what denomination, were horrified at the massacre and ashamed of it. Though these men did not forsake the old religion, they recognized the Reformation as the rational individual's protest against mass convention—as his demand to be held responsible for his thoughts and actions, in sharp contrast to the Church's claim to relieve him of that responsibility. It was recognized, too, that this sovereignty of the individual would some day come to pass, just as would the sovereignty of the people.

As always in times of crisis, when private conflicts become unimportant and even unreal, contemporary writers occupied themselves almost exclusively with this question of individual sovereignty. It naturally made little headway among the masses, but enlightened readers agreed and were passionately interested. Of the long list of names on the roster of such brave intellectual champions, the most important was that of a Frenchman of German origin, Francis Hotman. He had escaped being murdered in 1572, was a professor of law in Strassburg, a great scholar, a flaming political writer, a restless and revolutionary zealot, often vain, often rash, but true to the cause he served. In his principal work, the *Franco-Gallia,* he recalled the old Frankish times when the people in mass elected the King, and pointed out that free people were not meant to submit to despotism. The *States-General,* he contended, stood above the King. The highest power, *le pouvoir souverain,* belonged in the hands of the people who elected him, with certain stipulations, and if he did not fulfill them, he could be deposed like any one else. Hotman's ideas were not new. They had been advocated in Italy and discussed in France even in the reign of Henry II. But in Hotman's work they were for the first time methodically presented and logically founded, and their effect was enormous. His theses penetrated even down to the illiterate, became common property to such an extent that the Court considered them a danger and fought them with counterblasts and pulpit propaganda.

Gradually the character of this upheaval became clear. The Reformation was no mere deviation from Catholic dogma, it was a political struggle. The results, shown in the secularization of Church lands, as demanded by the notables at Fontainebleau and the preachers in Poissy and carried out by the Huguenots in every district under their control, were revolutionary. The sale of these lands and the distribution of the proceeds among the poor signified a sweeping change; an immense wealth was released from mortmain to flow into economic life.

The full import of this change became clear when it was

enforced in an entire country, England. There the Church was radically expropriated. More than two-thirds of the nation's total real property had been in the hands of the Church. By turning monks and those others of the population who had lived on alms out into the street, millions of hands, accustomed to leisure and idleness, were brought into the general process of labor. This huge mass of new labor, voluntary or forced, caused unforeseen alterations in the social structure. The problem of paupers assumed a new aspect, for there were now two kinds of them in England: those who under Catholic rule had lived on alms and those who had distributed the alms. Their number was so great that new laws and regulations had to be made to cope with them. The majority stubbornly refused to work; the others could not find work. What was to become of disorderly people who went begging from door to door?

One must visualize this situation. The stroke of the pen by which England dissolved the monasteries created more than fifty thousand new public charges who were accustomed neither to work nor to subordination within the community. Working society did not know what to do with them. Although conditions in France were different, because secularization there had not been carried out to any such large extent, the problems were the same. Erasmus tells us that even before the reforms, poverty had reached inconceivable proportions. He describes floorless houses that stuck into the muddy ground like caves, beds that consisted of bundles of rarely changed straw, logs of wood that served as pillows. And Fortescue, who made several journeys through France, reported about the country people: "They drink water, eat apples they find on the ground.

make a black bread for themselves of rye, and do not know what meat is."

Now, though attempts were made to help these very poorest of the poor by selling Church lands and using the proceeds for the general welfare, there was no denying the fact that idle monks and former recipients of alms formed a new host of beggars. Distress grew instead of diminishing—inevitable fate of revolutions! By upsetting an order no longer worthy of the name, to set up a new and more rational one, chaos was first achieved. And yet history shows that catastrophes are overcome, that the final results, compared with earlier conditions, always constitute a definite step forward.

It is hard to exaggerate how much misery France would have been spared had the Reformed movement kept its promise and captured the bulk of the people, the working masses. There was less and less talk of taxes as burdens upon peasants and artisans. Whereas the Calvinist nobles had once called themselves "blackguards of quality, to whom thieving and killing are as food and drink," they gradually gave up self-criticism. With ever-lessening conviction they fought the expropriation of the peasants, which under the last Valois spread like wildfire. They showed far more zeal in the defense of their own position against increasing centralization.

Perhaps the country, not yet ripe for the new ideas, could not sustain any further steps of economic revolution. Perhaps decades of irregular warfare had exhausted its substance. We cannot tell now. An epoch can be judged only by its own standards and not from the point of view of later knowledge. In any case, so many tolerant and intelligent groups had become convinced that France was lost if it kept rending itself, that they gradually took the form of a third or middle party. They sought a reconciliation of extremes, a compromise which would lead the country back to united endeavor for the common weal. They were known as the "Politicians."

How did this party come into being?

First, through controversy. The proposition discussed was that national interests were more important than religious ones. In the view of growing numbers, the country could be saved only by religious tolerance; a continuation of religious war was bound to ruin it. This, of course, was evident. Who would deny it? Certainly not the people, except for those who were bribed, seduced, or deceived.

Two professors, Jean Charpentier and Denis Lambin, held public meetings which attracted large audiences. After all, were not the two scholars right? Would it not be more sensible to have order again, perhaps even enjoy a little prosperity, instead of getting bloody heads all the time on the Protestants' account? More and more men of stature thought along these lines. It was at the house of ex-Chancellor L'Hospital, mentioned before as a man of conciliation, that the new faction, "Le Troisième Parti," was founded.

Outstanding among its leaders were the Constable's two sons. In his old age, Anne de Montmorency had often wondered whether it was wise to turn the Protestants over to the fire and the rack, doubting whether his fanatical Catholicism had been the best way to serve the state. When his sons thumped the table and thundered against the Guises, their arch-enemies, when they shouted: "The

Guises are murderers, they are ruining the realm!" the old man did not always contradict them. Although he himself stayed in the fight against the Reformation to his dying day, he understood what they meant. "Perhaps you're right. I'll certainly do nothing to hinder whatever you do."

His older son, Francis de Montmorency, who had fallen heir to the marshalship, became the head of the new faction. But it was his younger brother, Henry, who had inherited the governorship of Languedoc, who was to be of the greater importance. He called himself Henry Damville after his family seat, and is known by that name in history. He was a real man, hewn from a single block. His sympathies, which were moderate, did not bloom from one day to the next, and, moreover, were anything but stable at the outset. He defended them against his father but this did not prevent him from manifesting orthodox intolerance a few years later. Ambition, no doubt, played a prominent part in these shifts.

Damville became governor in his middle twenties. He knew exactly what he wanted. He wanted to rule like an independent sovereign in the south of the realm, with the anemic Valois mixing as little as possible in his affairs. It was Catherine who sensed that he was dangerous and made the mistake of sending him away from Court, down to Languedoc, where he was expected to re-establish the royal authority. Damville, a resplendent, courtly, chivalrous young gentleman, set out with full entourage and decided first to establish his own authority. He rode from town to town in his domain, receiving homage everywhere, and petitions from deputies and presents from officials. After a close inspection of Toulouse, his chief Catholic city, and Montpellier, the chief Protestant one, he set out to buttress his position with the Catholics, by treating the Huguenots with such outstanding brutality that complaints about him reached the Court.

When his rule was secure, Damville changed his tactics. He began by receiving the Protestants, to talk things over. By 1568, at the outbreak of the third religious war—when the Guises, the foreigners whom he despised more than anyone, were back in power—he had become a full-fledged member of the Politicians. Coligny, aware that this uncrowned King of Southern France would never be a Protestant, was contented with his adherence to the moderate group.

1573 arrived, and the siege of La Rochelle. Damville's brother, Marshal Montmorency, head of the Third Party since St. Bartholomew's, became the center of discontent in the besieging army. The Queen Mother had him arrested, and Damville replied by officially putting Catholics and Protestants on an equal plane in Languedoc. He even gave them equal rights to government positions, a move which made him the sensation of France and automatically the new leader of the Politicians.

He had matured by then. He knew now what he had only sensed before. He was in constant touch with eminent theologians in both camps but remained convinced that there had to be a unity of state, monarch, and people. He boasted of this unity: "I could bring it about more quickly than you think." When he was reminded of the Valois he replied that if they could not grasp the truism, if they kept rekindling the civil war, so much the worse for them. His own Languedoc, at any rate, was to be spared the misery.

Damville maintained that Catherine was behind attempts

to put him out of the way. Her emissaries were not allowed to come near him. He had a bodyguard of men personally loyal to him; he had a tamed wolf without which he never left the house; he shared a room with the giant Captain Aragon, the strongest man in France. The Queen Mother tried to transfer the governorship of Languedoc to another, but Damville sent the man back to her with his respects, and bound his province even more closely to himself by a simultaneous alliance with both religious parties. The Huguenots in Languedoc had organized themselves after the massacre and seized the best towns and castles, and Damville found a dependable following in them. When he demanded the renewal of the peace edicts, he had the support not only of them but of the Catholic nobles who were tired of senseless feuds. An almost independent power grew up in the south and southeast of the realm: Catholics and Protestants lived side by side, not without friction but without threat of hostilities. One was tempted to think the world could get along in peace.

When Anjou, in distant Poland, heard of his brother's death, he quit his kingdom in the dead of night. He left the palace in Cracow on his best horse, secretly and alone. His subjects noticed his decampment too late, pursued him in vain. He reached Austrian territory, after sixteen hours in the saddle, barely alive; and the horse dropped dead.

From then on he was in no hurry to be King of France. Vienna was different from Cracow. Once in Venice, he could hardly tear himself away from the amusements. He had to be urged to approach his throne, for after Charles's death the condition of the realm had grown more desperate and insecure. With Henry of Navarre still in the hands of the Queen Mother, the Huguenots had elected Montmorency as provisional leader and young Condé, beloved for his father's memory, as the nominal one. Uncertain what to expect of the new King, they kept their powder dry. Damville ruled Languedoc like a sovereign; Alençon, the King's brother who had conspired with the Politicians, was also a prisoner and his mother wondered whether to release or kill him; the Cardinal of Lorraine insisted on continued and conclusive execution of the policy inaugurated on St. Bartholomew's. In addition, the demands voiced by assemblies and synods for abolition of simony, convocation of the *States-General*, and tax reduction were growing louder.

Henry of Anjou arrived in Piedmont eventually, brimful of good intentions after his debauched journey, and met with Damville to discuss means of restoring peace. How enthusiastic, how excited he was about all ideas of the shrewd, self-confident governor! The *States-General?* He had never desired anything more than the *States-General.* A balanced budget? Why, it headed the program he had himself drawn up. Freedom of worship? It was to be his great deed. Damville was delighted with the new ruler and arranged for popular celebrations.

But in Lyon, where Anjou met his mother and Cardinal de Guise, he agreed just as whole-heartedly to all their points. Besides, he had something better to attend to than politics: there was money enough now to buy lap-dogs, and if he heard of a fine specimen which was not for sale he simply had it stolen. He reached Paris, still in the company of Catherine and the Cardinal, and his first public statement showed their effect on him. In an address to a deputation from Guyenne, he announced that he would continue his brother's policies unchanged: no public worship for others than Catholics, and no peace without unconditional surrender.

Inevitably, hostilities started all over again. Montmorency called upon the nobles of France; they flocked to him and declared for Damville's aims. Their party gained added prestige when the Duke of Alençon, having managed to escape from Court at last, joined its ranks, and made their complaints his own. They did not trust him, to be sure. After all, he was a Valois and an unprepossessing one, at that, with a pock-marked face lacking form, strength, and expression. Why should he be less deceitful than his brothers? But the old argument that had once saddled the movement with Anthony of Bourbon-Navarre, prevailed again: for the moment, at least, it was of supreme importance to have a member of the Royal House as leader. Fortunately, before Alençon's inevitable desertion, a better one appeared.

15

HENRY OF NAVARRE'S IMPRISONMENT AND FLIGHT

HENRY OF NAVARRE had been a prisoner for three and a half years. Attempts to dispose of him quietly had failed. So had all efforts to win him over in all sincerity to the side of the Court. He had never ceased thinking of freedom and his former co-religionists. He concealed his plans well; in three and a half years, he had become a master at dissimulation.

He was the cleverest of them all. He was playing Hamlet, melancholy, ineffectual, with d'Aubigné, the only man he trusted completely, as his Horatio. His Ophelia was Charlotte de Sauves, but she had only beauty in common with Shakespeare's. Otherwise she was a little baggage, on intimate terms with the opposition and an active spy of the Queen Mother's; but Henry adored her. Then, of course, there was also his wife.

He hardly knew her, hardly noticed her beauty, of which the celebrated Don Juan d'Austria said: "More divine than human, more apt to lead men to damnation than to paradise." She was no worse than the rest. She hated her brother, the King, no less than he hated her; professed a wild and glowing adoration for Alençon, her other brother; and treated her husband with a playful, somewhat condescending good-fellowship. She was most at ease in sordid company, picking the women with the worst reputations to flit with her through the dark streets at night, with their faces masked.

This Court no longer knew a way out of its decay. It no longer had a choice, only its morbid charm. The women were dressed like pages, while the men wore earrings, high coiffures, and décolleté clothes, and plucked the hair from their bodies with tweezers. Royal favorites shifted quickly; only Sieur de Guast remained, the evil spirit of the Louvre, a born intriguer who could not bear to see people in agreement. He was kept informed of Henry's every step by eavesdroppers behind all curtains, spies who opened all mail, stool-pigeons among all servants, and never failed to juggle facts or poison the air.

And so young Henry watched inactively and impotently from afar, while a fifth religious war started, a new sacrifice of thousands, while the Huguenots seized one place after another, and the soft-headed Alençon, mindful only of his own advantage, headed the party now strengthened by flocks of disgruntled Catholics. He watched from afar how the best Protestants, La Noue among them, followed this Alençon; how fortresses sent him humble delegations. He heard that the little Prince of Condé was doing his part like a man, had joined Prince Kasimir, the Palatine Elector's son, on the German frontier and commanded 14,000 German and Swiss foot soldiers, 3,000 French riflemen, and 8,000 horse. He clenched his fists in silent, helpless rage when he heard the news of the battle of Dormans, where the Huguenots were beaten and cut down by the King's vastly superior forces. He had to look pleasant when the Court went mad with joy over the glory of the young Duke of Guise, who was hit by a bullet in the cheek just as his father had been, and, like him, received the honored name of "Le Balafré" for his scar, thus winning all Catholic hearts.

The days passed in love-making, drunken orgies, intrigues, at best in hunting or gaming, with fools, softheads, gamblers, poison-mongers, harlots, and spies. The twenty-two-year-old Henry could stand it no longer. He had depressions, crying fits, lay unconscious for hours on end. His servants spied on him. The Queen Mother and the King tried incessantly to win him over. They dangled the honor of a lieutenant-generalship before his eyes, but he became emaciated and sick. He had only three men who were true to him, who could not be bribed: d'Aubigné, Armagnac, and Jonquières.

Agrippa d'Aubigné, the dyed-in-the-wool Protestant, was the best of all. He had never forgotten the cruel sight of the withered heads at Amboise and the oath his father had made him take then. As a mere child he had fought in skirmishes with the Catholics. Once, as a half-grown boy, he was taken prisoner and locked in a tower, and the Inquisitor tried to frighten him into the Roman Church. Led to the stake, where the executioner had already lit the fire, Agrippa was called on to renounce his heretical beliefs. Boldly he replied that he did not fear the fire, and began to dance and sing a Huguenot psalm. He was returned to the dungeon to be made more tractable by hunger and thirst, but a Catholic nobleman, who had admired the child's courage, helped him to flee. Immediately Agrippa threw himself into the fray again. His body became covered with scars. In his leisure hours he wrote verse praised by contemporaries and posterity alike. He was summoned to the Court by the Queen Mother to write mythological ballets and occasional poems. Time and again he ran away and picked up new wounds; popular ditties celebrated his swashbuckling pranks. But once he had joined Henry of Navarre he did not leave him again.

It had long pained d'Aubigné to see his protector, the leader of the Huguenots, disgracing himself at this disgraceful Court, thinking only of love-affairs, seeming to forget the mission for which his mother intended him. One night when Henry had gone to bed, Agrippa and Armagnac received some news and, not knowing if he was still awake, took off their boots and softly entered his room. There they heard Navarre fervently but quietly praying behind a curtain, repeating the last verse of the 88th Psalm of David, the one from which the Huguenots drew comfort and strength. At first Agrippa would not believe his ears. He tore the curtain aside and saw the young face wet with tears. Yet he did not soothe him but shouted reproaches: "What are you? Shall I tell you what you are? A whoremonger, a rotter, a worm grovelling before women, lying in bed with them while your friends die in battle!" The youth did not answer. Now d'Aubigné knew that Henry had never ceased thinking of the hour when he would head the party once again.

On February 2, 1576, seven trusted persons were advised of the date for the flight, February 20. By nightfall of the first date it was already apparent that one of the seven had informed the King. At a new conference—long after midnight—it was decided that if the Court had been warned about the 20th, it probably would make its own arrangements some days earlier. There was only one thing to do, act at once and flee in the morning.

Henry's wife constituted a danger. One could never tell where she stood. She was contemptuous of her husband's faith, contemptuous even of himself, who seemed to her unkempt, unwashed, unappetizing. At Court she had been out of favor since Alençon's flight, in which she was charged with connivance; constant threats had so put her in fear of her life that she was ill with recurrent fevers, her face swollen from weeping. It was hoped that she did not notice the preparations for the departure, although she slept in the same room with Henry. His early rising was not likely to surprise her because he always got up before she was awake, in order to meet Madame de Sauves at the Queen Mother's levee.

Henry asked and received the King's permission to go hunting early. At the gates of Senlis, after some miles of pretending to look for a stag, he found fresh horses waiting. Someone whispered to him: all has been betrayed to the King; immediate action is necessary.

Henry knew that two of his companions were spies. Armagnac wanted to kill them but Navarre had a better way. He commanded one to ride back to His Majesty and ask him not to listen to any rumors: he, Henry of Navarre, had no intention of flight; no hunt in the world meant so much to him that he would not return at once if the King wished to hear his defense. The man dashed away. A little later Henry called the other: he had just heard that the King was not in Paris but in Chartres. The second spy was sent there, with the same assertions.

In this simple way the flight succeeded; the little troop of faithful raced westward. They rode for a day and a night, finally reaching Alençon, a Huguenot town. Indescribable was the veterans' surprise and joy, when they found that the muddy, sweat-stained stranger who slid exhausted from his horse was their own Henry of Navarre.

A new life began for him. Awaking in Alençon on the morning of February 7 to the sound of arms and trumpet calls he thought he was dreaming. His body was chafed and sore from the long ride. But the voices he heard in the next room were those of his friends.

16

THE WAR DRAGS ON

AS THE forces were now aligned, avoidance of further belligerent action was out of the question.

Once again England had given money to the Huguenots while Germany, on the promise of the return of Metz, Toul, and Verdun, gave men. The Protestants had three leaders of rank: first, young Condé, who brought the Germans from the eastern frontier; then Alençon, the nominal commander-in-chief; and finally Navarre, who had solemnly recanted the conversion to Catholicism forced upon him four years before. He was busy in the south executing the economic program of the Protestants, recruiting troops, reading Plutarch, and at the same time carrying on a number of love-affairs, all with his own peculiar adroitness.

But the Court, too, was well prepared. It too had German cavalry and Swiss mercenaries, besides its own trained troops. The command was in the hands of a brother of the Duke of Guise, Sieur de Mayenne, who was then coming to the fore and gradually growing into his future important rôle. He was a born soldier, a capable and prudent officer, not a genius but reliable, alert, and cautious; a little drab and lacking in luster, but raised in the army and attached to it.

These were the years of waging war without enthusiasm, of making peace without conviction; one fought a few months, rested a few months. As time went by, Alençon's fame was overshadowed by the brilliance of Condé and Navarre, who jointly exercised the actual command, leaving Alençon only the title. The Queen Mother knew her children, knew not only from hearsay but by instinct how matters stood with Alençon. She traveled to his headquarters and amid embraces, biting insults, and tears, suddenly offered him three of France's most fertile districts and an annual pension of 100,000 ducats. He discovered his ardent Catholic heart and went home. Then the German Prince Kasimir was given 14,000 ducats plus the whole outstanding pay of his army, amounting to another 1,200,000, whereupon he discovered his homesickness and marched back to Germany. Meanwhile deputations from the provinces were entertained, allowed to prattle about the grievances of the subjects and sometimes given a few promises which were never kept. These were uneventful years.

Too large a part of the people were simply tired of war, tired of discussions, tired of distress. The peasants wanted to plow, the townsmen to ply their trades. The glamour of arms, fame, the slogans, how unimportant they had all become, how everybody longed for quiet. Much had changed since the first Calvinist generation had gone to their graves. True, those nobles had fought also for their special interests, but they had made the people's cause their own and their hearts had been in the Reformation.

What was left of this early, dawn-like purity? Condé, who had a German Protestant wife, was known to place religion above everything; but of how many others could that be believed?

Calvinism, over the years, had become a movement dominated by the aristocracy and upper middle class. The beautiful thoughts of earlier days, when according to the letter of the Gospel all men were to be free and equal, had experienced a strong oligarchical correction. The movement's center of gravity had shifted from the small artisans, who had provided the first martyrs, to the landed gentry and the urban bourgeoisie. The secularization of Church lands benefited the poor less and less, and the Protestant feudal lords more and more. Sermons against all nobles, Catholic or Protestant, were already being preached to the lower classes; sermons bitterly demanding that nobles, clerics, and judges be expelled from the country. It meant a split among the Huguenots themselves, for those who clung to the conception in its original purity were ranged against the younger generation, which viewed the religious war as a means merely of settling their political differences with the King.

It was an oft-interrupted, ever-resumed, but always unwillingly fought civil war. Waged with the old weapons, French and German, it consisted of an eternal exchange of strongholds; and it was always La Rochelle which ultimately offered protection to the attacked. Referred to as the War of the Three Henrys—for Henry Valois, Henry of Navarre, Henry de Guise—it marked the lowest point in the history of French royalty in centuries. Weak, hysterical, perverse, wavering between repulsive excesses and equally repulsive contrition, such was the monarch whom everybody, Huguenot and Catholic alike, was really fighting. Henry III no longer knew how to deal with the hostile parties. A slimy coward, yet sometimes exhibiting strange dignity and wisdom, he bowed first to the right, then to the left, sneering at the people one day, wooing them the next—and in the wake of his shifts followed ever again war and respite, respite and war.

From all this weariness there might yet have emerged something resembling final pacification—a co-existence of the denominations and a gradual increase in the power of popular representation—had not a change occurred just then within the Catholic Church. So violent and invigorating was this change that the Popes could think of taking the offensive. It was as if the threat of disintegration had brought the Church to its senses. It listened, late but not too late, and arrived at a new evaluation of the trend of the times: what was taking place was no passing revolt but a requisite, inexorable change in the social scheme. At last the Church understood. It understood that it had sided with the declining forces of feudalism, long since devitalized, while the Reformation had embraced the rising urban populations who could not be subjected again because their monopoly on industry and commerce was sweeping them to power. The Church saw the situation far more clearly than did the Huguenot nobles, who still hoped the Reformation would win them their special demands. They gave their lives and fortunes to its cause, but in reality, as demonstrated in England, Switzerland, and Holland, Protestantism had gone beyond their reactionary interests and turned into a religion of urban capital. The

Catholic Church by then had made its decision: if it wanted to win back the *bourgeois* deserters, it had to renounce its own aristocratic character.

In short, it had to beat the Reformation on its own grounds—meet the reform it represented with another reform. Protestantism could no longer be fought with contrary tendencies. It had to be made superfluous, by adopting the same tendencies and presenting them more shrewdly, more firmly, and at the same time more attractively. For this, the most decisive transformation the Church had undergone in many centuries, its existing statutes and institutions, based entirely on feudalism, did not suffice. To make itself heard by the mass of this new bourgeoisie, the Church first had to change the training of its priests. They had to learn the Protestants' ascetic unworldliness, learn their realistic discipline of daily toil. A new monastic order was assigned this task: the Society of Jesus.

Ignatius Loyola was the founder. His was a unique talent, combining an iron will with a rigidly logical mind, pitiless severity, bold imagination, complete lack of illusions about human nature, practical sense, and a gift for organization. His order was a military body, an ecclesiastical militia, a legion of God.

Equality among members, such as prevailed in other orders, was out of the question. A rigid scale of rank pervaded the Society, headed by a general with absolute power, who was responsible to God alone. Of the three monastic vows, that of chastity was casually mentioned and that of poverty skillfully evaded. The only one stressed was that of obedience. This law, however, was so clearly and pitilessly thought out, it made such blind tools of subordinates, that the order received an impetus surpassing that of any military institution since the armies of the Roman Empire. The will of the individual, his opinion, his conviction, ceased to count. "If the Church defines as black what our eyes see as white we must declare immediately that it is black," is the thirteenth rule of the *Exercitia Spiritualia.* It was the most striking contrast to the individualism of the Reformers. Nothing was left for man to decide for himself; all he had to do was to submit.

The first Jesuit generals were either Spaniards or loyal allies of the King of Spain. Their influence supported Philip in all his plans. In France it was the opinion that the order had been founded only to promote Spanish interests, for the founder himself had declared it as the duty of Jesuits to pray above all for the King of Spain. Soon, however, they spread all over the world. No barrier could hold them. Their missionaries visited the smallest hamlet; to them, a teacher, bookkeeper, or artisan meant as much as a baron. And the French talked of "*cette épée dont la poignée est à Rome et la pointe partout.*"

Under Jesuit urging the moderate, conciliatory policy lost ground in France, step by step. The danger of the realm's destruction by Protestantism was painted in the darkest hues from pulpits and in pamphlets. The end of unity! The end of society! The collapse of civilization!

The volte-face took place swiftly. All of a sudden those who thought they had the upper hand were again in peril. The forces in conflict swayed back and forth, making total victory unlikely for either side. Confusion reigned. So tangled were the events of those days that even from our vantage point in time they seem like a planless mêlée of opposing parties, with each on occasion borrowing the other's arguments. They traded arguments, and kept faith only with their hatreds.

By December 6, 1576, when the *States-General* met at Blois, the Protestants found that their hope for a mutually just agreement had been frustrated. The electoral system had been devised by Cardinal de Guise—and, lo, among the deputies there was but a single Protestant. They had been tricked as never before. The King was beaming when he opened the sessions; he made no effort to hide the fact that his sole purpose was to get anti-Reform resolutions.

His plans were so radical that at first even leaders of clergy and nobility urged moderation. They vetoed a motion to banish all Protestants from the realm. Gently, the Queen Mother worked back-stage, talked to the deputies in private, and with all sorts of promises brought them into line with the King's view. The Third Estate was more obstinate. It had also sent a purely Catholic delegation, but it was not interested in antagonizing the Huguenots. Its troubles had reached a point where all religions seemed irrelevant. Transubstantiation this, transubstantiation that—if only we had enough to eat again! This was the mood which had brought forth the *Troisième Parti.* And the *bourgeois* delegates had to be subjected to threats before they would join those of the other Estates in a plea to the King to tolerate but one religion henceforth.

War was at the gates again. The Huguenots, embittered by disappointment, came forth in arms from their castles and towns. But now, aware that he had gone too far, the King hesitated. He had no money, and the *States-General* had convinced him that popular distress admitted of no further increase. Several plans were discussed: a shift from indirect to direct taxes, to be levied on every fireplace in the country; a war loan of two million; even a sale of the feudal domains. But the opposition which had yielded on the religious issue stood firm on the financial one.

It seemed as though war might yet be avoided when the King's Council met in February, 1577. There, however, the Cardinals, supported by the Guises and spurred on by the Jesuits (who advertised the war as a crusade), so forcefully urged the creation of religious unity that the war party gained the upper hand. Marshals de Biron and Cossé, who favored negotiations, were shouted down.

Catherine long avoided taking sides. Everyone waited to hear from her; everyone knew that she was still the King's mentor and that he would do nothing without her approval. Once again she radiated a charm undiminished by years, listened, said nothing. Not until the envoys she had sent to Henry of Navarre confirmed the Huguenots' preference of peace to new wars did she join the moderates, with light talk but weighty arguments.

"You make long-range decisions," she said, "and overlook what lies under your noses. People are hungry, not even the Court has money—and you want to make war. With what, if you please? At the *States-General* you knew no way out. Have you found one since? If so, I have not heard of it. Here I see some honorable gentlemen so concerned about the faith that they would rather see the nation ruined than the Protestants tolerated. I do not mind saying frankly, I am not so pious a soul. To me, the preservation of the state is the main issue. If I may advise the King, I should ask him first of all to save his kingdom; then, I am certain, God in His infinite wisdom will one day bring the religions together again."

And the King, who so recently had urged war upon the *States-General*, adopted her view. Yet before he could finally make up his mind for peace, hostilities broke out. The Guises, who had raised two armies, stormed forward rapidly, took two of the most important Protestant fortresses—La Charité and Issoire—entered Poitou, and were laying plans for a new siege of La Rochelle.

The fitful tension could not conceal the fatigue underneath. The Queen Mother's words came true: money was lacking, and the unpaid armies grumbled. In the Protestant camp the situation was not much better; the leaders' only thought was to call a halt at any cost. Damville, head of the Politicians, had split with some Huguenot generals and secretly was working on a reconcilement with the King. And Navarre, matured in his years as Governor of Guyenne, a Protestant whose love of the faith was outweighed by his love of torn and bleeding France, pleaded ever more anxiously with his friends to reduce their demands for the sake of peace.

Negotiations began at Bergerac, were continued at Poitiers, and there, as plenipotentiary of his side, Henry of Navarre first showed the diplomatic skill which later was to smooth his way to the throne. He actually succeeded in concealing the weakness, the impending dissolution of the party from its opponents. By casual remarks he managed to create the impression that the Huguenots were raising new, menacing troop levies. To him belongs the chief credit for the peace that was signed at Poitiers in 1577—the most important, perhaps, of that entire series of covenants.

The treaty consisted of seventy-four articles. It dispelled the Catholic fear that the Reformation might overrun the whole country; and it satisfied the Huguenots, who had expected less than they received. Public worship was permitted in the localities where it was exercised on the day peace was made, but it was limited to one place in any single district, and altogether prohibited in the capital. Huguenots would have the right to hold any office. The King publicly and solemnly expressed regret and condemnation of the excesses of St. Bartholomew's. He removed all blemish from the honor of Admiral de Coligny and other murdered leaders, and reappointed all governors and officials to the posts from which they were dismissed. He recognized the King of Navarre and the Prince of Condé to be his faithful subjects, and finally granted the Huguenots nine strongholds.

The peace of Poitiers filled everyone with joy and hope. The King called it his peace, the King's peace. When the Prince of Condé was told of the ratification after he had gone to bed, he was so overcome with happiness that he ran out to the soldiers half dressed, and had a torchlight parade held that same night.

But the fond dream that France might now enjoy an age of peaceful reconstruction remained unrealized. For some time already a new power had arisen beside the Royal House. Allied with the Jesuits, it refused to sheathe the sword while a Valois sat on the throne and a Frenchman professed the Reformed faith. This power did not rest; it made the peace an excuse to strengthen its organization.

17

THE FOUNDING OF THE LEAGUE

ALTHOUGH the peace had been forced on the government, it strengthened the Crown. It demonstrated the King's independence of foreign powers, his intention to do as he saw fit in his realm, without tutelage, to the point of tolerating heretics. It was an affront which neither Rome nor Spain could bear in silence and which in France itself could not be acceptable to the great party growing up round Guise. What made this party grow was not alone hatred of the bourgeoisie. More frankly and justifiably than ever, it was hate of the Valois, whose last scion was the rottenest of Catherine de' Medici's brood.

Foppish Henry III led his country into the abyss, while indulging in perverted relations with youths to whose insatiable, extortionate greed he could refuse nothing. At first there were ten or twelve of these, but gradually a quartet managed to win its way into the King's especial favor: Arques, Caumont, St. Luc, and d'O. At Court they were called the Four Evangelists. The country, which they furnished with material for ceaseless homosexual gossip, called them *mignons*. The King frequently retired with them to one of his castles, for extravagant amusements, droll fashion shows, and girlish games, and each time it appeared on their return that the young men had used the occasion to get new spoils.

All still in their twenties, they rose to positions for which they had shown no aptitude whatever, as when Arques one day became Duke of Joyeuse and Governor of Normandy, and Caumont blossomed out as Duke of Epernon and Governor of Metz, Boulogne, Calais, and Provence. Of course, this happened at the expense of better men. For example, Charles de Guise, Duke of Mayenne, was singled out for the honor once held by Coligny, and then bought off with 80,000 talers so that Joyeuse might hear himself addressed as Admiral. Whereupon Epernon felt slighted: could not he have been made Admiral as well as Joyeuse? To quiet him, Henry took the Lord-High-Stewardship from the Duke of Guise and gave Epernon its functions together with the post of Colonel-General of Infrantry, from which, to be sure, Count de Brissac first had to be ousted. Thus men who had worked hard and served well were shorn of their power and dignity and recompensed with money they did not want; those who had not yet aligned themselves with Guise turned to him now. In a few years his became a party of insulted grandees. And many gleefully recalled the Guises' own brutality twenty-five years earlier: they now were receiving from Joyeuse and Epernon the very treatment which under Francis II they had dealt out to Bourbons and Montmorencys.

The *mignons*, ill-bred, lazy coxcombs, were shrewd enough to hide behind the royal skirts—no mere metaphor, since His Majesty loved dressing as a lady. They wore their hair like streetwalkers, in long curls under little velvet berets. They powdered, danced, strummed guitars, and rattled a bit with arms otherwise unfamiliar to them. They had delightful ideas; people without ideas did not count. They attended public games as amazons, with Henry as their "Queen." At one of his banquets the service was by ladies of the Court—stripped to the waist. On another most amusing occasion he and his friends raced through the streets of Paris disguised as monks, the whole cavalcade flogging passers-by with steel rods.

Bizarre, repulsive extremes of unscrupulous monarchy! For in the intervals of such behavior the self-same King would walk to church barefoot, ashes on his head, rosary in hand. When the people greeted him with jeers and cries of derision, he seemed to bear it in patience as well-earned humiliation. Actually, his ridiculous devotional exercises aroused more hatred than his orgies. To public affairs he no longer paid the slightest attention. It was known that in each year of his reign the government had spent twice its annual income. Often the officials went unpaid for months, and then new posts were hurriedly created and sold to the highest bidder. The Italian usurers whose interest bills could not be met were driven over the border. There were attempts at reform, too; economy measures were announced. They remained mere talk. The sums paid at the same time to the *mignons* upset every budget.

How different was the Duke of Guise! A man, first of all, a real man: big, strong, purposeful, and daring; a soldier, an excellent horseman, a fine speaker, amiable, democratic, a lover of camp life who had been seen to swim upstream wearing full armor. His politeness extended even to the fishwife. And how good-looking he was! When he walked through the streets—slim, with fair locks, curly beard, flashing eyes, with the famous scar on his cheek, dressed in white with a black satin cloak thrown over his shoulders—the people of Paris thronged about him, threw flowers from windows; women touched him with crosses which they pressed to their lips. And always with him, a devoted aide, was his sister, Madame de Montpensier, who told anyone willing to listen that she hated the King like the plague, and organized a group of clergymen to curse him from the pulpit.

The crisis was brought on in June, 1584, by the death of Alençon, Catherine's youngest. For some years past he had waged his private war with Spain in the Netherlands—whether with or without the King's approval, was not clear. He had had his share of successes and failures; was never popular but, as heir presumptive, always in the center of interest. Now he was gone. Spain's waning glory showed a new, threatening gleam, with her generalissimo, Grand Duke Alexander of Parma, amassing victories. And the doctors said the King's marriage with Louise of Lorraine would remain childless.

What would happen after his death? Under the law the throne had to pass to the outlaw, Henry of Navarre. A grandson of Margaret Valois, Francis I's sister, he was the only living descendant of Louis IX, the canonized King of France who appeared in the old coronation formula: "Rise, O son of Saint Louis, and ascend thy throne!" Should the heretics' leader take the oath required by the Salic Law, to guard and defend the Catholic faith against all heresy?

The two interested families, Habsburg and Guise, slowly drifted into a questionable relationship. First, innocent-looking visitors arrived from Madrid, and the

Guises poured out their hearts. The constant annoyance to which they were subjected, that they were used to, and what did it matter? But the disregard of the only true faith, was it to be tolerated indefinitely? The Spaniards coldly raised their eyebrows and kept silent. The Duke of Guise became so frank that his brother Mayenne felt uneasy; he told of warnings he had sent to the towns against admitting royal garrisons, lest they be at Navarre's mercy if he should inherit the Crown. And why should he, anyway? Were the Guises not descended from Charlemagne who had ruled France centuries before St. Louis?

Whereupon the Spaniards remarked that some day their King might desire revenge for the way France let Alençon fight alongside the Dutch rebels, and recognized and encouraged them even now. And John Moreo, a Maltese Knight who mingled with the malcontents on orders from Madrid, hinted that Philip II, in certain circumstances and if the situation should require it, would help.

The mask was dropped, and Guise beat a slight retreat. "Would not that be rebellion against my sovereign?" In a day or two, very cautiously, he asked, "How about first obtaining the Holy Father's approval, to ease my conscience?" The Maltese might well have answered with the Jesuit vow, "*Per omnia et in omnibus*"—with all means and in all fields—but it was unnecessary. At this moment of indecision Henry III committed a new outrage. He sent Epernon to Navarre with word that if only the Béarnais would turn Catholic, he, the King, would designate him as his successor.

The departure of Epernon and his magnificent retinue was insolence itself. He took leave of every person at Court except the Guises, whom he purposely snubbed.

The time had come for decisions. At the Lorraines' ancestral castle of Joinville, in a tiny back-room, "The League" was founded, in January, 1585. Moreo and Tassis negotiated for the King of Spain; the French signatories were the Dukes of Guise and Mayenne and a representative of Cardinal de Bourbon.

In brief, the agreement ran as follows: First, no heretic must ever be King of France; with Navarre thus eliminated, the Crown would go to the Cardinal, his uncle, the late Anthony de Bourbon's brother, a devout Catholic and stout foe of the Huguenots. Second, the common goal must be the utter extinction of Protestantism in the Netherlands as well as in France. Third, Philip, for the first year, gave a subsidy fixed in the treaty at 1,000,000 escudos; and the French on their part, as though already able to dispose of the power of France, pledged full aid in suppressing the Dutch, and renunciation of the Turkish alliance planned by the present government. They also would cede to Spain all Navarre's possessions beyond the French borders—meaning Lower Navarre and Béarn—and would assist in the subjugation of Portugal.

The League's first manifesto, issued in April, was full of fire and pathos, and directed mainly against the misrule of the *mignons*. They had deprived meritorious men of honors and offices, and made them their own. Not only had they ignored the resolution of the last *States-General*, at Blois, to lead the whole of France back to the Catholic faith, they had subsequently instituted the most malicious persecution of all true believers. They alone had prevailed upon His Majesty to name a Calvinist as his successor. If ever Navarre should come to power in the most Christian realm, Frenchmen would be in duty bound to rise up against the usurper. And the manifesto's specific demands —for measures against unemployment, tax reduction, sessions of the *States-General* every three years, trade subsidies, aid for the Third Estate—made it read like a Huguenot program.

However, a comparison of text and real motives revealed a glaring discrepancy. All the League members were disgruntled individuals who concealed their true interests behind defense of the faith. There was Louis de Gonzaga, Duke of Nevers, pained because his merits had not brought him a governorship. There was Guy de Lanssac, once a royal favorite and now shunted aside. There was de Villiers; as a reward for various services, notably the capture of the Count of Montgomery, the King had promised to make him Governor of Caen, but failed to keep his word. There was La Châtre, Governor of Berry, who would have liked to be Governor of Blois as well but had been turned down. The list could be prolonged.

The League was perhaps the first political organization built on Jesuit principles. To win mass support it told the people what they liked to hear; but it was concerned only with the aggrandizement of its own leaders. Although in its manifesto it claimed to speak for "the better and healthier part of the nation," this did not keep it from cooperating with its hereditary enemy against the nation. Religion was pleaded as excuse for everything; though at the time it would no longer convince the people, it still offered oily phrases to cover the contradictions in the program.

18

VICTORY AND DEFEAT

THE King was in a dilemma. He felt danger mounting, the ground trembling under his feet; the very air he breathed was charged with hatred. He did not suspect the scope of the conspiracy. That subjects of his, scions of the greatest houses of France, might be taking Spanish money to unleash a new civil war—he would not have dreamed this, and even Catherine apparently failed to grasp the full import of events. But they both understood this much: with Guise's party steadily gaining in strength, one had to join it, to avoid being caught in a vise.

Henry asked his mother to undertake the negotiations. Catherine agreed, though tormented by gout, coughs, and fevers. Of late she had come to hate her son-in-law Navarre, who held his own Court at Nérac, dividing his time between work, study, skirmishing, and love-affairs, just as if nothing could deprive him of final victory. Only the worst was to be expected of him. His marriage with her daughter was a terrible failure; he insulted Margaret at every opportunity, and she was in contact with his mortal enemies; some of his councilors advised having her killed.

In her stormy career Catherine had suffered many humiliations. But now at Charri where, bent with age, she went to see Guise, it was the first time that she, the Queen Mother, found herself looked down upon as a petitioner. She was not even allowed time to consult with her son. The League demanded immediate opening of war against the Huguenots; and when Catherine hesitated, Mayenne sent part of its army against the King's Swiss Guards. To prevent their slaughter, the Queen Mother quickly yielded on a few points. Besides, perhaps old Cardinal de Bourbon —past sixty, stupid, and worn out by debauchery— seemed to her a less obnoxious aspirant than her son-in-law. Of course he was no more than a puppet of Guise; still, what mattered was to avert the immediate threat to her royal son. Where there is life, there is hope.

As a result of the negotiations the King and Guise declared themselves friends again, though in truth more bitter enemies than ever. And the Huguenots had to foot the bill. Again, as how often before, all solemn promises were broken. All previous pacification edicts were revoked, all grants of strongholds rescinded. It was long since the Huguenots had been so harshly treated. Not only the practice of their religion was prohibited, but the creed itself: "We have commanded and command that all who confess to the new religion must leave it, and within six months confess to the Catholic, Apostolic, and Roman faith, or, if they refuse, withdraw from Our Kingdom." And, as in the days when the Sorbonne ruled in matters of religion, confiscation of property and death were the usual penalties for non-compliance.

Of the three Henrys who now faced one another, only Henry de Guise was happy. The King was aware of the inferior rôle imposed on him, and of the violence done his ideas. If he had had his way, attempts to draw the rightful heir and his following over to the Catholic faith would have continued to the last. Nothing, of course, could have pained the League party more; its purpose was to exclude Navarre forever from succession, to destroy the Huguenots and appropriate their lands. And Henry of Navarre saw the superior foe in whom he had ceased believing suddenly rise again like a black cloud rolling toward his gay, sunny province full of song and scent of wine. It was another of many crises in his life, when all that mattered was to keep his neck out of the noose. The news of the agreement overwhelmed him. For a time he sat dazed, answered no questions, was unaware of his surroundings—perhaps of himself. What was to be done? His army was small; he was poor. His friends told him to flee to Germany, not to return until he had strong German support; but he would not yield. "They have me surrounded," he wrote in a letter, "like a hunted deer; but I will fight my way out over their bodies."

Already reports came in of the pernicious consequences of the Catholic pact. The cruel executions of Henry II's time had been revived. In Paris men and women were burned, their children sent to notorious institutions. When the victims' widows begged the King for permission to retire with the children to some designated corner of France, their requests were rejected. He would only promise to have them sent to England. Some of the Protestants tried hiding behind a formula, such as "Whereas the King desires that . . ." meaning thus not to disavow their faith but merely to express obedience to the government; but it was of no avail. The bishops only treated them the more harshly. To fill the cup to overflowing, Pope Sixtus V excommunicated Henry of Navarre and the Prince of

Condé; their estates were forfeit; they were forever guilty of heresy; anyone who did their bidding came under the ban.

By then, however, Henry had found himself. He answered the Pope with a manifesto full of scorn and confidence and had it posted in Rome. Next he proceeded to find out on whom he could count. Damville, who had flirted with the Court a while, came out strongly for him. The Reformed cantons of Switzerland, aware that neglect to help in the fight against the French-Spanish Catholic alliance would doom themselves, supplied three regiments, 16,000 men in all. And Germany? There we meet Beza again, the preacher of Geneva, Calvin's friend and successor, who had been so helpful to the Huguenots in their beginnings. Then full of youthful, robust humor, we now find him white-haired but as resolute as ever. He traveled personally to the Palatinate, and succeeded in persuading John Kasimir to send a new auxiliary corps. Before its departure the German wrote Henry III that the action was aimed not at him but at the League, an evasion of existing facts which, as like half-measures, ended in disaster. In command of the German army this time was not John Kasimir himself but a Prussian Junker, Fabian, Burgrave zu Dohna, a convinced, right-minded Protestant, skilled in combat but far too inexperienced in generalship. Lastly, Elizabeth of England supported the uprising with money for coldly selfish reasons: the busier the League and the House of Lorraine were in France, the less likely were they to trouble English and Scottish waters.

At the last hour, while everywhere men were arming for war, Catherine journeyed to her hated son-in-law. Near Cognac, at the castle of St. Bris, she made one more effort to bring him round to Catholicism. But her Italian wiles remained ineffectual.

There were two theaters of operations in this campaign, both near the Loire. The King himself marched against the Germans, to cut them off from the troops of Henry of Navarre. In command of the second army, which was to engage the Béarnais, he placed his favorite, Joyeuse.

Anne de Joyeuse, with Epernon the most beloved of the *mignons*, was related to the King through his wife, Marguerite de Vaudemont, a sister of the Queen. This dubious character, whose annual income exceeded a million écus, allowed the King to keep him and at the same time inclined toward the Guises. Whether Henry now made him a general in the hope of regaining his affection or because he thought it wise to remove Joyeuse from Court and the League's influence, or perhaps even because he anticipated the other's defeat and death—no one will ever know. Thus far, at any rate, the twenty-six-year-old Joyeuse had never had an opportunity to prove his military genius; it was not even certain that he could lead a squadron.

The contrast between the two armies that met on October 20, 1587, at the little river Dronne, near the village of Coutras, was extraordinary. Joyeuse's men wore helmets of silver, adorned with plumes and flowers; their weapons shone with chased silver; broad pennons fluttered from their lances; embroidered on their sashes were the love protestations of courtesans. The Béarnais's army was small and poor—old veterans from earlier Huguenot wars and half-grown boys hastily recruited in Gascony—but though the battered armor was rusty the men inside it were sinewy and straight.

And Henry of Navarre was no aide-de-camp here, as at Moncontour. Here he was the commander. He had proved himself in the meantime, in the small wars of the south, had stood knee-deep in blood several times and fought like a common soldier, hand to hand, for every inch of ground. He had also studied the military works of great generals. He surveyed the terrain now and made his dispositions accordingly. He deployed his artillery so that it dominated the field and gave every platoon a definite assignment. Then he turned to his cousins, Condé and Soissons: "You are Bourbons; I need say no more. As for myself, I will show you that I am your senior."

At this moment, with the soldiers waiting for the signal to begin the battle, Duplessis-Mornay—later one of the great men of Protestantism—stepped up to the King and addressed him loudly and roughly. "Sire, you know we love you. But we cannot answer to God for letting you lead us like this, soiled with all the dirt you have wallowed in, in a battle for Jesus Christ. Look at your soldiers, Sire. You will not find one who regards you kindly. I'll not detail the amours with which you were pleased to scandalize your followers. Enough that you acted as you did just now in La Rochelle, bringing shame on honored houses, causing grief to God-fearing folk. Before taking up arms, we demand that you do penance. But perhaps there is not time, so ask God to have mercy on you if you die."

Startled and confused, Navarre sought to answer, but could find no words. He fell to his knees before his men and prayed aloud. And the soldiers knelt with him.

When the Duke of Joyeuse saw the praying army from afar, he exclaimed: "They're afraid, the peasant oafs!" But the veterans on his staff knew better. "Gentlemen," said an old officer, "when the Huguenots pray, they are ready to fight like heroes." He proved to be right.

The engagement began at nine in the morning, with cannon fire from both sides. The Huguenot artillery peppered the center of the Catholic infantry, causing a great slaughter and shattering the front; while the Duke's gunners aimed their pieces so low that all the balls hit the ground. Lavardin, the commander of the royal light cavalry, not wanting to wait until his troop too was decimated by the fire, resolved to charge at once. He headed for the enemy cavalry, rode them down, attacked the cuirassiers with such force that he cut right through their squadron, and in triumphant pursuit of the fugitives raced on to Coutras, where he knew the Huguenots were keeping their supplies. This had been Henry of Navarre's precise intention. His supply train had arrived at Coutras with so well-staged a secrecy that it could not remain hidden from the Catholics. The ruse involved the cold-blooded sacrifice of his cuirassiers, but it succeeded: Lavardin's cavalry had left the field.

Now Henry began his own attack. He let his corps of noblemen with short lances advance, slowly, step by step; when they were quite close to the enemy's heavy cavalry, they suddenly broke into a quick run, with lances extended before them. The King's men charged in haste, and their horses, startled by the sudden command, plunged into the lances; others overshot the attacking line in the disorderly start, and were cut down from behind, before they could throw their heavy horses around. In less than half an hour it was all over. Only dead and wounded men and fallen, bleeding horses remained on the field. The Duke of Joyeuse in his uniform of velvet and silk had also been unhorsed. He begged for his life and offered 100,000 talers' ransom, but he was killed with three pistol shots.

The Catholic infantry met with no better fate. They were attacked on all sides with the cry: "Remember St. Bartholomew's!" The Huguenots' thirst for vengeance was not to be quenched; they killed as men mow grass. The bloody struggle lasted for three hours. The artillery, all the flags, the entire supply train of Joyeuse's army fell into the hands of the victors, who with derisive laughter held up the articles of luxury and effeminacy which the royal warriors had taken into battle. It was a great victory. Of the Catholics, 3,500 remained on the field, and nearly half the army were made prisoners. On the King of Navarre's side, the dead numbered less than 200 and not one of the leaders was among them. Navarre behaved as he would during his future reign: always pardoning immediately. Wherever he went he ordered an end to the carnage, treated prisoners kindly, and honored the brave among his men.

That night the large hall of the castle of Coutras, its walls bedecked with captured flags, saw a delirious, endless feast. On tables in another hall lay the bodies of Joyeuse and his brother. It was the Protestants' greatest victory since the beginning of the religious wars. The air was heavy with the turbulent triumph of the captains, as they came in directly from the battle, sweating and mud-stained, threw lances and armguards on the floor, dropped staggering into their seats round a table laden with food and wine. Roar, din, laughter, torch-smoke. And amid all, Henry, quite the Gascon again, a gamin fit to burst with joy, telling the tallest tales in his native accent.

This was the great victory of Coutras. But its hoped-for fruit—the disastrous weakening of the League—was wanting. It was wanting because Henry failed to exploit his victory, and because the other Huguenot force was not so fortunate as he.

The King had occupied both banks of the central Loire, to intercept the Swiss and Germans. Fabian Dohna walked right into the trap: he marched deeper and deeper into hostile country, and was more and more tightly encircled. The October rains beat down on his soldiers, drenching their quarters; dysentery killed them off like flies. Even so, Henry III was not eager to match his men against these Teutonic giants. Cunning was always more in his line than a fair fight; his store of tricks was inexhaustible, as he had proved before and now proved again.

When he heard that the lansquenets still thought they were marching only against the League, not against the King, he asked that one of their detachments be sent to his camp so he could talk with them. And when they saw him in his ermine and, startled, sank to their knees, he graciously bade them rise. "My dear men, what are you doing? You think you are fighting for me, don't you? You have been deceived. You can see, you are fighting against me."

Was he really the King?

"Yes, yes," he smiled, "I am really. This is no ghost standing before you; you may touch me, and make certain that I do not vanish."

They declared they would not draw their swords against the Crown of France. Henry paid them their wages, long overdue, and without listening to their officers they started east toward their homes, which few were to see again.

For the Duke of Guise did not keep promises made by the King. He struck the returning army from the rear wherever he found them. When Dohna's troop took refuge in the fortress of Anneau, Guise bribed the inhabitants; they opened the gates, and the ensuing rout sealed the Germans' fate. Dohna saved himself only by fleeing over the roofs. The further up the Loire they came, the faster they were destroyed. They fled with lowered flags and tattered uniforms, without horse or cannon, covered with shame. Fever, hunger, dysentery finished what the sword had left undone. They were no longer human beings, but creeping skeletons. If they collapsed on the road, the peasants killed them slowly and cruelly. One peasant woman, using a knife as for pig-sticking, stabbed to death eighteen sick Germans who had crawled into her thatched hut.

What point had there been in all this butchery? France's balance of power was unaltered, and its internal problem was no nearer to solution.

19

THE END OF THE VALOIS

BUT the troubled times allowed no respite. Events pressed upon one another.

The Duke of Guise soared in popular favor. Nobody mentioned the King's share in the victory over the Germans; all praised the Gashed One. The Pope sent him a consecrated sword, and Guise reciprocated with a statement to the effect that the Inquisition, so startingly successful in Spain, ought to be introduced in France as well: "It is the only way of eradicating heresy—provided its officers are foreigners." Congratulations, dripping flattery, arrived from Philip II and the Duke of Savoy. And the Parisians, goaded on by the priests, called Guise "the savior."

Their enthusiasm led to the memorable Day of the Barricades, May 12, 1588. For about a year an organization had existed in Paris for the purpose of defending the Catholic capital against a possible Protestant attack. The clergy did not shrink from concocting a tale that the King was plotting with the foreign enemy against his own people. The League alone could not stop the army of heretics, reported to number 300,000. Sixteen men, one for each municipal district, led this society, of which the Duke of Guise was a charter member.

Paris was in a state of dangerous ferment. Insubordination rose wherever authority tried to assert itself. Speakers harangued the masses until jails were stormed; posters called the King a traitor and caricatured him as a girl. Street riots occurred, at which prisoners were torn from the hands of the police. And the Duchess of Montpensier, Guise's sister, posed as the King's public accuser and boasted that her propaganda was more effective than her brother's sword. Occasions to poison the air were not lacking. One of these was Joyeuse's death at Coutras, which vacated the governorship of Normandy. Guise demanded it from the King, but the King smiled disdainfully and gave it to Epernon.

Then there was the sudden demise of the Prince of Condé. The vicissitudes after the defeat of his proud German army had undermined his youth, destroyed his vigor; he lived in exile in London, where he met Charlotte de la Trémoille, the apostate daughter of an arch-Catholic family, and married her after his first wife had died. Charlotte, devoted to Calvinism with a romantic extravagance, lay at the young hero's feet, solicited aid for him in London society, and spent her own fortune on an English flotilla whose guns guarded his return to La Rochelle. On re-entering his native land Condé knelt to touch the soil. But in St. Jean d'Angély he died untimely, at thirty-four. The doctors had noted strange symptoms and an autopsy strengthened their suspicion that the Prince had been poisoned. His widow was charged with the crime and with having feigned conversion to aid her family in hounding Protestants to death; she spent years in prison but the mystery was never solved. In any case, Condé's governorship of Picardy was now also claimed by the Guises. And again the King dared to affront them by handing it to another, this time the Duke of Nevers.

The Guises were so flagrantly slighted at Court that the Queen Mother felt compelled to put in a word for them. The result was a violent altercation.

"Madame, I do not want your advice any longer. I cannot find that listening to your wisdom did my brothers much good."

"So you think you, in your twenties, can govern a country like France better than . . ."

"I must ask you once and for all to stop meddling in my affairs." Red in the face, abruptly turning his back on her, he ran up and down the room a few times. But when she had sufficiently recovered from her surprise to answer, he withdrew in haste.

Paris, meanwhile, grew more restless from day to day. The King, of course, had the power, he had the guns; but what good were they? Could they be trusted? He who rules with guns is dependent on what their bearers think of him. And public opinion in Paris considered Henry, who clung to old and decayed but at least French things, a traitor; while Guise, who took Spanish money to make his country a puppet of the Habsburgs, was thought to have the salvation of France at heart. Already the city was overrun with suspicious characters. The authorities tried to deport the newcomers—in vain; the lower functionaries were largely in the pay of Guise. The King, growing anxious, ordered Marshal de Biron to call in Swiss troops and post them in outlying villages. The number of the guards was increased; all leaves were canceled. The forty-five noblemen who watched over the King's person stayed with him day and night.

Paris was one vast, sinister, rumor-filled den of conspirators. Suddenly a report spread that the King would have all prominent citizens arrested and executed. People trembled for their lives. A plea for help was sent to the Duke of Guise, urging him to hurry to the defense of the true Catholics. When the King heard of it he sent a message to Guise, explicitly forbidding him to enter the city.

Guise thought it over. To disregard the royal command was open rebellion. To obey it meant that the lives of his men in Paris were no longer safe, and he might lose his following. Was this perhaps the great hour for which he and his forebears had waited so long?

The Duke of Guise rode into Paris at noon on May 9, accompanied by only seven men on horseback. But his train grew, as a tiny snowball rolling down a mountain grows into an avalanche in its descent. People left their work, left houses and shops to follow him with cheers; before he reached the center of the city, his seven companions had increased to thirty thousand. Their shouts rose to the skies; many kissed the hem of his cloak; others folded their hands to worship, as if he were a saint. Flowers were flung from the windows. The Duke rode through the crowd with bared head, smiling, greeting, jesting, waving his hand. He rode straight to the St. Eustache quarter, near the Queen Mother's palace, and immediately paid his respects to her. Catherine had not expected him. She stared as at a ghost, trembling, perhaps for the first time in her life, when the Duke knelt down before her. "I am glad to see you," she said finally, "but I should much rather have seen you at any other time."

The King sent him an invitation to a conference. But as Guise had heard that Epernon was awaiting him with forty-five dagger-bearing catchpolls, he took along four hundred noblemen who were not exactly unarmed, either. This pleasant parley produced no result, of course. The King screamed at Guise, demanding to know how he could dare come to Paris contrary to royal command. The Duke, without hiding his contempt, offered a few general protestations of loyalty but left the question unanswered. The parting was even more hostile than the meeting. This was on May 10.

On the following day, the King ordered Marshal de Biron to take precautionary measures. On the 12th, at dawn, twenty platoons marched with fife and drum through the gates and occupied the district round the Louvre, the Cité, Les Halles, and the Place de Grève. When the troops appeared, the people closed doors and shops, took up arms, and rushed to the quarters held by Guise. The tumult grew as the sun rose. Suddenly speakers announced that the royal municipal government had been overthrown and replaced by one composed of representatives of the people.

Now, with storm bells ringing, the citizens started building barricades in the streets, thirty paces apart. They worked at such speed, in such silence, and with such discipline that the barricades seemed to grow out of the ground. Before the King's men were aware of it, they were hemmed in on all sides. Only then, as if on command, did the shouting begin: "Hew the troops down!" Both sides fought bravely. But the organization of the League forces was perfect; after a short while, the Swiss called for a truce. Their weapons were taken from them amid derisive laughter, and the Duke of Guise rode unarmed through the streets with a white marshal's baton, ordering his men to cease attacking the royal soldiers and merely to hold their ground.

The King, however, when the fall of the Louvre seemed imminent, had stepped into the garden as if to consult with his marshals, donned peasant clothes, and escaped by way of the Porte Neuve. He fled as far as Chartres, at full gallop, and in twenty-four hours the whole Court assembled there. Guise's *coup d'état* had succeeded in the capture of Paris, and then failed when the chief opponent got away. He was now ready to negotiate a compromise which on the day before he would have rejected. The concessions made by both sides were of little consequence. All that mattered to Guise was his appointment as commander of the army and the King's solemn promise to convoke the *States-General.*

Henry opened the meeting in the great hall of the castle at Blois, with all the display of vain dignity that he prized. On the top step of the throne, which was covered with a gorgeous canopy, sat his mother. At the foot of the throne sat the Grand Maître, the Duke of Guise, baton in hand, clad, as always, in white satin, proudly surveying the obsequious assembly.

The King's oration was prolix and elegant; as in all such speeches, there was much talk of honest intentions, sleepless nights, cares, peace-mindedness, and love of the people, and of responsibility to God and man. If he and his mother had their way, France would enter upon glorious times; but the parties were evil, indolent, and cowardly. This led to a scene, after the first session, between the King and

Guise, who felt offended despite Henry's assurance that he had not been meant. On the second day the deputies took an oath to the League, as it were; and the King swore to continue in the Roman Catholic faith to his last breath, to do his all to uproot heresy, and never to let a heretic be his successor. And to steal Guise's thunder, he appointed himself head of the League.

A dogged, sneaking, creeping struggle went on between the two, with much mutual bowing and scraping. Guise made proposals from which he expected a further rise in his popularity. He demanded a reduction of taxes and the abolition of most custom duties. The King replied with such fine pathos that he himself was moved to tears: he was in a lamentable position, did not have enough for the upkeep of the Court, sometimes lacked the few cents needed to dispatch a courier. He showed the assembly his clothes, every suit of which had to last him three months. He said he had long ceased to be a spendthrift but would in future be satisfied with even less: if two capons were too much at table, he would make one do. The delegates, adamant, threatened to leave Blois unless the *taille*, at least, was reduced. After days of wrangling, Henry yielded with one of those sly tricks which never failed him.

"Of course, I now expect the honorable assembly to find ways and means to make up this loss to the exchequer. The present income, gentlemen, totals 9,500,000 écus. With sharp retrenchment, I think the country can be administered on 5,000,000. I am ready to do all I can to reach that level. But I beg you, in the name of the people, get us the 5,000,000."

Now nobility, clergy, and bourgeoisie were at a loss. It turned out that no one had studied the complex machinery of government in sufficient detail to make practical suggestions. When it was proposed that the deficit be covered by the personal guarantees of the richest members, the motion was carried, but subscriptions were deplorably meager. The deliberations became hopelessly entangled, and it was easy to predict that they would end as they had begun.

There was no longer a bridge between this King and his people. They were too far apart on fundamentals. Now and then the King might concede a point, but ever present underneath, incorrigible and yet unconsciously prophetic, was one idea: "I am King by the Grace of God, responsible to God alone, above any law by virtue of my calling. If I beg you to give legal force to your resolutions, I do so because I choose, not because I must; not compelled by any constitution but because I care for the people. I will swear not to violate the laws you put into force, but my oath is a voluntary act."

The deputies, on the other hand, were frankly determined to uphold a form of government in which the powers of the sovereign and his advisers depended on the popular will. They considered the power of the people superior to that of the King; in their view, resolutions passed by the *States-General* became law automatically, whether or not the King approved them. He was to be no more than their executive arm.

How different was the meeting held at the same time by the Calvinists in La Rochelle! The King of Navarre, with two other high-born Protestants, presided. Authority was respected as a matter of course, and in full harmony regulations were worked out governing the administration of justice, finances, military levies and discipline, and community work. And to Henry III a petition was sent asking, with great dignity and without self-abasement, for a renewal of the latest peace edict.

The *States-General*, however, by then had been shocked by the news that the Duke of Savoy, in accord with Spain, had used the party strife to seize the French town of Saluzzo and incorporate it in his realm. Now the sorry condition of the French Estates became apparent. A foreign prince, without the shadow of a right, had occupied French soil—a prince, moreover, whose military strength was negligible—and the course of action might have been considered plain. But national interests were represented at Blois only by the King and his small following; the League was in no mood to break with Savoy, who was one of its members and maintained close relations with the Pope. It wrapped itself in flaming zeal and urged war—upon the Huguenots!

Attempts have been made to picture the League as the forerunner of Richelieu's policy of centralization. Even if the thesis could not be refuted otherwise, it would be untenable in view of this laxness of the organization toward national interests when Spain, the Pope, and the Savoys set out to dismember France. Morally the League cannot be justified, no matter how one may try. It convicted itself, not by its program, nor by its brutal fight against the Reformation, but by its very "achievements" for the state, which always turned out to be achievements against the common welfare. They did not even benefit a certain upper class, but solely a clique. No ideology guided the activities of the League; it did not contribute a single productive idea to the rise of France.

The King grew more and more helpless before the pointed, withering, breath-taking offensive of the Duke of

Guise. He sensed that soon he would no longer receive consideration; and as on the Day of the Barricades he feared an attempt at forcible seizure of his person to compel him to sign whatever was needed. Already his and the Duke's retainers were fighting, even soldiers and lackeys. One afternoon, in the palace yard, there was a squabble among pages, and if more thoughtful men had not intervened there would have been bloodshed. To the King, this much seemed certain: Guise was planning another coup. A final private talk with him was fruitless; the Duke wanted no agreement. During the conversation the King controlled himself, but back in his room his rage found vent in a screaming fit. "He must die, he must die at once!" Running round like a hungry beast in its cage, he kept repeating: "Die, die, die."

Guise was warned, as Coligny had been warned. But he merely laughed. "The King? Never. He is as cowardly as a rat."

On December 18, 1588, the wedding of a niece of the Queen Mother was celebrated with a banquet in the castle of Blois. While the guests were chatting in the salons Henry III sent for Crillon, the colonel of a regiment of the guards, and began bluntly: "Do you think the Duke of Guise deserves to die?"

"Yes, Sire."

"I have chosen you to have him killed."

"The sentence, Sire?"

"My dear Crillon, if we wanted to wait for the sentence . . ."

"Pardon me, Sire; I am a soldier, not an assassin."

The King pledged him to secrecy and summoned Loignac, one of his chamberlains, whose "pleasing" manners had almost raised him to the status of a *mignon*. Loignac did not hesitate; he promised to commit the murder with some of the forty-five royal bodyguards at his disposal. The pious King advised the deputies that he would spend Christmas in religious meditation at Notre-Dame-de-Cléri, and did not again appear at the sessions. On the evening of December 22 the Duke of Guise, sitting down to supper, found a note under his napkin: "The King wants to kill you." He threw the paper under the table.

On December 24 the deputies met early in the morning. Though Guise was late, he nevertheless stopped at the chapel for his morning prayer. When he entered the great hall he appeared nervous, apologized for not being fully awake, and sat shivering by the fire. He had had no breakfast and asked one of the valets for something to eat, raisins, perhaps, or some rose jam. The valet brought him plums, of which Guise ate only one when his nose began to bleed. His brother, already a cardinal despite his youth —the great Cardinal of Lorraine had recently died—was talking to the Archbishop of Lyon.

Then the Secretary of State, Rivol, brought word that the King desired to see the Duke. Guise put on his coat, hat, and gloves, crossed the adjoining room, and greeted Loignac and his companions politely as ever. They followed slowly, as if to escort him. When he reached the door, one of them stabbed him in the neck and the rest set upon him from all sides.

"Merciful God!" Guise cried, then dragged himself into the King's private room, blood streaming from his body, and collapsed before the King's bed. He was still sighing: "Oh, my friends, my friends . . ." when he died.

The King had watched the scene from behind a curtain.

"Finished?" he asked, coming out. "Finished," said Loignac. Henry approached the victim with evident satisfaction. He regarded him curiously. "He did not look so big when he was alive." He kicked the corpse in the face. If a spark of life was left in Guise, his last thought must have been of Coligny's death.

When Cardinal de Guise heard the excited noise in the King's room, he knew what had happened. Together with the Archbishop of Lyon he jumped up and ran to the hall door to summon aid. The door was locked. A moment later they were arrested by Marshal de Retz.

The Archbishop was pardoned by the King. Cardinal de Guise, however, was beheaded on the next day.

Thirteen days following the murder, the Queen Mother died after a long illness. Behind her she left her last son with a broken crown, the kingdom divided, the people on the brink of ruin. She had lived long, worked long, yet only the curses of the Calvinists and the horror of the Catholics followed her to her grave. "No one cared about her death, as no one had cared about her illness," wrote Estoile. "It has aroused no more attention than the death of a goat."

How could any heart be moved by the passing of an old woman—whom people spoke of as a witch, who was charged not only with every intrigue and calumny but with black magic and poison-mongering—so soon after the glamorous party had been robbed of its idol, the handsome Duke? Slowly, after days of numbness, Frenchmen began to recover from the first deep shock. Bedridden old Cardinal de Bourbon, Prince Charles of Joinville, the Dukes of Elboeuf and Nemours, even the mother of the Guises had been arrested; in Paris, the seized men included the Provost of Merchants, and several deputies and officials. Papers found on Pélicard, Guise's secretary, disclosed the conspiracy with Spain: there were statements of the sums received from Philip. Many members of the League sought salvation in flight.

But it was too late to hold the people in check. Orléans rose after Paris, then Chartres, then Blois. As long as there was a Valois left, treacherous and senseless killing would continue. What had happened under Henry II, Francis II, Charles IX, was legend already; but the legend lived, every child knew it, no one had forgotten it. The masses packed the churches during sermons. Seventy divines of the Sorbonne declared all Frenchmen absolved from their oath of allegiance. A procession of one hundred thousand children was arranged; they carried burning candles through the capital and then, extinguishing them underfoot, cried in chorus: "May God let the Valois breed be soon extinguished, like this." The Duke of Mayenne, brother of the murdered Guise, came to Paris to lead the revolt; whole provinces rose up against the royal assassin. The League demanded that the case be tried in court, and a Papal bull came from Rome, threatening Henry III with the ban if he did not release Cardinal de Guise within ten days. But the Cardinal had long been dead when the bull arrived. Above all, people raged against the Politicians, who were accused of being friendly to the King. More and more towns revolted, in Picardy, Normandy, Champagne, Provence, and Burgundy.

The King fled to Tours, as to a last refuge. Who was to aid him? Was he really lost? Now, in this most desperate situation, Henry III turned to the Calvinists, who were holding the country beyond the Loire. After the death of the Duke of Guise, Henry of Navarre had addressed a manifesto to the three Estates of France, passionately calling them to unity: "I entreat you all, Catholics, servants of the King or not; I appeal to you as Frenchmen. I implore you to have pity on this land and on yourselves. Have we not fought and suffered enough? Has God not yet sufficiently chastised us to bring us back to sanity and sate our anger?" Now, with the King forced to appeal to him, Navarre saw the day of reunion finally dawning.

After some hesitation, distrust was allayed; the royal and Protestant armies united. A national French feeling arose, perhaps for the first time. The two fraternizing Kings were bankrupt—their officers had to take up a collection—but in the field they scored success after success. A raid by Mayenne on Tours was beaten back. At Senlis, La Noue enveloped the Parisians under the Duke of Aumale. 15,000 Swiss joined the 30,000 Frenchmen. The strong and growing forces quickly approached Paris and encamped before the city; Henry III took up quarters at St. Cloud, Henry of Navarre at Meudon. Preparations were made for besieging the capital.

But no siege occurred. On Tuesday, September 1, a Dominican monk named Jacques Clément asked to see the King, to deliver important news. The King had often been warned; he knew that the priests called from the pulpits for his assassination, praising it as a deed pleasing to God which would be rewarded with eternal salvation. But he feared no evil from the wretched, frail, humble young man who came shuffling in now. Asked to step nearer, Clément leaned forward as if to whisper something in the King's ear and thrust a knife into his belly. Henry cried out, and the murderer fled into a far corner of the room to stand with his arms out against the wall like one crucified. He was killed instantly.

Henry III died during the night. In his last hour he summoned the Catholic nobles and commanded them to accept Henry of Navarre as King.

20

THE STRUGGLE FOR THE CROWN

HENRY OF NAVARRE'S winning of his kingdom after the Valois died out has inspired numerous works of history and fiction. It is the story of a ceaseless, wearying struggle; of a man without royal might, authority, or revenue, a mere pretender, with a claim founded on an old law, prevailing in the end against superior foes; of his rise to power, and his gift to France of a unity already a hundred years overdue. It was a thrilling achievement by a courageous, supple, and unusual talent. But it belongs only indirectly to the story of the Huguenots. Though a detailed account would be interesting, we shall have to crowd eventful years into a few pages.

For more than a generation France had taken the extinction of the House of Valois for granted and come to regard it as a just disposition of fate. Even Catherine de' Medici, whose only goal in life had been the aggrandizement of this house, could hardly retain any illusions when one of her sons after another died without issue. A tale was told that one night, at Chaumont-sur-Loire, she arranged a spiritualist séance to find the answer to the question which troubled her so deeply; she always thought much of magicians, astrologers, and palmists. The roll of the French kings was called, and each spirit rounded the magic circle as many times as his reign had lasted years. Henry II, her husband, was followed by her sons, Francis II and Charles IX, and finally by Henry III, who was still among the living. "How long will you reign?" The phantom walked round fifteen times and vanished in the darkness. Tension gripped the spectators. And when the magician called into the silence: "Who will inherit the crown?" the King of Navarre appeared, as strong and agile as he was in life.

The prophesy had been fulfilled. But the kingdom that fell to Navarre was disintegrating, the majority of his subjects hated him, and his capital was in his enemies' hands. He had not only to conquer this realm but to re-establish it. He had to restore peace and order, justice and morality. The Catholic notables refused to be bound by the oath they had sworn to the dying Henry III unless Navarre returned to the Catholic fold. And so grotesque was this Court that, to plead for their religious demands, they chose the Marquis d'O, the most corrupt of the *mignons*, the despicable and generally despised leader of those male courtesans. And d'O, whose cynicism was famous, now declared in the name of the notables that he would rather fall upon his sword than see the Apostolic faith debased in France.

"Gentlemen," replied the King, "if I were ready now, because you wish it, to change my religion, I should prove only that I have no religion at all. Do you really wish to serve a godless king, an atheist? If such a king called you to battle, could you follow him with clear consciences?" After long discussions he promised only to let himself be instructed by Catholics of standing, and to give his final decision after six months.

In those days, to be sure, such a promise meant more than its language indicated. A sovereign could do nothing under duress; if known to be displeased with a politic course of action, he must let himself be convinced of its merit so that he might seem to follow it with pleasure. To play the dialectician, so as not to be deemed an opportunist, was a king's only way of changing his mind. Both parties knew the meaning of the formula. To the Catholics it was a promise, and to the Huguenots it left a slight hope that ways and means could yet be found to prevent its fulfillment. As for Henry himself, he seems to have decided even then to be guided more by events than by learned men.

For the time being, his situation looked more difficult every day. Among the Catholics the view gained ground that heretic was heretic, regardless of any publicly staged conversion. Many joined the ranks of the League. A large part of the nobles played a waiting game, frankly unwilling to battle for the King before his kingship was certain. Most of the Huguenots had gone back to the provinces in disappointment; and his Catholic partisans demanded such exorbitant promises of money, land, and honors, that he would be stripped before he could begin to fulfill them. After some weeks the royal army had shrunk until it hardly counted; of the 40,000 Henry had led toward Paris 6,000 were left. Unable to maintain his position in the heart of France, he had to withdraw to Normandy.

The most faithful were still the Huguenot leaders: the Duke of Bouillon; Francis de Châtillon, Coligny's son; Jacques Caumont, Agrippa d'Aubigné, La Noue, Sully, and Duplessis-Mornay. Some of them had sacrificed so much for Henry, had placed so much of their property at his disposal while he was prince, that by leaving him now they would have abandoned themselves as well as their faith in his star. But what good were 6,000 soldiers to a King of France? He had never been so weak. If the desertions continued, he might soon have not a thousand with him.

The feudal lords, fortified in their pursuit of independence by each progressive weakening of the Valois, now used their full power to promote their own interests. They undertook to set up provincial satrapies. The towns, perceiving a chance to establish themselves as free communities, displayed like tendencies. The League still had the support of the wealthiest and mightiest princes and of the Papal Court. There could be no doubt as to the outcome of this unequal struggle; the only question was how soon the King would collapse. Mayenne would dispose of him in short order, after chasing him from refuge to refuge. Soon, perhaps tomorrow, Navarre would be a prisoner or, with luck, might catch a ship bound for England. At the moment, of course, he still held a prisoner himself: his uncle, old Cardinal de Bourbon, whom the Parisians had proclaimed King Charles X. But the Cardinal was a marionette. There would be a few more months of civil war; and then either Mayenne or a foreign prince would become King by unanimous consent. Perhaps Spain would supply the prince; in which case, while the Lorraines' century-long quest for the Crown of France would end in failure, they probably would get a state of their own in the east. Such a buffer state between France and Germany might even have advantages. And the incorrigible south, hardened in heresy, would then be taken care of by the Inquisition.

Henry was aware that constant reorganization of his feeble forces would only wear them out and himself, too. As so often before, he must stake all on one throw. He appealed to his former companions-in-arms, to their hearts and consciences, and not a few returned. He appealed to England's parallel interests, until the island decided to send troops. "To win," he said, "we have too little, but that is the very reason why we must win."

Suddenly, to the surprise of everyone, he stood at the gates of Paris again and took a few suburbs—a bluff, of course, for to dare more would have been suicide. He whirled about to pounce upon the towns along the Loire like a bird of prey. There he was surprised: the *parlement* of Tours voluntarily recognized him as King. He turned the campaign into a steeplechase; losing one place, he simply took another. He did not march, he flew. In two months, with heavy artillery, he covered five hundred miles.

On March 14, 1590, battle was joined on the plain of Ivry, one of the great cavalry battles so apposite to the French military style. Henry's opponents were so far superior that they had only to advance against his force to overwhelm it. His white standard was seen to fall ever farther back; his ranks were beginning to dissolve. He had lived through many moments when all seemed lost, but this was the worst. He called out: "If you don't want to keep fighting, cowards, at least take one more look and see me die!" and plunged into the thick of the fray. His entourage, shamed and stirred, went after him. The plume on his helmet was their standard; in its wake, they threw themselves on the enemy. The front of the League cavalry broke, and in its flight upset the infantry; soon the whole army was scrambling to escape. The French and German troops were wiped out; the Swiss surrendered. Suddenly, quite unexpectedly, the road to Paris was open. Henry besieged it, cut all its communications with the vicinity, and aimed his guns at Montmartre.

In later years he often talked of his feelings at the time when he encircled Paris and tried to starve it out. Walking through his camp in the evenings, with the walls of the city before him, he would sink into abysmal despair. What hurt most was not that he had to fight for his capital, but that its people had nothing to put up against him but the power of Spain. Here he was, a Frenchman, of the best French blood, in the prime of life, full of bold plans and intentions—and they rejected him, loathed him, preferred a sick old Habsburg who did not know France and did not love it. It was incomprehensible, unforgivable.

On the other hand, if the Parisians locked their gates against him it was not only because they detested the heretic. Another reason was that Spanish-Papal propaganda spared no lie to prove that Henry came only to avenge St. Bartholomew's. He was said to have sworn to plunge his arm in blood to the elbow. The new Papal Legate, Gaetano, worked hand in glove with Spanish Ambassador Mendoza. They had all municipal officials put on oath never to pay homage to a King who was not a Catholic, and the people had to repeat that oath in the several quarters of the city. The less food there was, the cruder grew the lies; with famine increasing, there remained no outrage of which the Béarnais was not said—and believed—to be capable.

Yet Paris was saved. Philip II ordered to its relief his most illustrious general, Alexander of Parma, then on the point of subjecting the Dutch provinces again. Parma obeyed, albeit reluctantly, and invaded France with the greater part of his army. Since Henry was unable to face him and at the same time keep Paris surrounded, the siege was raised. But the issue of the war remained unsettled, for Parma, seeing his mission accomplished and himself victorious without fighting, avoided battle. He returned to the Netherlands; soon, winter and lack of money made further operations impossible.

By then, Philip had got the entire anti-Navarre movement into his hands. The French people were weary of civil war; they preferred even an end with horror to this horror without end. In God's name, let the King of Spain rule, or someone designated by him. Mendoza had done his work well. He could induce the Sorbonne to petition Philip: would he be so kind as to accept the throne of France? The Jesuits supported the plan. The preposterous decision was made to declare all opponents of Spain guilty of high treason.

As not all the provinces were willing to go along with Paris, the war continued. On the one hand, Parma kept frightening the Protestants with his splendid, superdisciplined army; on the other hand, Elizabeth of England kept frightening the Catholics with troops and money. When Parma died and the scales turned in Navarre's favor, Philip balanced them with increasing pressure on the League. He now revealed the bent of his peculiar genius by asking the French throne for his daughter Isabella and the man she married, whoever he might be. Improbable as it sounds, this scheme was seriously debated at a meeting of the *States-General,* called by Mayenne as though he were the legitimate ruler. Philip suggested a match between the Infanta and Archduke Ernest, brother of Emperor Rudolf. What a prospect: France and the Netherlands united under a Habsburg couple, who in turn would have to lean on the Habsburgs' Spain! It was too much even for the League. If Isabella would be Queen of France, she should wed the young Duke of Guise, the son and heir of the one murdered by Henry III.

Public opinion stirred at last. There was a change, an upsurge of national feeling. Pain gripped the hearts of townspeople, soldiers, merchants, scholars, peasants. No one had any illusions about the meaning of dependence on Spain. A subject unthinkable only a short time before was now discussed daily: did or did not Frenchmen owe allegiance to him who by the grace of God was legitimate heir to the throne, even if he should persist in Protestantism?

Long past were the six months after which Henry of Navarre had promised to declare himself. He had been in the field four years without interruption and without decisive progress. He felt his energies waning; the trials were too many for a single life. At last, the Catholics sent him an ultimatum.

During these years the King's struggle with himself was more trying than the war against his enemies. Yet those who thought him incapable of renouncing the Reformed faith a second time did not know him. Henry was not only the son of Jeanne d'Albret, he also was the son of Anthony de Bourbon. At heart he had always been a

Catholic Protestant. His mother, who had made Calvinism dominant in her tiny country, had raised him on her own fanaticism, had him tutored by the great Huguenot Florent Chrétien, taught him to sing Marot's psalms; in his first combats the example of Coligny, the unwavering, had been before his eyes. But when he grew up, his actions and demeanor showed a deep, pagan zest for life, a Latin-Gallic humor, a prodigal *laissez faire;* at bottom his character was wholly alien to Calvinist asceticism.

Returning home after years of imprisonment in Paris, he made only half-hearted efforts to dispel the reputation earned him by his past life: that of a frivolous, irresponsible, unstable young man. The plain-spoken d'Aubigné, who came to him as master of the horse, remained his constant exhorter. From the start, he fought against the King's speculations whether religious neutrality were not the most sensible attitude for an heir presumptive to the French throne. In his amusing satire, *Confession catholique du Sieur de Sancy*, d'Aubigné reviled Henry as an ingrate and debauchee, and went so far as to disclose many of the King's love-affairs, darkly picturing them as threats to the Reformed cause. Among those mentioned were: one Catherine du Luc d'Agen, a Demoiselle de Montagu, the ladies Rebours and Fausseuse who also appear in the memoirs of la Reine Margot, Fleurette, the gardener's daughter, and a certain Esther Imbert; then a baker's wife from St. Jean, who was followed successively by a Madame de Duras, the concierge's daughter, the Viscountess of St. Magrin, and the two sisters de l'Espée. In between was the great love, the Countess of Gramont, alias Corysande, whom Henry really intended to marry —something which, as a rule, he was satisfied merely to promise. In addition, there were several liaisons which d'Aubigné felt obliged to pass over discreetly. His anger often prompted him to bid the King farewell forever, and he actually did leave him at times. But he was always drawn back by Henry's charm and indispensability. A dominating talent is easily pardoned; a talent clearly created not for itself, but for many, will be forgiven almost anything.

The King's mastery of life was unique, and so was the magnetic force which drew men to him. His reign in Nérac was serene, imaginative, purposeful. Miraculously, in that era, it raised no problems that had to be solved with dagger, poison, or assault. People understood one another. They were quick to agree. The blessing of the southern sun humanized the strict Calvinists; the others were no angels, either, not even dry, sober Sully. The sole exception was Duplessis-Mornay, who never adopted the Court's light Gascon tone; which makes it the more remarkable that he, particularly, always retained faith in Henry. "It takes a camel's patience," he told him frankly, "to stick to you. But I know you alone in France are born to greatness, and now that is more important than those other things." And he wrote: "What the world needs, what it is thirsting for, is a real king. He is here. He has but to step forth to be recognized."

To Henry's generation, the political problem was already of greater import than the religious one. As King of Navarre he would never have changed his faith; as pretender to the throne of France he saw a duty rising out of his right. If he was to save the monarchy and the nation, he could not reject the only means at hand. He could calculate exactly how much longer Protestantism would survive—now that the first religious ardor had cooled and it was confronted with the Jesuit reform of Catholicism—unless at last a central power was established that would stand up to the forces of reaction. Continuation of the rift would doom the state.

At heart, Henry always belonged to the Third Party, to the Politicians who cared nothing about religion when France was at stake. Everything urged him toward conversion. The seed sown by Calvinism had ripened; he wanted to live to be the sickle that reaped it. Distinguished advisers stood ready to assist him. The political ideas of the Reformation—that the feudal monopoly on power had outlived its day, that at least in financial matters power belonged to the towns and the productive agrarians—had permeated large groups; the many revolts over purely economic issues proved it. In Paris, significantly, the bourgeoisie had joined the working class in an attempt to exclude the aristocracy from the city government. A pamphlet entitled *Discours sur la comparaison et élection de deux parties qui sont pour le jourd'hui au ce royaume* declared: "Why should the poor, unhappy people care what religion rules, so long as it is not one whose teachings let the marrow be sucked from their bones? We see only a jumble of conflicting, hostile, ambitious parties, gathered to swallow a morsel that ought to choke them."

Bitter words, but true; they were not to remain true. The Third Estate had furnished the most dauntless fighters; it had earned the right to support. By aiding it, the provincial satraps could be broken. The most truly royal fight, against the independent tendencies of the nobility, could be won, and a united France created. The King would have to resurrect the old coalition first entered into by Francis I, with towns and gentry against the great lords—who would have to be absorbed, as it were. These were the tasks before him, Henry of Navarre. He sensed them clearly; and Sully and Duplessis-Mornay did their best to keep his feeling alive and to strengthen it.

Philip was making ready to have his daughter proclaimed Queen of France.

On July 23, 1593, the Archbishop of Bourges talked with Henry. Their discourse lasted from six to eleven in the morning; it was the last of the Catholic instructions with which he had been plagued almost daily. He interrupted the Archbishop only to ask for explanations; when their opinions differed, he always closed with the words: "I submit entirely to the authority of the Roman Catholic Church." It was a beautifully prearranged scene.

On Sunday, July 25, the King, escorted by the princes and officers of the Crown, appeared before the great portal of St. Denis at eight in the morning. The prelates awaited him with cross, Gospel, and holy water. "Who are you?" asked the Archbishop of Bourges.

"I am the King."

"What do you wish?"

"I ask to be admitted into the Catholic, Apostolic, and Roman Church."

"Is it your sincere wish?"

"It is."

The King knelt down and repeated the stipulated formula. The Archbishop imparted absolution and benediction. High Mass was sung.

The stage for peace was set, but it did not come immediately. The Papal Legate, furious about the attitude of the French church, addressed an open letter to French Catholics, threatening any cleric who would visit Henry with severe ecclesiastic punishment. He also had the gates of Paris closed to keep the people from going to St. Denis, but they stormed the gates to be on hand for the ceremony that was to end the national misfortune. The League was disunited, and gradually its ranks dwindled by defections to the King's side.

Henry's march to his capital began. The Spanish representative, the Duke of Feria, tried to the last to stir up resistance, but his power over the Parisians was gone. When word came of the King's approach, expectation mounted to fever heat. People were in the streets from two in the morning. The Spanish troops in the city were locked up. Then the bridges came down and the royal guards marched in, through the Porte St. Denis, the Porte Neuve des Tuileries, and the Porte St Honoré. As the sun climbed higher and the day broke clear, the thoroughfares became thronged. Everywhere glistened white sashes. Cries rose: "Peace! Peace! Amnesty! He forgives us! Long live the King!"

And then the King came. He came on foot, sword sheathed, head bare, laughing happily. Jubilation welled over—this was deliverance from a nightmare that had lasted for decades. The King's laughter was infectious; people laughed back, gained confidence, opened their shops. The King stood before Notre-Dame, where he had married Margaret Valois; since then he had not been allowed to enter the city, and that was twenty-two years ago. The crowd surged toward him till the guards could no longer hold it back. "Never mind," he said. "They are starved for the sight of a King."

The difference with the Pope still remained to be settled. But Clement VIII, too, was eager to rid himself of Spanish pressure, which had so tormented his predecessor Sixtus V. He also feared that France might leave the Church as England had done, and so grasped the hand Henry offered, absolving him from the ban. Only then did the Duke of Mayenne acknowledge that his day of power had passed; he submitted to the King.

Of all the enemies only Philip was left. He continued the war against France for three more years, but his position grew weaker from month to month. The two Protestant sea-powers, England and Holland, concluded an offensive alliance against him with Papist France; attacked by their united armies and fleets, he had finally to abandon his world-wide plans. Unable to understand an age in which religion had ceased to reign supreme, he could no longer handle even his own country, plunged into untold misery by incessant war. He had come to the end of his days: an old, sick, evil man.

The Pope mediated, and peace was made between France and Spain at Vervins in May, 1598. Henry's Protestant allies fought to the last to prevent it; they regarded his separate pact with Spain as a base defection. The English Ambassador called to remonstrate.

"I can't help it," Henry said. "Words cannot explain how weary we French are. We are sick at heart. We need rest."

21

THE EDICT OF NANTES

NOW that the Huguenot leader had become King of France, should not the first result have been general fraternization?

Such is the pattern in fairy-tales: delusion vanishes; everyone's better, more beautiful self reappears, and people end up in one another's arms. But the true world, that of the poets, is not the real world.

The King was not master in his own house. He had to pay whenever he wanted a sword drawn; his associates were watched; his old friends were kept away from him. What could he do without the Council's consent? And what good were the edicts drafted by the Council if they were not promulgated by the *parlements?*

So Henry put the Protestants off with fine words, year after year, while trying to buy the Catholics with governorships, benefices, and revenues. At times he managed to see the Huguenot deputies alone, and then he assured them that he had not changed, that they still had his full confidence. To justify the privileges which he granted the Catholics, he cited the parable of the prodigal son, for whom the father had the fatted calf killed. Answered the deputies: "Can you say you are treating us like the good faithful son, to whom the father said: 'All I own is yours'? Surely the Gospel does not teach us to rob the good son of his rights, so as to give them to him who spurned parental authority."

The King turned away, gazed off into space, tugged at his graying beard. When he had regained his composure, he turned back and said, a shade too loudly: "You will have satisfaction as soon as I can give it. I can't say more. Be patient."

But under the circumstances it was difficult for the Huguenots to be patient. They were still excluded from all offices, still ill-treated and persecuted, and never sure of their lives. They finally decided, with heavy hearts but with the King's tacit consent, to take matters into their own hands. They resumed their political meetings. There is no doubt that the King conspired with them, against himself; he advised them to rebel, so that he might bring pressure to bear on the Council and the *parlements*, by playing on popular fear of a new civil war. Without being bitter, he knew men; and he knew Machiavelli. He had learned from him and from his own experience that most men will agree to a new order once they see its necessity; but that they will never see the necessity save in actual danger.

The first political *Assemblée* of the Protestants took place at Sainte-Foy in May, 1594.

These Assemblies are not to be confused with synods. Synods serve ecclesiastical purposes; in them, clergy and laity are represented equally. In the Assemblies laymen were the vast majority. The Huguenots divided France into ten districts, each of which nominated a deputy for the General Council. Like the *States-General*, the Protestant Council represented three classes and was composed of four noblemen, four members of the Third Estate, and two pastors. Under the General Council were provincial councils, consisting of from five to seven members each. The General Council received suggestions and complaints from the provinces, passed them on to the King, and negotiated with his representatives. Though definitely a state within the state, the arrangement can be called unjustified only by those who refuse to consider how far the Huguenots still were from sharing in general justice. Catholic dogma treated them as un-French—aliens, really enemies; and public opinion regarded them as criminals. How could laws apply to them of which they were not deemed worthy?

The first Assembly at Sainte-Foy achieved a temporary compact, but the *parlement* of Paris refused to ratify it. The King was disregarded entirely; besides, he had enough troubles of his own. The Catholic lords were blackmailing him with threats of secession; economic distress, which Finance Minister Sully's most ingenious decrees could not relieve from one day to the next, had led to peasant revolts; efforts to have the ban lifted were being obstructed; Savoy, in concert with Spain, was ravaging the south-eastern frontier; and the League raised its head again under the Duke of Mercoeur. Enemies and adversity on all sides, and at Court nothing but insinuations against the Huguenots; even beloved, beautiful, tender Gabrielle d'Estrées, whom the King wished to marry, had little liking for them. Henry found himself being pulled hither and yon; everyone demanded, no one would wait; he was to unravel instantly what had been artfully and artlessly confused in fifty years. In this continuous, tiring self-defense he aged faster than he had in combat. He sought refuge in a hearty, boyish humor, in a hearty, boyish affection for Gabrielle. He sought refuge in interviews with Huguenot delegations—meaningless interviews, but Heaven-sent opportunities for furtive handclasps behind curtains.

But the Huguenots refused to be appeased by his friendly phrases and the slick polish of his Court, while in the country persecution went on as if nothing had changed. During the fruitless negotiations, acts of violence increased in number. At Châtaigneraie, on the border of Poitou and Brittany, League forces, incited by the Duke of Mercoeur, attacked the Protestants at divine service. Two hundred men, women, and children lost their lives. One of the victims was an infant about to be baptized; a boy of eight offered the ten sous he had in his purse as ransom for his life, but the killers preferred his blood to his money. The lady of Châtaigneraie insisted on counting the dead herself. It was a repetition of Vassy, a savage, bestial outrage which roused even the King's reactionary councilors to the point of barring the instigators from an amnesty proclaimed at the time. And yet this was but one crime out of many.

For years, now, Henry had done nothing but make promises. That the Huguenots put little stock in them is evidenced by the fact that even under this, their very own King, they kept leaving the country. Since the days of Henry II, a steady stream of French emigrants had poured into the Protestant parts of Europe: mighty nobles rode into Geneva, to beg the Seigneurs Magnifiques of the Council to admit themselves, their families, friends, and entourages; tradesmen and artisans came to the Netherlands by stage, in farm carts, on foot, to settle in Amsterdam or Leiden; vintners from Champagne and Burgundy crossed the border into the German Palatinate, where they could follow their trade and where divine service was held in the manner they deemed right and proper. In the four last Valois reigns, with the bulk of the Huguenots battling to remain both Protestant and French, increasing numbers had preferred to bid their native land farewell; and Navarre's accession had not halted the trend. Whatever trust in him the Calvinists had retained after his apostasy was shattered by his failure to speed aid for them once he was King.

The Assembly at Loudun considered re-establishing a formal opposition, waiving all peace edicts and preparing to take the consequences. The motion was rejected at first. But when Duplessis-Mornay wrote his name under the document, others followed. "May the Assembly resolve not to adjourn until we have a good edict!" he cried into the hall. "The gentlemen at Court must be taught a lesson! Perhaps they think we are not the same any more, that our fighting spirit has died since Henry deserted us. Let us show them that they are mistaken!"

The siege of Amiens, which had been reconquered by the Spaniards, proved opportune. Depressed and desperate in his camp before the town walls, Henry said he saw he was not yet King of France; he would have to be the King of Navarre once again. The Huguenots were needed now; he invited them to join the besieging army. They, Frenchmen in spite of everything, felt they could not fail their country. And when Amiens was back in French hands, the King informed the Council that he would not return to Paris until the edict for the Protestants was assured.

It was proclaimed at Nantes in May, 1598.

These, roughly, were the contents of the "secret articles and brevets" of the Edict of Nantes: complete freedom of conscience for every house and every family; public worship wherever it had been allowed in 1597, and in the suburbs of all other towns; permission for all high officials to hold divine service for co-religionists in their homes, and the same for the noblemen in their castles. The lower nobility also were permitted to have private services, provided not more than thirty people were present. Also decreed were the eligibility of Huguenots for all public offices, of the children for schools, of the sick for hospitals, and the poor for alms; the establishment of mixed commissions in the *parlements*, composed of members of both denominations, to adjudicate civil disputes between Catholics and Protestants; and the latter's admission to the civil and criminal jurisdiction of the King's courts. The Edict provided four academies for training in sciences and theology, authorization to call synods, and, finally, a number of strongholds.

The Edict of Nantes did not bring full religious freedom. It did not even bring full tolerance. In every respect Catholicism was still the state religion; there were still two armies, two kinds of justice, separate districts assigned to each party, in a country that should have belonged to them both. But what efforts had been required to attain that much, and how difficult it was for people to accept! When Henry IV's councilors submitted the Edict to the Paris *parlement*, there was directed against it the same agitation which for forty years had vented its spite and malice. The feudal nobility knew well what this peace meant. The Calvinists' policy would undergo a complete change; they would combine to protect the power of the King as in the past that of the Bourbon princes; the bourgeoisie would be driven into their camp by fear of mob violence and the peasantry by fear of an aristocratic restoration. So the Duke of Mercoeur tried to halt what could no more be halted, and it was astonishing how much resistance he still could arouse, always in league with the Jesuits. For a few days there were whisperings in Paris of a second St. Bartholomew's. Three individuals hired to murder the King were arrested. But Henry was retreating no longer. He had recovered his former firm determination; he had dared the leap, and now had to stand his ground.

He summoned the refractory members of the *parlement*, then received them quite unceremoniously in his house robe, emphasizing the private nature of the talk, and reminded them of the horrors of civil war. Did they want to start it anew? It was up to them. He, for his part, wished to be a peaceful King; he was awaiting the riots in the city very calmly; he had surmounted much more forbidding obstacles than they could erect. And so he spoke a long time, gesticulating with his old fire, quite the Béarnais again, the man of the South. The Catholic faith, he said, was indispensable to the realm—no doubt about it; but he, Henry de Bourbon, was equally indispensable. Or wasn't he? Did anyone wish to differ? Nobody? All right, there was agreement on that score. The difference between Catholics and Protestants? He did not question it. But they were all Frenchmen. They had not been told this often enough; he told it to them again now. And, he said, he had long thought of a plan—if God let him live he would carry it out—of reuniting the two denominations. But as the time was not yet ripe for this, he advised the Catholics first to end the abuses discrediting their creed; that would make the execution of his plan very much easier.

With the same frankness he talked to representatives of the *parlements* of Rouen, Bordeaux, and Toulouse. The last he accused so violently of conspiracy with Spain—in other words, treason to France—that they preferred to withdraw. Gradually people calmed down; the Edict of Nantes became effective under the King's supervision. The 250,000 Protestant families living in the realm henceforth had a place in the body politic.

And what had been the cost of the pernicious maxim that mankind might have but one faith? The financial loss caused by the religious wars was beyond calculation. But one thing was certain: 2,000,000 people had lost their lives. Stake and ax had killed for seventy years, and civil war had raged for thirty-five. France was devastated, half its towns and castles lay in ruins, the fields were so ravaged that thousands of peasants had emigrated because the soil that had nourished their fathers no longer bore enough to sustain them.

A relatively untroubled period began for the Calvinists, permitting the change-over from warlike activities to productive work for which they had been striving in recent years. Their revolutionary flame had long since expired. They were content to have achieved at least part of their program: proclamation of freedom of conscience and worship, elimination of Guises and *mignons* from the government, recognition of the lower nobility and bourgeoisie as entitled to a share in public life, and assurance of the independence of rural communities from the feudal lords.

For decades before the Edict, their leading representatives had no longer been poor, unassuming preachers and hot-headed artisans. The Huguenots were now ordinary, often prosperous citizens who wanted to work, earn, and worship in their own way. They were ready to compromise in all directions, to realize their economic plans for town and country. Pietists and pacifists, they were chiefly interested in setting up their churches, academies, and parish schools without interference and in directing the country's wealth into industry and agriculture rather than armaments. To them it seemed monstrous how public funds had been squandered for generations, with criminal irresponsibility.

One must remember that the reigns of the last Valois coincided with the great era of the American gold mines. Year after year galleons returned from Mexico laden with gold. In Spain, while poverty reached incredible proportions, the government had more money than ever before. It used the gold to finance wars, to seek supremacy in Europe, to raise huge armies which then lived on the country. Hardly had the soldier left a cottage with his loot when the policeman entered it; two or three times a week the peasant was required to satisfy these rascals' insatiable appetites. Philip's Spain imported gold not to increase prosperity but to wage war. Instead of augmenting the country's wealth, the gold exhausted it. The Protestant princes, on the other hand, unable to match Philip's financial power and yet obliged to pay their soldiers, sought the equivalent in the pockets of their subjects. They cut off production at its source, drained the life-blood from their states, inspired hatreds precluding even a domestic peace. The *States-General* at Blois furnished a list of desperate cases, of strangled priests, murdered soldiers, tortured townsmen, hanged peasants, and raped women; all this was the fruit of gold.

Centuries were to elapse before at least a small group of intelligent men perceived the true, pacific value of the American discoveries. But a vague inkling had already dawned in Calvinist heads. Of all the parties which time and again unleashed civil war, the Huguenots' was the only one to do it under compulsion, against better judgment.

The Calvinist mentality combined shrewd business sense with profound devotion. Wherever Calvinism established itself, it soon attracted the circles engaged in productive work and money-making; most of its proselytes were artisans and merchants. The monastic life was of no value to the Protestant, for worship of God was no longer sufficient to guarantee salvation. In its place came the demand for good works, to wit: all forms of Christian, neighborly love, which finds its most tangible expression in daily labor for the common good.

We have discussed the doctrine of predestination and election by grace, according to which every human is damned or chosen from the beginning of time by God's eternal decree. We have seen how this doctrine, denying that the individual could in any way influence his or her destination for heaven or hell, leaves only one means to make even half-way certain of one's own election: untiring Christian work; for probably only the chosen can perform it. True, Calvinism does not say we cannot be saved *sola fide*, by faith alone; but faith alone is exposed to so much self-deception, to so many misleading ecstasies, that it can never afford *certitudo salutis*. Life in and for the community, on the other hand, can be held strictly to account. It is quite possible to distinguish what merely looks like a good deed from what actually is one. And, in the long run, good works are impossible without God's help; thus he who performs them must possess the divine strength which is granted only to the elect. With the appearance of Calvinism in history, the phrase, "God helps him who helps himself," acquired meaning.

Inevitably, this philosophic revolution was also an economic one. By laying primary stress on a man's daily labor, by denying the bishop precedence at the pearly gates over the clerk or the weaver, it permeated public life with the ideology of work. It declared that only he who works shall eat. Its method of self-surveillance trained the individual in the employment of all his capabilities, indirectly guiding him to self-improvement and education. It drove the passivity out of the masses and replaced it with discipline. The century's achievements were put to use; the printer's art, which quickly spread, became a new weapon; intellectual changes were followed by surprising industrial ones. Calvinist logic penetrated every phase of daily life, as when it instigated work on cattle-breeding, which changed the commercial structure of Holland by inducing the Dutch to eat more meat and cheese and catch less fish. Sailors took up farming; soldiers raised the stock instead of hiring out for wars. The distressed masses gradually perceived what was at stake; it dawned on them that the productive work of everybody freed them of the necessity for living on alms.

So the social structure changed in the Protestant countries. The workingman made room for himself, forced his way into the area of the hereditary landowners. The middle class widened and strengthened its towns by means of financial transactions, which it had learned to view as work like any other. The rise of the Calvinist Reformation became one with the rise of capitalism. The countries which joined it registered an undreamed-of upsurge; from that time on, England, Holland, Switzerland, and, later, America came to the fore. In France the dams built by orthodoxy and reaction broke under the Edict of Nantes, and the flood of progress poured freely through the break for almost a century.

Yet even the beginning of this revolution bore the seed of its end. The power of capital was hardly established before its possessors had to think about maintaining and fortifying it. The brakes were applied to the rise of the Third Estate as a whole as soon as its upper stratum, the bourgeoisie, was politically and economically in the saddle. As a corporation, it was not at all interested in having the power of its old members weakened by the influx of too many new ones. Thus Luther and Calvin alike barred further evolution: both, in their writings, declared it to be the task of the state to keep the masses poor so as to keep them tractable. In Germany, when order was restored after the Iconoclast and Peasant Wars, Luther approved it as an order willed by God. Those who had come out on the short end of it had to submit to fate, to the Divine Plan; as peasant, a man could contribute no less to the glory of God than as prince. Obedience to the Lord required everyone to perform his allotted task, and, consequently, to defer to the authorities set up by the Lord, no matter how imperfect or evil they might be.

This was a far cry from the original tendencies. And it made inevitable what later doomed the Protestant political movement, although in Henry IV's time it was but faintly noticeable: the inner split. Many of the Huguenot aristocracy—noblemen or *bourgeois* patricians—had made their peace with tradition. When the lower classes persisted in the earlier policy, the gentlemen dropped out. They wanted henceforth to stress the spiritual aspects of the movement, and retain of the political ones only a vague libertarian trend. By liberty, however, they did not mean individual liberty, freedom as such, but a number of special liberties like class privileges, "no taxation without representation," and cultural non-restraint. The original line was upheld only by the lower strata, artisans and laborers.

The world had taken a step forward from feudalism to capitalism, but no more than a step. The rigid social structure of the Middle Ages had been shattered, the circle of property owners somewhat widened, the multitude of disinherited somewhat diminished. The numerical relation of the classes had been altered; much had happened and yet not enough by far. But man fears nothing so much as his own boldness.

22

THE KING'S MINISTER

THE new type of man who came to the fore at this period, unprecedented in his combination of Christian ethics with business acumen, has never been better personified than in Henry IV's Minister of Finance, Maximilian Baron de Rosny, later Duke of Sully.

Maximilian de Béthune was born at Rosny Castle near Mantes in 1560, and was thus seven years younger than his King. At the time of St. Bartholomew's he attended school in Paris. Both his tutor and his servant were killed; but he himself, though merely twelve years of age, kept his wits about him. In his pupil's uniform, a lecture schedule as passport under his arm, he walked right through the murderous bands as far as Bourgogne. There he asked a schoolmaster for sanctuary, and for three days remained in hiding in a barn, behind tools and straw. When still a youth he joined the King of Navarre, followed him to Court at Nérac and into the field, where he proved himself a brave soldier. Henry found the right assistant in him. Good sense, a fearless heart, and the iron will with which he pursued his aims made him the King's perfect complement. He lacked Henry's faults as well as his virtues; his strong and weak points were distinctly his own.

Sully had the sort of mind peculiar to Protestantism: a mind which sees in work that produces income not a mere means to an end but an end in itself. Even as a soldier in the service of the Prince of Navarre, he took the best possible care of his master's standard of living; and he liked transactions which cleverly replenished the cash drawers of Nérac while leaving him a neat profit on the side. He married a rich heiress, and was not above war profiteering—as when he bought up horses cheaply in Germany and sold them in Gascony at a vastly higher price. The King had his unreserved devotion. Once, when Henry was in financial straits, Sully had his own timber at Rosny cut and put the proceeds at his master's disposal. He remained an ardent Calvinist all his life, yet it was he who advised the King to turn Catholic, because, as he put it, "just now, Sire, it is the best religion for you to end the war." Henry once told Venetian Ambassador Priuli that he considered Sully his most faithful and dependable servant; and as far as we can judge, centuries later, Sully was exactly that.

He was not a pleasant person. Virtually no one felt real affection for him. He was frigid, gruff, inconsiderate, caustic, cynical, and vain; a crusty individual who took pride in his crust and delighted particularly in being rude to the King. People went out of their way to avoid him, and after the King's death Sully was soon made to pay for the antipathies he had aroused. But he was indispensable, the backbone of the state, and on the whole a great man.

As soon as Henry became King of France, he appointed Sully a member of the Finance Council. In the beginning the experts disregarded the newcomer, but it soon turned out that the King had chosen well. First Duplessis-Mornay declined the financial portfolio, on the ground that his humane and benevolent temperament disqualified him for a post requiring a strong dose of brutality. The reconstituted Finance Council was found to be lining its own pockets; then, Harlay de Sancy failed lamentably to balance income and outgo. So the King put the thankless, herculean task up to his old friend. "You know best what you will find, my dear Baron," he told him; "nothing but debts. I can give you no advice because I know too little about the subject. The one thing I can say I really need not tell you: if we do not put the state household in order we shall shortly starve, and Spain will dine off the remains."

In 1596, data on the financial crisis were compiled for an assembly of lords at Rouen. They made a shattering picture of the devastation wrought in a state which was run too long by megalomaniacal amateurs. The funded debt totaled nearly 100,000,000 écus—about $50,000,000—and the annual deficit was estimated at around 6,000,000 écus. The situation was desperate, and no economist could think of a way out. The suggestions that were made quickly proved impracticable. One was to lower the interest rate on the national debt by two percent. Another was to annul a part of the capital obligation equal to the sum of previously made interest payments; this meant a declaration of bankruptcy, but at least a fresh start could then be made. A third proposal envisioned an increase in taxes, to be levied mainly on the towns; a toll, like the one collected in Paris, was to be introduced in every town in the country.

Noteworthy suggestions, but how should they be carried out? Reduction of the national debt, capital or interest? The men who had to vote on it were largely those who had lent the money to the state. They did not dream of taking cuts. They preferred tax increases—for others; their own private property certainly must not be touched. On the contrary, they complained of the *rente* being in arrears and demanded that henceforth it be paid regularly and without delay. As in all previous discussions of the kind, the national budget had to defer to the private ones.

Such was the situation when Sully, already Governor of Poitou and of the Bastille in Paris, was appointed to the Ministry of Finance. And the outstanding fact about his administration is that he did not so much blaze new trails as make order along the old ones. Of his many plans for radical fiscal reform hardly any were put into practice; most were thwarted by the resistance of the propertied groups. The bourgeoisie, faced with the prospect of financial losses, intimated to the masses, which could expect only good from the reforms, that actually they would be the ones to suffer. Often Henry took the part of his Minister, but had to retreat again because the Council, made up of men of wealth, held that the capitalists could not be forced to waive deeded rights. Sully did not even succeed in lowering the *taille*, a measure which every session of the *States-General* had advocated for decades; he only managed to extend it to the circles of the Third Estate which so far had been exempt. A true, great reformer, like Colbert in the following century, Sully certainly was not.

Where, then, lay his merit? It lay in a fact which sounds almost absurd: he was the first to put into effect the theory that the finances of a state should be administered thriftily, in an orderly manner, and according to methodical, fixed rules. He brought into the treasury the full revenues, whereas previously a third had always vanished into the collectors' pockets. He further accomplished a considerable decrease in expenditures, a feat which brought him into conflict with virtually all classes of the population. The chief objectors, of course, were the lords at Court, who for years would gather in his anteroom, threatening loudly, refusing to see that the age of blindly scattered gifts was past. But the King, whose traditional extravagance fully matched that of the nobles, also demanded such vast sums for his love-affairs that more than once he seriously imperiled the budget. On the subject of money, however, Sully was hard of hearing; at times he left the King standing in the middle of a discussion, and slammed the door. His third and greatest achievement, finally, was the rapid utilization of the years of peace for productive effort.

There was no more trusting to chance. Sully moved into his department and immediately spent days and nights there, studying obligations and sources of revenue. His main principle was to create a revenue for every disbursement, to separate all items punctiliously, never letting revenue A be diverted to purpose B. The tax-collectors were sharply called to task after a control commission found that under Henry III only 30,000,000 écus, out of 150,000,000 paid by the subjects, had reached the treasury. Henceforth grave punishment awaited those officials of noble birth, the bailiffs and seneschals, as well as the *trésoriers* who had connived with their subordinates, and all the castellans, provosts, forest, water, and customs officials, and their expert aides. Even the courts of exchequer were roughly handled. Unnecessary departments were abolished; and many involuntarily retired office-holders had to be paid high indemnities although they no longer did any work.

The reforms were costly, but through them the Crown daily regained some of its sovereignty, got more financial and economic authority back into its hands. While enforcement of the measures was difficult, it was much less so than keeping those circles directly affected from turning against the government. Repeal of the exemptions from the *taille* was bound to arouse the bourgeoisie, which had enjoyed them. The new controls were bound to arouse the financiers, who lost huge profits. It took extraordinary skill to keep all three Estates from rebellion and at once instill confidence that everybody's sacrifices would be made up soon by universal prosperity.

Sully took the view that to enrich the King one must enrich the subjects. His principal care was lavished on the improvement of agriculture, which he regarded as the primary source of a nation's wealth: "The raising of crops and the breeding of livestock are the two breasts on which France feeds; they are the real mines and treasures of Peru." To this dictum may be added Henry IV's remark to the Duke of Savoy: "If God lets me live, I shall see that every peasant in my kingdom has a chicken in his pot." For support in their partiality toward the peasantry, the King and Sully drew upon the science of Sieur Olivier de Serres, whose *Théatre d'Agriculture*, published about 1600, is still one of the most informative agricultural textbooks. Every day, Henry devoted an exactly fixed half-hour to its perusal.

Naturally, the peasants did not grow rich at once. The

ruined state could not manage without heavy taxes, but gradually, at least, these were being lowered. If Henry had lived ten years longer, the rural French population might have risen to relative affluence; and even now it could work securely under the protection of the state. The punishments Sully decreed for looting and ruthless billeting were so draconic that the military's abuse of the peasantry, the worst plague of the century, was all but eliminated. From year to year the world looked brighter to the farmer, who received not only crop and stock subsidies but government aid in exporting grains, wines and liquors, especially to the Netherlands.

Today it is difficult to understand Sully's failure, throughout his term of office, to recognize the importance of manufacturing. He professed the aristocrat's contempt for trade and the indifference of Calvinist philosophy to luxury and ease; and his refusal to learn sprang from the unfortunate fact that he was quite as stubborn as he was shrewd. No one could ever budge him from a preconceived idea.

Henry IV was particularly intent on a plan to introduce the culture of silkworms in France, and this caused the two men to quarrel so violently that they would not speak to each other for days. The soldier in Sully came to the fore then as much as the puritan. "How can a people be kept strong," he wrote in a petition to the King, "if they are given a silk industry? You are leading them away from a life of hardship and labor. France needs her army, and it is well known that sturdy peasants and skillful artisans make the best soldiers; if you replace them with people who know but one job, which a child could perform, you will soon find them useless for soldiering as well. At the same time, while unnerving the peasants, who are in every respect the backbone of the state, you will introduce luxury with its whole entourage: license, softness, laziness. Those are urban qualities, dangerous for people who now have little and are satisfied. My God, have we not enough such futile citizens in France, who hide their unmanliness behind gold-and-scarlet clothes?"

But in Olivier de Serres and Barthélemy de Laffemas the King had two vigorous champions of his pro-industrial policy. At Laffemas's suggestion, chambers of commerce were created in the principal towns. The foundations for the silk manufacture which was to make France famous were laid in Paris, in Lyon, in Tours; the workers were paid well and aided in developing their skills. Linen mills were set up in Picardy and Champagne; a lace-making industry was established in Languedoc, and a veil-net industry in Reims and Amiens. After the textile factories came factories producing rugs, tapestries, crystal, mirrors, watches, and perfumes. An astonishing number of the unemployed were put back to work.

The new industries, however, do not begin to tell the story of French progress during Henry IV's reign. Sully covered France with a net of broad, surfaced highways to facilitate the flow of commerce. He spent an amount equal to the cost of the roads on canal construction, and reorganized and safeguarded the mail- and stage-coach system. The army now became an orderly institution, in which the soldier received regular pay and knew that his widow and orphaned children would be cared for should he die in battle. Military academies were built in Paris and at La Flèche; the artillery, Sully's particular hobby, was improved; about twenty large towns were fortified. The port of Marseille was revived, to become a center of the Levantine trade. A colony in Canada—of which more later—flourished after the settlement of Port Royal in 1604. Schools were modernized. A medical college was founded. The Jardin des Plantes of Montpellier was created. The royal library was housed in a new edifice. Scientists and poets were subsidized. And this list indicates but a fraction of all that was done; it seems almost impossible that so much achievement could have been crowded into a scant twelve years.

In the Paris Arsenal one can still see the cylinder on which Sully used to wind his bills and files in order to have them easier to hand, the exquisitely wrought iron chest in which he locked the revenues of the French Crown, and the marble desk on which he wrote. The room is rather low, with paneled walls and ceiling. Here worked the man who brought a mortally sick state back to health. His success was due to a new kind of discipline, which may well be called simply Huguenot discipline.

23

AMERICA

ON THE ancient ramparts of the port of St. Malo stands a statue of its great son, Jacques Cartier, the discoverer of Canada. It faces west, where the sun sets in the Atlantic. And every sunset seems to bring the hard face to life: the changing lights of the western sky play on it, and roundabout it roar the storms which sweep this land of a lost cause. Many sailed away from this coast, never to return. Their country had banned them. Their strength, talents, and energies, lost to France, helped the New World achieve its progress and glory.

Nothing could quench their thirst for a free existence across the wide ocean, neither the disaster which befell Fort Coligny, that first settlement in Brazil, nor the stigma placed on the entire colonization idea by Villegagnon's betrayal. Fort Coligny had been a painful experience. But are not experiences given us that we may learn from them? One would have to try again as soon as possible, and prepare better.

The next attempt was made seven years after the Rio de Janeiro catastrophe, and again Coligny was the patron. This time he chose his captain with the greatest care, after painstaking investigations; and luck was with him. Jean de

HENRIK DE VIERDE BY GENAAMT DE GROOTE KONING VAN VRANKRYK EN NAVARRE ETC.

HENRY IV

MAXIMILIAN DE BETHUNE
Duke of Sully

Ribault was honest and devoted to the Reformed cause. He set his course for the American mainland north of Spanish Florida, dropped anchor in the St. John's river, and led his men ashore. They called the place Charles Fort, fortified it at once, built magazines for munitions and supplies, kept discipline and tightened it. Everything seemed to augur well, and Ribault appointed his second in command as deputy and returned to France to gather reinforcements. They arrived, in three ships, under René de Laudonnière to found Fort Caroline.

Yet for this colony, too, a frightful end was in store. It had begun under friendly stars, on fertile soil, under responsible leadership, with hard work cheerfully done by Catholics and Protestants laboring side by side, with Jesuit exercises mingling with Marot's psalms. But to the Spaniards who claimed this entire coast such amity meant nothing. The Viceroy of Florida, Pedro Menéndez de Avilés, who hated hell less than he hated Protestants, massed his forces for a crusade against the French. For one scant year Ribault, Laudonnière, and their men had seen their colony prosper, when they were set upon and butchered like cattle, or rather, unlike cattle; the tortures devised for them would never have been inflicted on mere beasts. Very few escaped.

And now, for decades, colonization actually came to a standstill. During the civil wars after St. Bartholomew's the Huguenots did not again try to find peace overseas. The Admiral, whose unflagging, driving spirit had been behind the early, ill-fated voyages, was no more. Besides, however great the lure of a distant haven might be for the persecuted, the disruption of everyday life for all, even seafaring men, was greater. Who, in this chaos, would have put up the huge funds needed for any such enterprise?

The vision lay dormant until the reign of Henry IV. He, however, had inherited it from his teacher Coligny; and he also had the Admiral's suspicions of all pipes of peace. The Edict of Nantes, his great creation which assured the civil and religious rights of Protestants in France "forever and unalterably," continued to encounter vigorous opposition. He feared it would not long survive him. American colonization, a last hope in Coligny's day, reappeared as an insurance scheme. Though Henry's friends were divided on the idea—some were enthusiastic, while others were discouraged by the failure of the previous undertakings—the King himself never gave up Coligny's ancient plan.

The man whom he finally put in charge of a new expedition was Pierre de Guast, Sieur de Monts, a man of honor and patriotic zeal who had often fought at Henry's side. Any who spoke of him emphasized his integrity. As his destination, he chose the spacious peninsula to the south of the Gulf of St. Lawrence, on maps of the period called either L'Acadie or La Cadie—the Nova Scotia of today. Discovered seventy years earlier, it was praised by explorers for its fertility and mild yet bracing climate; and de Monts himself had been there on a former voyage and thus could draw on personal experience. In the settlement which he had in mind, Catholics and Protestants were to live together with full and equal rights.

The year was 1604, an important date in the history of human freedom. In the end, of course, the Acadians shared the tragic lot of French Protestants as a whole;

but about their start, at the instance of the greatest King of France, one stirring fact remains: it was then that, consciously and in documents of record, the New World was assigned the task of proving here on earth that before God all men are equal.

Early in March two well-equipped ships set sail, with one hundred and twenty passengers and crew. It was a motley crowd of emigrants, among them peasants, artisans, scholars, vagabonds, nobles, ne'er-do-wells, and paroled convicts. The Protestants were led by a minister, the Catholics by a priest. Two of the noblemen were de Monts's old companions-in-arms: Samuel de Champlain and Baron Poutrincourt. Both were to play a great part in the exploration and early history of the Northern Hemisphere.

Champlain has described their quiet, uneventful crossing, the leisurely investigation of the bays and rivers of the peninsula, where frequently they met the lonely boats of trappers and fishermen from Normandy or Brittany. He tells how they came down from the north to the Bay of Fundy and there found a most delightful place, a wide, quiet valley surrounded by sunny hills and dense forests with foaming waterfalls, and how Poutrincourt was so enchanted that he decided to stay and settle on the spot.

It was not its beauty alone which delighted him, for those emigrants were realists. Chiefly, Baron Poutrincourt was guided by practical considerations. He had seen the salt marshes extending along the coast and recognized their commercial possibilities. He had also noticed the advantages of the harbor: large ships could enter it and lie at anchor, and yet the channel was narrow enough to make easy defense against undesirable strangers. In fact, from whichever angle the Baron looked at it, he could see nothing that was unfavorable: the soil was rich, the rivers teemed with fish and the woods with game, a mountain range to the northeast warded off the Arctic storms. For a settlement nothing better could be desired. He called the place Port Royal; today it is Annapolis, N.S.

De Monts, agreeable to dividing the expedition, sailed on with Champlain and their men, always close to the coast. Champlain drew the first map of the district, showing the trails and camps of the natives besides rivers, bays, and lakes. They rounded the top of the bay, and on its western shore selected an island for their colony, calling it St. Croix.

This choice, which proved calamitous, was dictated mainly by strategic reasons; it is easy to see why the leaders, mindful of the massacres of former settlers, wanted above all a good defensive position. The island controlled the river, and it was a natural stronghold; but it also was an infinitely strange and lonely place. The first night ashore all felt heart-sick. Between them and the Pole was not one group of people to talk to; no hearth, no roof existed in the terrible desert of rocks where nothing grew but grass. Gray autumn came early. Soon endless snow buried the endless forests. Icebergs floated past. Sickness came, then epidemics, then famine. Valiantly Champlain tried to keep up the men's spirits; not until about half of them had died did the remainder finally make their escape to Port Royal, to join their comrades under Poutrincourt. From there, some years later, Samuel de Champlain went on up the St. Lawrence, and on its right bank founded another settlement, Quebec.

The history of these Huguenot settlements in French Canada is a replica of events in the mother country, on a smaller scale but no less cruel. Ever new hopes, ever new conciliations, work, prosperity—but Catholic hostility would not die. Some day, Jesuit fanaticism would reach across the sea and follow them into every hidden corner; again and again these industrious settlers, the King's most loyal and right-minded subjects, were ruined. Even flourishing Port Royal collapsed after "Good Henry's" death; all the privileges he had granted his faithful de Monts, with the title of "Vice-Roi de la Nouvelle France," were taken away from the town and placed into the hands of a company headed by the Marquise of Guercheville. Under this zealous tool of the Jesuits Port Royal soon became a purely Catholic community.

Once the great King was gone, there was no halt to the Jesuit triumphs. None of the tiny settlements established here and there in future Quebec Province and in Newfoundland was too small for ruthless destruction by the reactionaries. A few Huguenots had only to succeed in earning their and their families' daily bread when along would come a monk, with other monks following in his wake. First they would only preach; then suddenly they would produce papers from the King in Paris empowering them to restrict Protestant worship here and there. After a while such worship would be discontinued altogether. Later, more monks would arrive and quickly build a monastery, and then it was never long before governor and police were under orders of the abbots. In the end a decree was published throughout the colony, commanding the original settlers to embrace Catholicism or leave their towns or villages within so many days.

By 1633, the entire St. Lawrence country was closed to Huguenots.

Not one of the French Protestant efforts succeeded in establishing a lasting colony on American soil. And though the settlers may have made mistakes, both Catholic and Protestant historians agree upon the blame for the fiascoes: the governments of Louis XIII and Louis XIV, which with grotesque political obtuseness persecuted people whose highest desire was to create a French colonial empire. After all, what was the big favor the Huguenots were asking? Permission to settle on virgin soil under the flag of their country, the France they loved in spite of everything and could not cease loving, whose tongue and customs they held sacred. But in seventeenth-century France clerical fanaticism, together with commercial jealousy and fear of competition on the part of the great merchant firms of Normandy and Brittany, destroyed all political sense.

Small wonder, then, that many French Protestant colonists, finally weary of this fruitless quest and martyrdom, resolved upon a complete break with their native land. They moved from New France to the parts of the continent owned by Holland or England—and the only really surprising thing is that not all of them reached this decision. For in New England or in New Amsterdam they were again the masters of their fate. There they were immediately granted the rights of citizenship, and any lingering anxieties removed by the warmth of their reception by their Dutch, English, or French co-religionists. Yes—French, too. It was in those possessions of foreign nations that Huguenot emigrants, traveling on foreign ships, had given abundant proof of French pioneering genius and made their contribution to the growth of Colonial America.

For instance, one of the men who made the voyage on the *Mayflower*, in 1620, was generally known by the Anglo-Saxon name of William Mullins. His daughter Priscilla later married John Alden after a courthip which Longfellow has made immortal. Mullins was a Huguenot refugee; his name originally was Molines. And one year later, on the *Fortune*, a nineteen-year-old French youth of noble birth arrived at Plymouth; born in Holland, where his parents had fled because of their faith, he had sailed with the Pilgrims from Delfthaven to Southampton, but when the *Speedwell*—intended to accompany the *Mayflower*—proved unseaworthy he had had to wait in England for another ship to be fitted out. His family's name was de Lannoy; among the *Fortune's* passengers he was listed as Philip De-la-Noye, and his descendants shortened the name to Delano.

To Virginia, also in 1620—ten years after the first French had arrived there, on the first ships which carried supplies to Jamestown—came a thirty-year-old Frenchman by the name of Nicholas Martiau. He became the original patentee of Yorktown and, in 1635, led the opposition against Governor Harvey, who urged submission to all measures taken against the colonists by the government of Charles I. Martiau declared it the colonists' sacred duty to make their own laws; his stand, called "the first opposition to British colonial policy," in fact reiterated only the old Huguenot demand for independence and self-government. But Nicholas Martiau's greatest importance to America lies perhaps in the fact that his great-great-great-grandson became "father of his country"; he was the first of George Washington's ancestors to settle on American soil.

But Huguenots also founded settlements entirely their own. Outstanding among those—this fact may surprise many natives of our generation—was the present city of New York.

About a hundred years had passed since Verrazano, the Florentine, had first set eyes on the Narrows and Manhattan Island (his voyage, made under the French flag, occasioned the later claim of the French to be regarded as discoverers and owners of the place), but little had been done here during that century. A trading-post of Amsterdam firms had been established, a few huts built—that was all. The "Great River of the North" remained a hidden, legendary monster until Henry Hudson explored it in 1609.

Then, in April, 1623, the *New Netherland* arrived from Europe, a Dutch vessel of two hundred and sixty tons. The thirty families on board spoke French among themselves: they were "Walloons," Huguenot refugees who had gone from France to Holland. The generally accepted theory that New York was founded by the Dutch is erroneous. It was not the Dutch crew but the French passengers who built the first houses there and lived in them. Their leader, too, was a Walloon. His name was Peter Minuit.

Unfavorable winds had forced the *New Netherland* to take a roundabout course via the Canary Islands. The poor emigrants, about one hundred and fifty in number, had lain closely packed in damp, diminutive, rat-infested cabins. Their joy must have been great when they finally beheld the "sweet and cheerful prospect" which explorers extolled: the wooded cliffs rising on either side of the valley, the wide sweep of the harbor. There was no wind; flights of birds skimmed noiselessly over the still waters in which large fish could be seen in great number. But —a painful surprise—lying at anchor in the bay was a French ship. Her captain no sooner saw the refugees disembarking than he hurriedly raised the Fleur-de-Lis on shore, taking possession of the country in the name of His Majesty Louis XIII. The few Amsterdamers in the post were in no position to protest; and the *New Netherland* was on the point of turning back to sea when her small Dutch escort, the sloop *Mackerel*, bared her cannon and the French ship disappeared.

Only now did the Huguenots dare look around. Slowly, laden with their goods and chattels, they approached the huts at the southern tip of land inside the bay. It was no settlement, only a post ready to be abandoned any time by the Amsterdam businessmen, a branch office at the end of the world. Not a patch of ground was cleared, much less under cultivation. But ten years earlier a child had been born here to European parents. The boy was sent for. He spoke French and sang French songs! He was Jean Vigné, the first white native of New York.

Not all the Walloons on the *New Netherland* stayed in this settlement, which they named New Amsterdam; actually only eleven remained. Two families pushed on to the east, to try their luck in Connecticut; four settled on the banks of the Delaware, not far from the future site of Philadelphia; eighteen went up-river with their ship, as far as present-day Albany. There they built a blockhouse and stockade—Fort Orange—and made friends with the Indians who brought them chickens and eggs.

They had come at a season when nature here is at its most lavish and extravagant. The American spring, of an abundance and suddenness unknown to Europeans, intoxicated them and aroused the boldest hopes. A letter which one of them wrote home in 1624 has come down to us:

"*We have found fine rivers here and lively springs in the valleys; lakes, on the plain, with fresh water flowing through them, and in the forest delectable fruits, such as strawberries, nuts, and wild grapes. Game abounds in the forest, and in the rivers there are quantities of fish. Above all, one is free to move, to come and go, without fear of harm at the hands of the savages. If we had cows and pigs and other livestock, which every day we hope to receive on the next ship, we should not wish to return to Holland; for everything we could desire in that paradise, Holland, we have found here. If you and yours were to come, you would not regret it. . . .*"

Soon, however, most of those who had gone inland encountered trouble. The Indians turned hostile, or the climate hampered farming with European methods, or internal dissension rent the groups. They abandoned their hopefully founded settlements and returned to New Amsterdam, contributing to the further growth of this colony, which counted two hundred and seventy inhabitants in 1628 and rapidly gained in importance. It had its own administration, responsible only to the West India Company in Amsterdam. Unlike the French possessions, New Amsterdam from the first was governed democratically: the local legislative, executive, and judicial powers were vested in the Council, of which the Director General was merely the chairman. And since among the settlers were not only God-fearing worshipers but many reckless fighters and unscrupulous adventurers, it was most essential that the chairman should at least possess a forceful personality.

The third Director General, in office from 1626 on, was Peter Minuit. We know more about him than about his two Dutch predecessors. He was a genuine Huguenot and liked to emphasize his French descent by signing his name "Pierre" instead of "Peter." Big, blunt and uncouth of manner, an autocrat who brooked no opposition and always preferred action to persuasion, he was the right man to keep the settlement in hand. He enforced iron discipline and was an excellent administrator.

One of his first official acts was the formal purchase of Manhattan Island from the Indians. Minuit did not wish his Walloons to be mistaken for Spaniards, whose methods of colonization were murder and rapine. Manhattan was acquired according to right and custom, in a mutually satisfactory bargain; and not until the treaty was signed by both sides was work begun on a fort to protect the village.

It still received all its house furnishings, livestock, pets, and clothes from home, in ships whose every arrival created a sensation; for aside from the supplies they carried, were they not the sole tenuous thread connecting castaways with a world they had left behind? And in yet another way those ships constituted the basis of the colonists' existence. In their bottoms went back what had moved the Dutch West India Company to extend its high patronage to New Amsterdam: the products gathered in the rapidly growing number of coastwise ships, sold by the Indians or brought into outlying settlements by trappers and woodsmen. As Wassenaer's *Historisch Verhael*, of November, 1626, reports, "The ship which has returned home this month brings samples of all sorts of produce growing there, the cargo being 7246 beaver skins, 675 otter skins, 48 mink, 36 wildcat, and various other sorts; many pieces of oak timber and hickory."

Thus began New York, a Dutch trading-center populated chiefly by Huguenot refugees: crude huts, of people stripped of nearly everything; the origin of a community; the treaty with the Indians; the fort. Rules were laid down, governing export and import. A large stone house was built for the Administration, and, in conjunction, regular divine services began: in the third year after the landing of the *New Netherland* a Dutch Reformed minister, the Reverend Jonas Michaelius, could be brought over. At that time, thirty houses stood along the east bank of the river. At that time, too, the two national groups—Dutch and French—had worked out a division of occupations, so that as far as possible every man should do what he was best fitted for by heritage and experience.

The Dutch, in the main, were farmers. They cleared the forests, tilled the soil, and raised cattle. The French found the going harder; they had been dyers or hatters or weavers, and a colony in the first stage of its development offered little chance to follow these or similar trades. There were locksmiths among them and brewers. Where were they to get their raw materials? Not to mention the vintners, who long refused to see the need for changing their trade. Many years they experimented with the thin, black-stoned, juiceless grapes found in the woods; only complete failure taught them that here they could not seek their old world but had to build a new one.

The reports on this first period of Huguenot colonization in America are scarce and summary, requiring much reading between the lines and rounding-out by conjecture. We know that in New Amsterdam an outstanding citizen was Jesse de Forest, the man who had conducted the negotiations with the Dutch which resulted in the voyage of the *New Netherland*. We know that Minuit's secretary was a refugee named Rasière, described as a good-looking, well-bred young man. We know that not much later a certain John de la Montagne arrived, who was a physician; as can be surmised, he became indispensable to the colony, and his descendants were to play a significant part in New York history. We know that Peter Stuyvesant, the one-legged Dutchman who became Governor General in 1646, was married to the daughter of a French preacher, Judith Bayard, whose brother Samuel married Stuyvesant's sister and became the ancestor of a great American family. We know about Isaac Bethlo or Bedloe, of Picardy, who gave his name to the small island on which the Statue of Liberty stands today. And we know of others—Toussaint Briell, François Crion La Capelle, Jean Casjou, Claude Barbier, Antoine Jeroe—who came to New Amsterdam about the same time.

But New Amsterdam is only one instance of many in which a Huguenot settlement grew into a Dutch or English colony, and eventually into an American city. Elsewhere, too, the first settlers were constantly reinforced by ships carrying Protestants from France. They all found their *terre d'asile;* they built houses and had children; they bore French names and yet became Americans more quickly than they knew.

Those early families—we hardly have the right to call them founders—lie mostly buried by now under the sands of time. A few have grown and prospered. Seldom were they called Huguenots, but rather the "Walloons." Their church was the Church of the Walloons. And correspondence still extant in government archives in London, Madrid, and The Hague also refers to them exclusively as Walloons: after the region on France's northeastern border to which the refugees had first gone from Normandy, Dauphiné, Languedoc, and organized themselves into congregations while awaiting their opportunity to sail for the New World.

The Walloons, however, were only pathfinders, trailblazers. Their descendants constitute but a minute fraction of the Huguenot strain in the American people of today. The great, decisive immigration of French Calvinists came many years later, after the curtain fell on the last act of their drama in France.

24

THE LAST YEARS OF HENRY IV

SOMETIMES, in quiet hours, Henry talked about having to hurry because he had not long to live.

He had changed little as King. It was not his way to reflect much; every mood was promptly translated into adroit, resilient action. If it is true that a man remains a child throughout his life, this one always remained a Gascon lad. He was never fully a part of the refined French Renaissance. He had primitive leanings, enjoyed being among the people. As a general, he would roll the dice with his soldiers and sing songs to bagpipe and drum; he still loved to sit about in taverns incognito and talk bombastically with fishermen and woodsmen, and what he heard there about the King was not always pleasing. It amused him to shop around country fairs and haggle vehemently over the prices, like a southern tradesman conducting his business with violent gesticulations. He loved to romp on the floor with his children; and when called away on matters of state in the middle of a game, he would wipe the dust from his hands and go laughing into the Council chamber. He never learned to handle money. What his lady-loves left him he lost at the gaming-table, and he was always much surprised when it was gone. Human nature he knew well, only too well; yet he was never bitter. He took people as they were, treating them with the irony and banter without which he could not carry on a conversation. He would mock anything on earth—with quick, caustic wit, sometimes cynically, sometimes tactlessly—just so long as he had something to make fun of. And he never nursed a grudge if the other sought his forgiveness. He forgave at once, and graciously drew former enemies back to his Court.

To his dying day, women remained his great weakness. He could not live without them, always had to have them near. His beloved Gabrielle—she of the beautiful bosom, high forehead, and white skin, whom a painting in the Musée Condé at Chantilly depicts so charmingly at her bath—died in her fourth childbirth. To Henry her death was a wound that never healed. Yet even after he crossed the delicate line between "man's best years" and old age, new infatuations continued to succeed each other. The most disastrous was that with Henriette d'Entragues, for there he fell into the hands of a cunning young *intrigante* used by her family to worm huge sums, castles, and domains out of him, as well as a written promise of marriage which the father flaunted at every opportunity to extort further favors from the King. And, worst of all, the lady spied on him for the Jesuits and the Spanish Court; what she heard in his arms was immediately communicated to a widespread conspiracy.

But Sully needed funds to administer the state. Lacking other means to raise a large sum of money, it was determined that the King would have to marry it. Without troubling to ask his permission, the Council made a pact with Florence arranging for Henry's betrothal to Maria de' Medici; the wealth of this dynasty of Florentine bankers, who had risen to the position of sovereign rulers and given France one Queen already, had long attracted Sully's envious eye. The little matter of the King's having a lawfully wedded wife necessitated a proviso: the pact was not to take effect unless the previous union, with Margaret Valois, were dissolved. But since the prospect of a link between Paris and Florence, counterbalancing Spanish pressure, was most agreeable to the Holy See, Henry was soon free of Margaret. She had been living in exile for years, anyhow, an eventful exile in a romantic robber-knight's castle in Auvergne.

Maria de' Medici, rosy and plump, was nearing thirty when she became Queen of France—no longer a young bride according to Italian standards. The King took her to wife without having seen her; and while the marriage was good in the beginning, it grew worse from year to year. Henriette was back in favor several times—although all her tricks had been exposed, although Henry had been forced to have her father and brother thrown into the Bastille, although she behaved scandalously. And in between there were always other love-affairs. The King now had a white, unkempt beard and wild, bushy eyebrows, disliked to wash, and often suffered from gout. It may just have been this approach of old age which led to his last, childish, cruel, and devastating passion.

Its object was Charlotte, daughter of Francis de Montmorency, who had become Constable like his late father. She was said to be the most ravishing woman in Europe, and the King was never to possess her. She was fifteen years old when he first saw her, in a ballet; playing one of

Diana's nymphs, she aimed an arrow at Henry's heart and while the arrow did not harm him, her glance did. Though promised first to the adventurer Marshal Bassompierre, she had been married to the crippled, enigmatic Condé, the son of Prince Henry and grandson of Prince Louis, who had none of the fiery qualities of his ancestors. Brought up at Court, he had turned Catholic and later was to be a merciless Huguenot baiter.

The King's desire for Charlotte proved truly ruinous. It undermined his health. He tried everything to win her, abandoned all restraint and dignity during violent scenes with Condé, until the Prince finally saw no way out but to take his wife in the dead of night to the Spanish Netherlands and place himself under the protection of the Archduke Albrecht. Henry demanded the extradition of the couple, which the Archduke refused with diplomatic correctness. Still, Condé felt no longer safe in Brussels, either, and went to Milan, where the Francophobe Fuentes ruled. The King suffered martyrdom. Old Montmorency played a rather doubtful role, transmitting Henry's letters to his daughter. She herself, not insensible to the honor, addressed Henry in her answers as "*mon cher chevalier*" and "*mon tout*." The Constable wondered whether to have Charlotte's marriage annulled, and the vain, coquettish child apparently did not object too strongly; her letter of May 9, 1610, left all possibilities open. It is improbable that Henry ever read it; five days later he was no longer among the living.

But we are anticipating. Moreover, this private royal affair would not deserve such detailed treatment had it not been connected in a strange, almost grotesque way with high politics and the religious question.

In March, 1609, John William, Margrave of Cleve and Jülich, died. Who was to succeed him as ruler of the tiny buffer state immediately became a burning question. The heirs, two German Protestant princes, moved in. The Habsburg Emperor, objecting to any increase in Protestant power, sent the Archduke Leopold with an army to eject them. The third interested party was France; Henry declared: "I shall not let the Archduke seize that country for two reasons—because the Protestant princes are clearly in the right, and because it is bad enough to have Habsburgs to the north and south. We can't have them in the northeast, too." But Leopold had already taken Jülich. If Spanish-Austrian might was consolidated there, it would have an ideal strategic position for checking the Dutch, the German princes, and the French. Henry decided on a plan which meant all or nothing.

Fundamentally, it was an old plan, many years old. The destruction of the House of Habsburg should be only the first step toward the realization of a bold and dream-like idea, that of a United States of Europe under French leadership. Signed alliances with a number of states were in Sully's files. In Italy alone, Henry could mobilize 60,000 troops—French, Savoyards, and Venetians—under Lesdiguières. Against Spain, two armies of 25,000 each. Against the Habsburgs, in Germany and the Netherlands, the following: 25,000 French, 12,000 Swiss, 28,000 Britons, Swedes, and Danes, 35,000 German Protestants, 14,000 Dutch, and finally 14,000 Hungarians, Bohemians, and Austrians, making a grand total of 238,000 men, with 200 cannon. The sums earmarked for this war exceeded 150,000,000 livres.

It was the most ambitious undertaking France had ever

contemplated. And for this plan, which would have changed the whole of Europe, dauntless romanticists have sought to blame pretty Charlotte de Condé! Their theory is that Henry wanted to avenge himself on the Habsburgs for the Archduke Albrecht's refusal to surrender the fugitives. Supposing he had been capable of such huge egotism —rather improbable in this peaceful King—did he ever have the power to start a war of such dimensions unless the Council and the Ministry of Finance found it necessary? But we need not go into any counter-arguments; the romantic invention can be disproved much more simply: *Le Grand Dessein,* as the plan was called, was already on paper in the year 1600, long before the crisis of the Jülich succession and long before Charlotte's appearance.

At that time, as shown by Sully's notes, it was far more closely connected with the religious question, one of its basic purposes being to give the denominations regional security. The fifteen countries in the European federation were not only to retain their frontiers, safe from aggression by Spain and by the Pope; they were also to guarantee one another the maintenance of the existing Catholic, Lutheran, Zwinglian, and Calvinist spheres. In 1600 Henry had ordered Sully to work out the *Grand Dessein* in detail, consider expert criticism, and decide on methods for its execution. He had watched the work with impatience. And now, when what so far had been a dialectic exercise, a diplomatic toy, a vision, suddenly assumed a tangible, large, ominous form, Henry was seized by a fever of unrest. The shadows of his life were growing longer. He felt anxiety about his country.

The *Grand Dessein* was not the only scheme he would leave behind unexecuted, fragmentary. He was worried, too, about the Huguenots, knowing that after his death persecution would begin anew; he had heard the concessions he granted them from time to time protested even by his closest associates. Few understood his sympathy for both parties, expressed in leaning now toward one, now toward the other. With these few, mostly scholars, he would debate ways and means to carry out his second great plan: the reconcilement of the creeds. Many a morning, sitting alone at a table, tugging at his white beard, half dressed, unwashed, he worked at the draft of a new edict which would amalgamate the Christian churches by fundamentally reorganizing both. And often, engrossed in this work, he shuddered, feeling his advancing age.

He clung to his life and his mission, but he was tired. He was an old man, so thin that his clothes hung loosely round him; he could not sleep, could not stay in one room for any length of time, had become afraid to show himself outside the palace. He constantly talked of feeling the point of a dagger between his ribs. For hours he conferred with Sully about his personal finances in case of his death; he was fifty-seven and had fourteen children living, six of whom were legitimate.

His departure for Champagne, to join the army, was scheduled for May 19, 1610.

On the 14th he went to call on Sully at the Arsenal. A man named Ravaillac had been waiting at the Louvre portal since sunrise. En route the royal coach had to stop in the Rue de la Ferronnerie, where some carts blocked the street. Footmen and runners were sent ahead to clear the way. The King was joking with the Duke of Epernon —the former *mignon*, since grown into a highly respectable grandee—who sat at his right, and the Governor of

Paris, the Duke of Montbazon, who sat at his left. Their loud laughter ceased abruptly when Ravaillac suddenly jumped on the carriage, stared fiercely into the King's eyes, and struck.

"It is nothing . . . it is nothing . . ." The second time, Henry said the words so softly they were hard to make out. The killer stabbed again, directly at his heart.

The King was carried into the Louvre, where he opened his eyes once more; then "good Henry" was dead.

What did it mean, whom did it comfort, that the investigation in the Ravaillac trial minutely exposed a web of plots, conspiracies, foreign and domestic opposition? The instigators of the deed were hunted but never found. Perhaps it was not intended that they should be found. Austria, Spain, Maria de' Medici, Epernon, Henriette d'Entragues, all were accused; witnesses came forward with evidence against each one of them. But it appears that in fact Ravaillac was only a pupil of the great school of theological fanaticism. He had read the Jesuit books commending regicide for the greater glory of the Church. Under torture, he screamed that he had waited years for the King forcibly to convert all heretics; he was convinced that the planned war would have been waged against the Pope and Catholicism. The most frightful tortures wrung no other names from him.

Ravaillac was quartered on the Place de Grève, and the police had difficulty in restraining the crowd that sought to lynch him. They were the same Parisians who, enraptured, like loving nuns, had glorified the slayer of Henry III as a saint. For this new assassin they wanted agonies a hundred times worse than could possibly be caused him.

25

REGENCY AND DECAY

WHEN the Huguenots learned of the King's death, it was as though at one stroke they had lost all arms, all strongholds, and all edicts. It was as though after a mild gray-blue day a single gust of wind had blackened the sky and swept it downward until the cowering earth lay at its mercy. Paris at once looked different. The bustling crowds in its streets heard the trumpets and drums of the funeral ceremonies with a tense, sensation-craving curiosity. And when Marshal Bassompierre, their latest favorite, rode through the city to make speeches, they ran after him and cheered.

Many Protestant families instantly left the city, as in fear of a new St. Bartholomew's. The prostrate Sully locked himself in the Bastille; for him everything was at an end. In the provinces the Huguenots massed in arms. They did not doubt that the dagger which pierced Henry's heart had also torn the Edict of Nantes. The King's eyes had hardly closed when Maria de' Medici asked the *parlement* to confer the regency upon her, according to custom, until Louis XIII came of age. And the *parlement* was still debating the procedure when Epernon appeared in its chamber, armed and spurred, and demanded instant settlement of the matter. Less than two hours after Henry's death she was given plenary power.

For the time being Maria retained her husband's ministers—Villeroy, Sillery, Jeannin, and Sully—and on May 22 she issued a declaration that the Edict of Nantes would be retained in full. But the Huguenots were not at ease. Was she able to do what she intended, granting that her intentions were sincere? And were they sincere? What was going on behind the closed and darkened windows of the Louvre? A Medici with a nine-year-old son! Catherine and Charles IX were still unforgotten.

Maria, then approaching forty, made a dignified but not pleasing appearance. Her walk was refined, her speech charming, and the ostentatious pomp of her attire, resplendent with diamonds and emeralds, was better liked by the people than her late husband's casual simplicity. But the expression of her greasy face with the puffy double chin was vulgarity itself, the vulgarity of a supercilious philistine. Later she grew so fat that even Rubens, an admirer of feminine corpulence, found it hard to do justice to this mountain of flesh; and it is a medal made of her by Guillaume Dupré which best depicts her stupidity, vanity, and malice. Henry had sought to teach her the business of government, but she considered it a waste of time. A true Italian, she spent most of her day curling her hair and painting her face. When the King tried to take his troubles to her, she silenced him with tirades repeating servants' gossip. She also rather enjoyed slapping his face. Now that he was dead, though, she seemed disposed to abandon her dull lethargy. "Save your tears for another time, Madame," Villeroy told her, whose eyes were perfectly dry, "you must be a Queen now, not a wife." She nodded, and from that moment on was very busy.

Above all, she had to think of remaining in power. Even before she could choose a magnificent Tuscan pose to strike on her throne, that throne was tottering. After the King's death, the Prince of Condé promptly became reconciled with his wife and father-in-law and returned from Italy. As Premier Prince of the Blood, he was entitled to a place next to the Queen Mother during a regency. He appeared in the Council as if he were lord of the realm, declared that the whole administration had to be changed, said he would see to it that the abuses prevailing under Henry IV were rectified. He thumped his chest. "Taxes will be reduced. I shall prove that it can be done. We have heard nothing but excuses; I shall not accept them. If the Regent opposes me . . ." He did not have to finish the sentence; the allusion to his close relations with the Spanish Court was plain. He also hinted that the southern provinces as well as the Loire region were ready to rise any time at his request. He demanded the Queen's written promise to make no decision without his consent, the chairmanship of the Council of Ministers, and the office of Constable.

He did not stand alone, either. The very first measures taken by the Regent had added to her unpopularity. Something which Henry IV had feared now happened: two Italian favorites she had brought with her from home —a certain Concini and his wife, who took the name of Galigai—dominated her completely. It is rather strange that Henry, before he met his future wife, in scanning the list of her suite had protested against this couple. His instinct warned him. When he first entered Maria's room it was Galigai who opened the door, and he, disregarding her low curtsy, ran past without hiding his revulsion. As long as he lived, the thin, olive-skinned little person was repugnant to him, and so was her husband. They were the prototype of the pairs of Italian schemers—quick, smooth, furtive, shifty-eyed, and given to black magic—so frequently met in contemporary fiction and later in opera librettos. But Maria loved them. There was no secret she did not discuss with these two, who played up to her silly vanity and hysteria.

Concini was quite an ordinary adventurer, who had had to leave Florence to escape his creditors. In France, thanks to the adroitness of his wife, he quickly climbed the ladder of a great career. Maria, as Regent, overwhelmed him with honors, revenues, and domains: he received Péronne, Roye, and Montdidier, was appointed Marshal, was created the Marquis of Ancre. Soon his clique controlled the Regent so exclusively that nothing could be decreed or accomplished which had not passed through his or Galigai's bedroom.

A regime of boundless incompetence. Maria meant to be a strong Regent, but the feudal lords, freed from Henry's firm restraint, aimed solely at a return to the good old days. Centralization of government, creation of a civil service, concentration of the financial administration in Paris, reorganization of the judiciary in the *parlements*—it was all too uniform, too royal. The nobility had been shunted aside, politically, but it was still very much alive. It had suffered economically, when Sully strengthened bourgeoisie and officialdom against it and reduced its income from imposts and from rents; but this had only kindled the longing for vengeance on judges, bureaucrats, and merchants, the longing to be lords in their domains again.

So the gentlemen descended upon the Court, to swear fealty if the Queen paid well or to threaten desertion if she did not. Maria paid. Neither she nor the Marquis of Ancre nor Galigai could think of anything else to do. She paid out of the public treasury, out of tax funds, uselessly and capriciously, merely to get peace. The millions administered so thriftily by Sully were thrown out the window. The Prince of Condé, always in debt, extorted one subsidy after another. The Duke of Soissons received Clermont, besides huge sums of money. Revenues which the Duke of Guise had pledged as collateral for loans were redeemed. Joinville, Epernon, St. Paul, all the Marshals had their incomes increased. But the beneficiaries remained rebellious as before; in a few months the great political edifice of Henry IV had crumbled.

Sully was still an obstacle to the extortioners. He was the man of the hated yesterday, the man who saw through them all, a constant reproach. Of his ideas they knew nothing. But they knew he must be put out of the way. Violent disputes occurred in the Council between him and Villeroy. Villeroy submitted his resignation; but as Maria did not want to lose him, Sully was forced to resign instead. He quit the Ministry of Finance, the Arsenal and the Bastille, wrote a farewell letter to the Queen stating in a few sentences what he had done for France, and retired to his *gouvernement*, Poitou. "Possibly I shall return," he told his friends. "But it is certain that the good days will not return during my lifetime."

All these events were only symptoms, however. More

important was the abrupt change in foreign policy. For abandoning the *Grand Dessein* Maria cannot well be blamed; she never would have been equal to its execution. But she turned the tiller right about, setting a course exactly opposite to Henry's. She was delighted to hear from the Count of Feria, sent to see her by King Philip III of Spain, that every reason for hostility had vanished with her husband's death; on the contrary, Spain would wholeheartedly welcome it—for the sake of Christendom and, consequently, of the world—if a *rapprochement* were possible today and a friendship tomorrow. The Queen Mother now revealed a plan to bind the two monarchies more closely than treaties could do. She proposed a double marriage between the older children of both ruling houses, and was presently told that the King agreed with indescribable pleasure. The negotiations lasted two years and were not concluded until 1612. Louis XIII, the young King of France, was to wed Doña Anna, the eldest Infanta of Spain; and Louis's eldest sister, Elizabeth, Prince Philip.

Fraternization and love—this was the tenor of the agreement. And surely nothing would better have served the peace of Europe than an end to the old strife between the two great Catholic powers. Naturally, however, such a peace policy was incompatible with tolerance. Already the Spanish Ambassador informed Madrid that the Queen no longer permitted Protestants in the Council, that all vacant posts were being filled with Catholics. Already the rights of the Huguenots were disregarded in the courts, and their sick no longer admitted to the hospitals. Already they were being blamed for any failure of government measures, as though the past twelve years of "irresponsibility"—as tolerance was now termed—prevented the restoration of order in France. Those Protestants who had persisted in the belief that Henry's widow would not veer from his domestic policies—their spokesman was Duplessis-Mornay—were disappointed. They took their complaints to her, asked for the amelioration of certain legal clauses and especially for more strongholds from which Jesuits would be excluded. Maria, embarrassed, at first replied timidly. But the Marquis of Ancre explained to her —correctly—that disunity had shorn the Huguenots of their once redoubtable power. Now, he said, one only had to show courage.

At the Assembly of Saumur the Huguenots vindicated his judgment. From the first session it was clear that the party was split; even the choosing of a chairman caused bad blood, distrust, and animosity. The Duke of Bouillon, resting on his past merits, thought he should be made leader as a matter of course. But a large part of the gathering no longer deemed him worthy of full confidence. His relations with the Court were too good. Sully and his son-in-law Rohan opposed him openly, and it was their influence which won the election for Duplessis-Mornay.

The Bouillon faction wanted at any price to avoid a rupture with the Court. So far, they argued, there had been no outright violation of the Edict of Nantes. There had been some cases of injustice; they might have been due to negligence, even ignorance; abuses could always be eliminated by mutual understanding. Take up arms? No. Compared with times before the Edict, this was still an era of peace. In which Catholic country were Protestants as well off as the Huguenots in France? A fight against the French-Spanish alliance was suicide.

After a comprehensive address by Bouillon, expounding

the advantages of trust in the others' loyalty, Sully rose in rebuttal. Irritation colored his delivery. His recent mania for viewing all general problems as revolving round himself, the stubbornness with which he took objective opposition as personal, made him seem older than he was. He could not get away from his own fate, could not forget his bitterness at having been driven from power and condemned to the inactivity of a pensioned official. "Loyalty!" he expostulated. "The ways of the Valois are revived by another Medici, and I hear the word loyalty! A pact is made with Spain, exactly as before St. Bartholomew's, and I hear the Regency has done nothing yet against the Reformation. Why, may I ask, was I discharged? Was my work unsatisfactory? Indeed not. It was an act of religious antagonism; they no longer wanted a Protestant in the government. What other violations of the Edict are we waiting for?"

Bouillon broke in noisily: Sully had been discharged not because he was a Protestant but because he was dishonest. Quite possibly there would be criminal proceedings . . . .

This was really not the Huguenot party of old. It required no political clairvoyance for Concini to dismiss these gentlemen as even weaker than he had assumed. He told the Queen Mother they would no longer be capable of concerted action: "I do not deny, Madame, that we, too, are weak at the moment and have enemies in every part of France. But we are united; that is what counts."

Aged Duplessis-Mornay tried to the last to reunite the Huguenots at Saumur. He reminded them how often during the religious wars their situation had been more critical than at present and yet they had stood fast. Once again, he was convinced, it would suffice to take a determined attitude, be strong in the faith in God and in deeded rights, to keep the Court from hostile action. But from session to session his support dwindled. Ferment increased. Young Rohan denounced the Duke of Bouillon as an illustration of where the pacifist trend led: no one could tell whether he was still a Huguenot or already a Catholic.

For the first time, on this occasion, thirty-two-year-old Henry de Rohan came to the fore. He was descended from a great line; his forebears, the Dukes of Brittany, had been virtually sovereign princes, at least in their own eyes, as evident from the motto on their coat of arms: "*Roy ne puys, Duc ne daygne, Rohan suys*"—"King I cannot be, Duke I deign not, Rohan I am." To France this family gave a number of brave men; the Duke of Montbazon, Henry IV's Governor of Paris in whose arms he died, came from one of its branches. Henry de Rohan had married Sully's daughter, Marguerite de Béthune. He was well educated, loved the sciences as much as soldiering, had traveled in several European countries, not for pleasure but to acquaint himself with their strength and characteristics. Simple and modest in his ways, intrepid, generous, daring in his decisions, he was a hater of compromise. He spoke jerkily, talked little, but what he said made sense. He was a convinced Calvinist; not even his enemies denied his devotion to the Reformed cause. True, it was matched by an equally strong ambition. At the Saumur Assembly he boldly leaped into his destined rôle, and it did not take him long to undermine Bouillon's position and emerge as the new leader of the party.

Many students of history attribute the Huguenots' downfall to their disunity. But disunity is never a cause.

Where the force of an idea is still strong, there is no disunity. Or, rather, there is no schism that cleaves the organism; at worst there are partial fissures, which heal again after unessential parts have been discarded and the wound has closed. Fundamental disunity springs from deeper roots; it indicates a sickening of the very substance. The Huguenots were no longer agreed on their cause. To only a few were religion and revolutionary aims still of primary importance. What mattered to the majority was highly personal interests.

It was the same all over Europe, in Germany, Holland, Austria, and Poland no less than in France. The pious believed and gave their blood for their faith, but the leaders used this faith to further their class purposes. This was the decade which set Jacob Böhme, a plain man from Silesia, to writing: "And the Lord said: Will you not feed those I have entrusted unto your care? Behold, I have placed you on Moses' chair and entrusted my flock to you, but you mind only the wool and not the lambs, and thus you build your mansions."

About the only possible description of Maria de' Medici's Regency is that everything was topsy-turvy and no conviction escaped damage. There is little point in relating the erratic, gloomy events here, except insofar as the Huguenots, oblivious of their real mission, entangled themselves in them. In 1614, it looked like war again in France. Condé had left the Court when his demands were refused. Together with the Catholic Dukes of Longueville, Vendôme, and Mayenne the younger, and the Protestant Bouillon, he set about the execution of long-fostered plans. The group published a manifesto against the government, demanding executive reform, Villeroy's dismissal, and the appointment of the Prince of the Blood to a position of authority. They also demanded immediate reversal of the pro-Spanish policy; the King should be independent of the Habsburgs and the Pope. Furthermore, their own feudal right to a part in governing the country should be confirmed, and the Third Estate should finally obtain some relief through reduction of the *taille* and the salt tax.

The Queen quite rightly denounced this demagogic program as a mere mask for selfish ends. The gentlemen's purpose was to destroy the central government created by her husband, so as to rule at will again over towns, troops, and judiciary in their districts. She mobilized an army against the threatened revolt, but when both parties saw that little could be gained, there was a swift reconciliation. The Court flattered all of Condé's vanities and, to appease his adherents, convoked the long-demanded, oft-promised *States-General*. It was opened in the Augustinian Convent at Paris in October, 1614, shortly after Louis XIII had been declared of age.

Condé had expected this meeting to support him and his plans. But, lo, the Third Estate had learned its lesson; it knew now that it had fruitlessly sacrificed its men and money in the feudal squabbles. Illusions had vanished. Slogans had lost their effectiveness. Jean Savaron, the leader of a delegation appearing before the King, talked only of economic questions: bread and wages. In a speech that was neither moderate nor smooth nor diplomatic, he said that since Good Henry's death famine had spread in Guyenne and Auvergne until people were eating grass. If the Queen were to see these emaciated figures, if she were to learn the child mortality, Her Majesty would weep. And in this situation the King was spending seven millions annually on the grandees, purchasing their doubtful loyalty in preference to that of his people, who would freely bless him if any part of this sum were applied to their support. Savaron uttered a warning: even in ancient Gaul the terrible burden of taxes had driven the people to throw off the Roman yoke by force of arms—the present situation was no less revolutionary.

The effect of his speech was general indignation. Maria de' Medici found it very indelicate to be told about people feeding on grass. The aristocracy felt offended; an exchange of insults followed. There was much commotion and no result.

It was not only suspicion of the phrase-mongers which urged the Third Estate toward *Realpolitik*. It was also the memory of the twelve years under Henry IV, when one had heard less of denominations and felt more of improvements. Sully's principles had since become as indisputable as laws of nature; it was of vital necessity to the *bourgeois* that these be not rejected again. Economically and politically, the bourgeoisie could prosper only if provincial autonomy was destroyed and national unity prevailed. Industry and trade could flourish only if all remaining regional barriers were eliminated, goods circulated freely, and local and corporate privileges were abolished. The feudal lords were still minting their own money, and if short of precious metals did not shrink from passing counterfeit; enforcement of universal respect for the value of gold and silver was imperative.

Thus a strange situation developed: the very same Third Estate which at Blois, against Crown, nobility, and clergy, had held the King to be a mere trustee of the people, who could claim obedience only while he justified their trust, this same Third Estate now took exactly the opposite view. The King, it maintained, was elected by God, accountable to Him alone, with neither Church nor nobility entitled to question his sovereignty. It is easy to see why the bourgeoisie reversed itself: only by elevating the King above the two feudal powers—especially by denying them the right to dethrone him—could it put him in a position to enforce reforms over their conservative objections. The bourgeoisie was more national-minded than they. It stood unequivocally against their aristocratic international ties. And while they were wasteful by nature, it was thrifty.

So now the *bourgeois* invited the King back into their old alliance, against First and Second Estates. The document in which they prayed that he set up an absolutist regime is one of the most extraordinary in history and deserves quotation in its essentials. "His Majesty is hereby requested to decree and proclaim the following as the inalienable and universal basic law of the state: the King is sovereign within the land. He has received his Crown from God alone. Thus no power on earth, be it spiritual or temporal, can have any right to his realm, or on any pretext whatever can deprive his consecrated person of his land, or release his subjects from their oath of allegiance."

The possibilities for intervention which this moment offered the Huguenots are incalculable. To stand unwaveringly by the King again, as Coligny had done, and with him thrust at Spain and feudalism! But they, too, had reversed themselves. Once, in the Guises, they had combated the faction which sought to seize power and overthrow the King. Now they made a common front with this same faction.

For when the *States-General* ended without result and the Catholic lords rose up to fight for more privileges, the Protestant lords did not wish to be left behind. They aligned themselves with Condé, whom they could not help knowing to be a rank opportunist and a fanatic Catholic besides, who would keep faith with them just so long as they were useful to his personal ambitions. Condé, the husband of the great Henry's last love, led a life about which revealing ditties were sung in the most squalid alleys of Paris; he was in debt up to his neck, and anyone who paid him well could own him. When he was short of funds, or his vanity was hurt, he had no qualms about high treason. One did not have to be a moralist to damn this alliance; for it is not true that a man's private life can be separated from his public one. Example means as much as preaching; just as a tyrant may be doubted if he himself cannot kill, so may a saint if his hands are not clean enough for benediction. A man need not be virtuous, but he must be himself. Condé was ever and everywhere on the fence. But the Huguenots, too, now committed the mortal sin of standing neither by their past nor by their present. They tried to mix the two.

As the few thinking people had foreseen, Condé soon made his private peace with the Court. He was given a fine governorship—that of Berry, a region in the center of the realm, fertile and with many strongholds—and most cordially invited to return to Paris, with the assurance that no decrees would be proclaimed without his signature. To the cheers of the populace he made his entrance into the capital. A new political balance developed at Court: the Queen Mother let the Marquis of Ancre rise from rank to rank, and Condé and his party laid the countermines.

Concini's power became a menace to the state. He might turn Maria's ambition against her son—there were rumors that she wanted to have Louis declared incompetent. The conspiracy against the Marshal made quiet progress, extending its network to the young King and his confidant, Luynes, who had always encouraged and supported him against his mother.

On April 14, 1617, Concini set out for the Louvre to see the King, who was preparing his departure for Normandy. On the bridge leading to the palace, Vitry, Captain of the Guards, shot him in the head with a pistol, and Concini fell dead.

On hearing the shot, the King had stepped to the window, and when he learned that the Marshal was dead, he raised both arms and exclaimed: "Now I am King!"

26

LOUIS XIII DEFEATS THE HUGUENOTS

LOUIS, not yet sixteen, was a melancholy, lonely, gloomy youth. He was under his mother's thumb until well into manhood. In her belated craze for power, awakened by Henry's death, Maria consciously denied the boy her love. He was rather ingeniously neglected, scarcely taught to read and write, kept in dreary, isolated rooms; any servant who came to enjoy his confidence would be removed. He seemed so devoid of resistance, so firmly in the grip of a silent, cringing fear of the mother—who still slapped the fifteen-year-old in front of the grinning Court camarilla—that people gave him up as hopeless. The consensus was that he would never be a man.

He was left to complete inactivity, and it was deemed an offense if anyone stayed near his apartment. His pastimes were puerile: he trained falcons and hawks, strummed a little on lute and mandolin, constructed toy fortresses, had the soldiers catch sparrows for him, which he hunted with falcons in his room for hours on end. When the terrified birds beat their wings against walls and windows, he laughed—a forced, stiff laughter. Then again he had his dogs draw cannon about the palace, through the reverberating corridors. He stuttered, was punished for it, stuttered worse. In the end he hardly dared to speak at all.

His health was always precarious. All his life he suffered from a lung ailment, and the physicians tortured him with bleedings, purgatives, hot and cold baths, and senseless diets. His skin was of a sickly color and he walked bent forward. His face was coarse, with a heavy chin and a long, fleshy Bourbon nose that touched a thin, drooping mustache. When he talked, his head moved jerkily.

He was joyless, and even later, as a strong and successful monarch, he could not master his melancholy moods; his lack of humor weighed embarrassingly on all those near him. For days and weeks he wrapped himself in silence; in this "*tristesse morne*" his eyes became opaque, remote, yet closely observant. Fundamentally bored, he sought escape in various selected cruelties, and ever again in the vastness of the woods, where he hunted the stag, passionately, untiringly. The restlessness apparent in the nervous twitching of his face gradually became unbearable. There came a time when he could not stay anywhere longer than six weeks. Women caused him agonies, because he loved but was too shy to conquer them. Even with his wife he never overcame his embarrassment.

To one man alone did he give his love, confidence, and affection: his master of the hunt, Charles Albert de Luynes, a handsome, personable, quiet man with no education to speak of, the King's senior by more than twenty years. He was so strong in his manly, harmonious assurance, such a good listener, so understanding, that with him the boy relaxed and gradually found himself. To Luynes alone Louis owed the sudden energy to join the murder plot against Concini, and from that day on he never took a backward step.

There followed years in which the disappointment of the lords—that Maria's dead favorite had been succeeded by one of her son's—gave rise to a still more widespread opposition. Its head was mighty Epernon. The playful *mignon* was now playing the provincial tyrant in his castles at Angoulême, Loches, and Plassac, which he inhabited by turns; he had learned the part to perfection, even maintained a well-paid standing army like a sovereign prince. The Queen Mother, banished after Concini's assassination, had lived for a time in the castle of Blois; but one night she climbed through a window, down a rope ladder—she, Henry IV's widow!—and fled to Epernon. She led her son's enemies into battle against his government, and took up the aristocratic demands for power she had so loathed as Regent. But something even more incomprehensible followed: she approached the Huguenot leaders, and they in turn did not shrink from calling the party to her aid. Bouillon went about with Epernon, and Maria de' Medici with Calvinist preachers.

All this makes a turbulent, magnificent, ultra-colorful story. There is more to it than the rope ladder; more than Armand de Richelieu, the dapper young Bishop of Luçon who flitted silkily from party to party as the Queen Mother's adviser; more than the bridge of Cé, where Louis besieged his mother and forced her to surrender to him. But it is not our story—except for one aspect: during this theatrical war the King grew convinced that the Huguenots would always stand against the state. The most pious of all Bourbons, he could not have had much sympathy for them in any case. He believed in Catholicism. He had a special *oratoire* for his collection of relics, and daily prayed fervently with his father confessor, Caussin. Yet he revered his father's memory, and surely would have inclined toward retention of his policy of tolerance, if circumstances had not turned him against it. His functionaries, in disregard of his decrees, perpetrated such outrages upon the Huguenots that for the latter to suffer them in silence could only have spelled doom for the Protestant cause. Once again they became foes of the Crown, and Louis faced a cleavage he had not wanted. But step by step now, under the influence of his spiritual advisers, he was moving in a direction exactly opposite to that of his father.

In Béarn, Jeanne d'Albret's country, Henry IV had left the expropriated Catholic church lands in the possession of Protestants. It was an act of piety toward his departed mother, and he had indemnified the bishops out of his own pocket. Now, it was one of the young King's first acts to demand restoration of these lands. There followed long disputes between him and the Béarnais, and instances of bloodshed. The King would not stand for the independent conduct of the province, and the Protestants would not stand for a resumption of their treatment as outlaws.

In 1620, war began anew. The King himself led his army against Béarn, which refused obedience despite harsh measures. The little frontier state, trusting to its geographical situation to halt any advance against it, was ill prepared. It put up only brief resistance, and the King entered Pau on October 5. He stayed only two days, because he found no church where he could attend Mass. But he brought the Jesuits back into a land where no Catholic parish had existed for fifty years. The cruelties of his troops he tolerated in silence, but to the rebels exemplary punishment was meted out: men were hanged or beheaded; women were raped. The constitution of Béarn was torn up; its provincial character came to an end; a Catholic, Navarrins, was left in charge, and in the courts the local dialect was replaced by the French language.

But in La Rochelle the Huguenots were arming. Their military leadership they offered to renowned Lesdiguières, formerly the general commanding Henry IV's Italian armies. He, who had always counseled peace, not only refused but shortly after joined the King, to fight as his field marshal against the Huguenots. Bouillon was approached next; he said he was too old and would be content to give advice. His son-in-law, the Duke de la Trémoille, also declined and began to curry favor with the Court. Châtillon's reaction was similar. From everyone came fine protestations with nothing to back them up. In the end, Rohan and his brother Soubise were chosen, but it was clear that they would not be blindly obeyed.

All were deluded. While they quarreled, afraid to admit their disunity even to themselves, they quite overlooked the trend of the times toward synthesis, the great synthesis of the Counter-Reformation, which was sweeping Europe. It was as if a flock of crowing cocks attempted to halt the onrush of a vast cavalcade. They kept claiming validity before the world, but failed to see that no religion remained valid, that now only national unity mattered, that not their creed brought the royal armies marching against them but their outdated political ideology which spurned that unity. When the King took the field, he declared that he would punish disobedience but would leave once-granted concessions to all those remaining loyal. And while his actions in Béarn were bound to sow distrust of his decrees, the Huguenots might yet have listened to Duplessis-Mornay, who wondered whether even the rape of Béarn had not become necessary to a sovereign royal policy.

With a sullen, embittered strength Louis XIII bore the hardships as well as the amenities of camp life. He would rather have hunted; to defeat the stag he did not need a general staff, or Lesdiguières, or Cardinal de Guise. Only he and Luynes understood each other. Soon, however, he scored a new success: the capture of the town and castle of Saumur, where Duplessis-Mornay had resided as governor since Henry III's time. Constable Luynes, in the name of the King, asked that the gates be opened: "We solemnly promise that Saumur's immunity will not be touched—by my word, which counts as if His Majesty had given it, and which Marshal de Lesdiguières guarantees." Mornay had the gates opened, but the royal troops had hardly marched in when the King declared Saumur as finally and fully his possession.

When Mornay made a protest, Luynes received him with all honors. "Believe me, Governor, His Majesty too would in this case prefer an amicable arrangement to the cheap fame of having seized a town. We are so deeply grieved to have to hurt a man of your merit that we suggest you remain at your post as our Governor and Marshal of France, with an honorarium of 100,000 écus over and above your present income. We must insist only on placing a garrison in the town."

"If I valued money as highly as you seem to think," replied Mornay, "I could have made millions under past regimes. As for the honor you offer me, I am of opinion that the greatest honor is to live honorably."

He resigned all his offices and went into retirement as a private citizen.

The royal forces met no more resistance until St. Jean d'Angély, where the Duke of Soubise was in command. This fortress, regarded as impregnable, had to capitulate after twenty-six days. Treason had a hand in it. Farther up the Loire, Gergeau and Sancerre fell easily. In Guyenne, the magistrates of Cartillau and Sainte Foy brought the King the keys of their towns.

Then the army came to the strongly fortified refuge of Montauban, above the river Tarn. Its citizens had always thought much of their local liberties; they were well organized in a military way and convinced Protestants. Their commander was the Marquis de la Force; Rohan had pitched camp near by and managed to smuggle soldiers and munitions into the town. Before this mighty fortress Louis XIII increased his staff. The Dukes of Mayenne, Angoulême, and Montmorency arrived; also famed Bassompierre, and the elite of the aristocracy.

The siege of Montauban lasted two and a half months, and all attacks were repulsed. The desperate defense was stiffened by news from outside, of anti-Protestant riots all over the country and of a new pulpit propaganda drive calling for extermination of the Huguenots, men, women, and children. Religious feeling in the people of Montauban blended with primitive fear for their lives. Rohan had inflamed them with speeches: defense alone could save the faith for them, else they would all be killed, or at least exiled; he had determined to fight on to the end; if but two Protestants remained on earth, he would be one of them; his mansions and estates had been taken away and only his sword was left, but he would use that to defend the faith.

And during the siege Montauban's thick-set, taciturn, tireless burgomaster, Du Puy, who talked the language of the people and, hatless, helped in the trenches, kept up the spirits.

By the time the rains came in November, 1621, the royal army had fired 20,000 cannon-balls at the heroic town, but the walls still held. The surrounding country had turned into a quagmire. When Louis was advised to raise the siege, he burst into tears. The hard, monotonous camp life, the failure, the deaths of some of his best men, had unnerved him. On November 2 he began the retreat. On the eve, one of his soldiers, secretly a Protestant, had played the opening bars of the 68th Psalm on his flute. Behind the walls, the Huguenots took the beloved melody as a sign of deliverance. And they were not mistaken.

The royal army avenged its defeat on other Reformed communities. The population of the neighboring village of Nègrepelisse was wiped out in a massacre which lasted but half an hour—after which time the streets were so heaped with corpses as to be impassable. In St. Antonin, where the women had fought with halberds, ten leading citizens and the pastor were hanged. Prisoners from other towns were sent to the galleys. In August, 1622, the rebellious region was subdued except for Montpellier, which resisted as Montauban had done. Loath to risk another failure, the King accepted the suggestions of intermediaries who proposed a peace with Rohan. The religious provisions of the Edict of Nantes were confirmed, but its political clauses were canceled in entirety: Assemblies might be called only with royal approval, the fortifications of Montpellier were to be razed, and the Huguenots were to retain only two strongholds—Montauban and La Rochelle.

This was a turning-point in their destiny, at the very time when the fate of the Protestants in Germany, too, was decided at the battle of the Weisser Berg. The Huguenots had proved in combat that their courage still lived. But combat had become a rare thing with them. Numerically they remained a minority; and despite Rohan's desperate manifestoes, too many of them, rich merchants and manufacturers especially, preferred suffering injustice to daring the uncertain fortunes of war. And how many could be bought! This decade saw the opening of a great campaign of seduction, by a Catholicism shining in new glory.

The gentry, the artisans and workers had taken up arms in honest determination. But this time there were no German allies, no valiant *Reiter*. Germany, involved in the Thirty Years' War, needed help herself. How could she give it to others? It was the beginning of the end. The Protestants in La Rochelle, beguiled by the example of the Netherlanders, set themselves up as a state within the state and thus brought about their own destruction; for this was the time that witnessed the forging of a state based on the union of all creative forces. While the Huguenots thought they were still moving forward, they were actually moving back. They talked of their past but could no longer understand it, because they were unable to divine the future.

27

RICHELIEU

AT 2 P.M. on Monday, April 29, 1624, Louis XIII met with his ministers at the old castle of Compiègne. Suddenly, to the amazement of the group, who had had no previous warning, he ordered Richelieu brought in and introduced him as a new member of his Council. The Cardinal did not state the policy he planned to pursue, nor did anyone ask him for a statement. After a brief, nervous session the King jumped up, left the chamber, mounted a horse, and disappeared for a week.

In summoning Richelieu, Louis had disregarded a strong personal antipathy. It was known, not only at Court but among the people, how patently he sought to avoid the Cardinal; his choice, now, occasioned general bewilderment. Perhaps it was a case of genius making its way with the help of even those who wish to suppress it.

For seven years, step by step, this prelate with the excessive ambitions had risen on his destined path. Armand Jean Duplessis de Richelieu, whose family in Poitiers was well connected at Court, had first embarked on a military career, but upon inheriting a claim to an ecclesiastic benefice, the small bishopric of Luçon in Lower Poitou, he changed over to the clerical profession. His delicate health may have contributed to his decision. He seldom resided at Luçon, but mostly at his priory of Coussey, where he devoted himself to the study of theology and politics, with special regard to the problems at issue between the religious parties. He became a bishop at an early age, presented himself in Paris, was encouraged by Henry IV, who recognized the young priest's unusual energy, received a doctor's degree from the Sorbonne for a magnificent disputation, and made his political debut at the *States-General* of 1614 which we have mentioned. His speech, upholding conservatism and championing the clergy, was so smooth, brilliant, scholarly, and charged with restrained fanaticism, that it attracted universal attention. It also aroused concern in the Council members, that this uncanny young man might have a future. From Paris, Richelieu withdrew again to the austere solitude of his study at Coussey, submitting to the ascetic Carmelite discipline but also turning his episcopal secretariat into a general foreign and domestic news agency. He never ceased broadening his education and practical experience. He dealt personally with everything that happened in his diocese, and opened a lively correspondence with the high clergy of the nation; these priests—Duperron, Sourdis, Casteignier, Aubespine, Duvergier—became his protectors, for they soon recognized what a trump card they possessed in him. And even at that early stage there appeared by his side a certain Father Joseph, who was never to leave and was decisively to influence him in all important matters of high policy.

Richelieu was thirty when the Marshal of Ancre drew him into his ministry. While the Cardinal despised the Italian gambler and upstart as much as every other Frenchman did, he masked his revulsion with deference, and served Concini and the Queen Mother to the best of his ability. The success was short-lived. When Ancre was killed, Richelieu was banished, first to his diocese and then still farther away, to Avignon. He kept in touch with Maria, who was likewise banished. Her escape from Blois led to the formation of an opposition Court, with herself as focus. A man was wanted to keep her affairs in order, a man able not only to cope with her caprices but also qualified to effect a reconcilement with the King. Richelieu was present and available. The Queen Mother received him as her savior, and a day later all the labyrinthine threads lay in his hands.

Maria's unconditional confidence became the stepping-stone to his career. It has never been discovered whether he was really on her side, or already seeking Louis's favor by sending him information. This much is certain: his advice led to the reconciliation without which Maria would have been lost. By restoring her to her former position he made a place for himself; he had become indispensable to her by now, and she insisted on taking him along to Court. Not only did the King mistrust him, but the Cardinal's precocious superiority and subtle finesse upset him, caused him an almost physical discomfort; when Maria first tried to bring Richelieu into the Council, Louis refused tartly: "Never! I hate him like the devil." A story was bruited about that one day, when Richelieu came toward him in the Louvre gallery, Louis turned tail, mumbling: "That blackguard again!"

This blackguard, this silky sneak—in bad health, suffering from constant headaches, rheumatism, and fainting-spells, deathly pale from prayer, depressions, overlong nocturnal studies—became the greatest statesman of the seventeenth century. His slim, unusually tall, wasp-waisted figure, his distinction of movement and gesture, his quiet, penetrating glance which remained fixed until its target was intimidated, his short, black, fashionably clipped Vandyke—this picture was to keep the Paris Court, then France, and finally all Europe breathless. While complaining that his headaches were killing him, he conceived the idea of a national state, the first in history, stacked the cards against Spain, joined German and Swedish Protestants against Habsburg and Bavaria, undertook the famous Valtellina campaign to thrust a strategic wedge between Austria and Spain, corrupted the French nobility with the most unscrupulous methods, made the King a responsible monarch and ousted his ever more intolerably scheming mother, to whom he himself owed his career. The realm, to which Maria was never to return, he extended to its famous "natural frontiers" and lifted it to the political, scientific, and artistic supremacy it would retain for centuries. In his mind there was room for little besides the national state; it is doubtful whether at heart this priest was not quite consciously indifferent to God.

To the Protestants he gave religious freedom, refusing to encroach on it even after he had forever destroyed them as a political party. His only life-and-death struggle was that for the power of the monarchy; if the Huguenots had not opposed him there, he would have let them live, pray, and work. His state was not improvised like that of his predecessor, Henry IV, whose plans he revived. It was constructed by an exact, scientific method; in this process, the miscalculation represented by the Huguenots in their communal and provincial petrifaction had to be corrected by eradication.

Once again there was deep, hopeless mutual embitterment, with excesses occurring on both sides. The unrest which stirred in all provinces was worst in La Rochelle, where the King had Fort Louis erected opposite the town and refused the town's urgent appeal to have it razed. He had to protect himself, or La Rochelle might some day be the gateway for an English invasion; but the townspeople saw in his refusal a constant threat to their self-government; it was peace in war, and war in peace. Lofty sentiments were expressed to the accompaniment of artillery maneuvers. It could not end well; that sort of thing never does.

The leaders were the old ones: Rohan, who had the Bible carried before him wherever he went, and his brother Soubise, hot-headed and adventuresome, planlessly starting premature local rebellions. To the Huguenots, majesty was no longer worthy of respect; they got more and more entangled in their particular partisan independence. They had equipped vessels under the pretext of a new attempt at American colonization; but when the fleet was ready in January, 1625, it attacked and seized royal ships at anchor in the harbor of Blavet and occupied the islands of Ré and Oléron off La Rochelle. The revolt spread along the whole coast.

Even this, in the view of the times, might still have been justified by necessity; it was never clear where danger to privilege ended and peril of life and limb began. The one deplorable and inexcusable step was the Huguenots' accord with Spain. How was this to be harmonized with their ideas? The heretics allied themselves with Jesuits, who promised to insure their safety and simultaneously called for their annihilation! It was grotesque. *Realpolitik* which is so realistic that it deserts its ideology is no longer *Realpolitik*. The argument that such abandonment of principle is temporarily required to stave off destruction is specious.

The Huguenot social program fared no better. An instance was the revolt of the "Croquants," as the peasants were called during its short, gory duration: for three years the oppressed folk of Poitou, Saintonge, Limousin, Marche, and Périgord tried desperately to escape from the clutches of tax-collectors, lansquenets, and their aides. The insurgents received help. From the Huguenots? Certainly not; it was the Dutch who had to back them up.

If the state, as foreseen by Richelieu, was the point of departure on a common road—a dynamic mechanism requiring the joint action of all separate forces—a party which refused to participate at all could no longer be allowed to exist. The growing unities for which he strove could not be endangered; universal collaboration was essential. Certainly, personal sympathy and antipathy played no part whatever in his conceptions; and that he wished to tolerate the Huguenots as long as possible is proved by more than one fact. But it is equally certain that these pietists were not only alien but profoundly embarrassing to him, the exponent of Catholic culture, the Renaissance man in the great style of Leonardo. He never understood this grave, gray autumn of the last great religious movement in human history. For any kind of pietism he had but a shrug. In his eyes, the Huguenots who fought for feudal privilege were rebels; and those who fought for their Protestant conviction were gloomy zealots, devoted to the joyless and austere. The fervor of their psalm-singing notwithstanding, it seemed that all warmth and beauty was dead within them. Their rigid self-righteousness struck him as mere emptiness of heart.

Richelieu, who loved no one after his mother's death, who had donned an impervious armor of icy aloofness, surrounded himself with all the luxury and refinement, all the pomp and ceremony of his baroque world. He walked in satin, purple, brocade, and gold, covered with jewels; he stared with unmoving, uncomprehending eyes at all who spurned the treasures of life and were content to have God near and to themselves. The holy images, the smell of incense, the harmonies filling the places of worship, hinting, promising, intoxicating, man-made yet inspirational throughout the ages: whether taken seriously or not—and he himself hardly took them seriously—they were part of his being. But that other thing was new, bare, freshly whitewashed, harsh toward the pitfalls and weaknesses of humankind, avoided by both muses and amourettes. And he wrapped himself more tightly in his glittering cloak when he passed it.

28

THE FALL OF LA ROCHELLE

RICHELIEU had been in power hardly a year when all things at once turned against him. The Protestants, subdued along the Loire only to rise in Languedoc under Rohan, received England's promise of aid. Buckingham, Charles I's favorite and dominant adviser, conspired with Soubise, who, in 1625, had taken the islands of Ré and Oléron off La Rochelle and captured five royal ships in the harbor of Blavet. Soubise was invited to London.

Anything Richelieu did could but add to the danger. If he attacked the Huguenots, England would invade by way of the two seized islands and La Rochelle, and the grandees, eager to overthrow the Cardinal, would probably join forces with the enemy. To meet them he would need to withdraw troops from the Swiss Valtellina; which was exactly what the Spanish were waiting for, to strike at it themselves. On the other hand, if he held onto Valtellina, his home forces would be insufficient to crush the domestic revolt.

Nevertheless, he had to do something. His power, and with it his policy, would not be safe while the Huguenots formed a state within the state, able to ally themselves with England or Spain, Savoy or the Netherlands, against their country. Any such alliance would have the use of La Rochelle, the powerfully fortified, the seemingly unconquerable, the perpetual gateway for invasion. To Englishmen as well as Spaniards this town, and the islands off its shore, would provide bases for a blockade of France or even a march on Paris.

La Rochelle was one of the kingdom's proudest and wealthiest towns. At high tide the harbor was navigable for all vessels, but no besieging fleet could long remain at anchor outside because of constant storms. Heavily armed watch-towers, emblems of dominion, and converging breakwaters easy to close with chains barred attack on land or by sea. Trading vessels sailed out of La Rochelle for the ports of England, Scotland, Flanders, Spain, Portugal, Canada, even Russia. A splendid, lavishly built town with rich arcades, wide streets, new churches and mansions. It was thoroughly Protestant: over doors, beside gates, Bible texts were hewn into the stone.

The inhabitants persisted in the tradition of discipline carried over from Geneva. Every citizen was as devout as a priest and as warlike as a soldier; and all were seafarers. Men liable to service were grouped in companies; all merchant vessels were quickly convertible for use as warships. Privileges, won in the twelfth century, were zealously guarded; a government by patricians, independent of the King, was the pride of the town. The people said they had been annexed to France, but had not joined it; their town was free, like the German towns of the Hansa. They underwent several sieges during the religious wars, and each time emerged triumphant. Condé, Coligny, Jeanne d'Albret, Henry of Navarre, La Noue—all had found refuge behind the walls of La Rochelle. Its independence was valued even by the feudal Catholics; whenever the monarchy planned to attack the town, it had to pay dearly for the gentlemen's succor. Besides, it helped to preserve this symbol of provincial independence—it was so perfect an object lesson in royal impotence, if only defiance was bold enough!

By July, 1627, the political situation was so tense that war seemed inevitable, awaiting merely the initial hostile act. Buckingham, with a fleet of a hundred sails, suddenly appeared in Breton waters. He landed on the Ile de Ré and laid siege to the royal fortress of St. Martin, defended by the valiant Toiras. To the people of La Rochelle he sent an offer of his sovereign's support, calling on them to take up arms in defense of their imperiled freedom.

This brilliant upstart who with his perfumed charm bewitched Charles I, as he did James I before him, appeared to be still at the height of his power, though the English hated him and cursed him in the streets. His fame still outshone that of his French opponent; little did he know what sort of man now faced him there across the Channel, always taking the long view. The scales seemed still balanced; soon one would rise, light as a feather, empty—and Buckingham had no idea that it would be his.

In La Rochelle they deliberated. They were not deceiving themselves; acceptance of Buckingham's offer would put the town in a position that was no longer equivocal. But despite its craving for independence, La Rochelle was loyal at heart, far more so than the Languedoc Protestants under Rohan. La Rochelle sought to avoid any impression that the fight for its privileges was a fight against the King. Once more it suggested that the government raze Fort Louis; then one could induce Buckingham to give up the

Ile de Ré, and peace would be saved. Louis XIII had to decline. He could not yield under pressure; to do so would have meant to recognize the King of England as the Protestants' protector, and might well have rallied restive Catholics to the successful Huguenot opposition.

Buckingham continued his siege of St. Martin, one of the more bizarre episodes of this baroque age: men bled to death at assaults and sorties, died of hunger, fell victim to epidemics, but never forgot courtesy. They never would thrust the lance into an enemy's belly without complimenting him on his heroic death. Prisoners were treated as guests. How at the last moment, on the evening when the fortress was ready to capitulate because not a scrap of food remained, Richelieu brought a flotilla with reinforcements and supplies through the fog, despite all precautions of the English—that is an adventure story replete with improbabilities, almost a legend. Toiras, revitalized, proceeded to destroy the English army, and Buckingham, robbed of both glamour and strength, fled home, where indignation at his ridiculous venture exploded in riots.

King Louis, only just recovered from a serious illness, was hard to persuade now to besiege La Rochelle in turn. Yet this had become Richelieu's *idée fixe*. His mind was made up; he would at any cost strike the great blow on which his position depended; he was ready to expend all the power of his genius and all the money of the Crown and his private fortune. He staked his destiny on the capture of La Rochelle—which, he was convinced, would break the Huguenot party, put the first families of the kingdom in their places, and leave only one power in France, that of the King. He was fully aware of the difficulties. He knew that the town's fortifications were regarded as impregnable, and that the inhabitants would fight to the last man. But failure to crush this revolt would encourage others; after all, the questions involved were largely social, with the workers in Protestant countries still believing that the Huguenots were fighting for the Third Estate. There had been riots in Amsterdam, artisans, sailors, dock-hands going on strike because of favors granted to French ships. The strike had spread to Plymouth. How long before such resistance would flare up in Brittany, everywhere in northern France, and put an intolerable strain on the foreign situation?

The terms Louis sent to La Rochelle were honorable and lenient. Its religious privileges were to remain untouched. But Providence seems to have doomed La Rochelle like ancient Troy; while the townsmen deliberated, in the main not averse to finding a formula for agreement, news came from Soubise in London which surpassed the wildest hopes of the advocates of resistance: Charles I of England promised all the help in his power; the town must hold out at whatever cost.

Meanwhile, in the south of France, the Duke of Rohan visited town after town, trying desperately to rally the Huguenots to a mighty effort in aid of La Rochelle. And how did these co-religionists react? To what decisions did they bestir themselves, now that their whole political existence was at stake? Rohan sped to Uzès, to Milhau, to Nîmes, the length of the Cévennes, from one end of Languedoc to the other; he found only timid minds and cold hearts, aside from those already bought by the King. In vain did he show them Soubise's letter, sent him by his mother, the old Duchess of Rohan, who had done much to inspire resistance in La Rochelle. He heard many excuses, but the only valid one was that at present one must not oppose royal authority. It was understandable, too, that many declared they had taken part in enough religious wars and had earned a rest. The worst, however, was the indifference of the youth, who had never fought and would not see that the fate of the men of La Rochelle was their own. It turned out that the Calvinist party was no more. An Assembly at Nîmes passed a resolution to send aid, but the towns refused to comply. "What business is it of ours?" they asked bluntly. "Each must fend for himself."

The royal army which was to besiege La Rochelle was placed under the command of Charles de Valois, Duke of Angoulême, an illegitimate son of Charles IX. Originally it numbered 8000 men and 24 cannon. Its mobilization was still disguised as maneuvers, and Angoulême still parleyed politely with the councilmen of La Rochelle. He offered terms under which the town need fear nothing if it proved loyal. But restrictive measures followed fast: no more provisions were allowed to enter the town, nor could the harvest be brought in from the fields outside the gates.

Suddenly, on Friday, September 10, 1627, shooting started on both sides. There was no real reason; masons at work on Fort Louis were said to have shouted insults at the halberdiers on the walls, causing the halberdiers to open fire and hit a workman. Tension, accumulated over a period of weeks, had itself created the incident for its abrupt discharge. War—the "last Huguenot war" of the historians—had begun.

The King arrived before La Rochelle on October 12. He took up quarters in the little village of Aytré, atop a hill of vineyards, and Richelieu in an isolated house in the vicinity, between the road and the sea. Weeks of gigantic labor lay behind him. Every detail had gone through his hands: he knew of every rifle and every piece of bread, he knew the morale in every tent and the qualifications of every lieutenant. At the same time he had set up a far-flung intelligence service, whose innumerable spies kept him informed about the events and the atmosphere at every European Court. He had worked too hard and soon fell ill; but what worried him most was the discord among his generals. They did not see what was at stake and, as of old, thought only of their private fame and pay. The King's mood, too, was constantly changing. At times he was all interest, only to be all ennui a day later. But Richelieu soon pulled himself together. He managed to raise the size of his army to 30,000, an unusual strength in that age. He improved their equipment, uniforms, and quarters, and for the first time in French history set up regular pay-days. He brought food prices in camp below the Paris level; but looting was punished by death. The greatest task, however, was to cut La Rochelle off from the English, their men and supplies. Richelieu had to defeat the sea.

In his lonely house he read the story of Alexander the Great, who conquered the island of Tyre by means of a dam built on the ocean-bed. A similar though fruitless attempt had already been made off La Rochelle a few years earlier; Pompeo Targione, an Italian military engineer employed on that project, was called back by Richelieu, but at flood-tide his dam burst a second time. Then Clément Métezeau, a Paris architect, advised the construction of a very simple boom, composed of huge boulders, wooden poles, quarry stone, and sunken vehicles. Late in November, 1627, work began on this plan. Four thousand laborers drew extraordinary wages for day and night shifts; and

Richelieu was with them many a night, cardinal's hat pulled down over his yellow face, swallowing medicine, defying wind and rain. The King, too, sometimes spent half the night at his side. But not until five months later was the boom completed, after all sorts of accidents. When the English warships and freighters arrived with supplies for La Rochelle, they had to turn back without having reached their objective. But that was five months later.

About the end of the year the weather turned more and more against the besiegers. The countryside became a bog as rain and snowstorms followed each other; the supply roads were washed out. The beleaguered Huguenots attacked, and their violent sorties inflicted discouraging losses on the tired royal troops. Discipline slackened. Epidemics spread. Louis's restlessness grew. He looked anxious, could not sleep, quarreled with the Duke of Angoulême, with Bassompierre, especially with his repulsive, corrupt, treacherous brother Gaston. When a fearful cold wave struck the coast in February, with the storm howling and crashing for days and the sea raging as at the world's end, Louis's will power crumbled. "I shall die in this horrible corner of France," he said, shivering and longing to be in Versailles. He began to avoid the Cardinal.

A rumor spread that the siege would be lifted. Louis wished to be allowed to go to Paris for some weeks to recuperate. Richelieu objected, fearing a complete collapse of his enterprise once the King had left. He implored him tearfully; he actually wept, wept over his own wasted energy. Gaston strutted about the camp and triumphantly, with many jests, predicted the early dismissal of this gentleman whose sole talent was presumption. When Louis gave his word to come back in a few weeks, Richelieu yielded; if he had not, the King and the whole crowd of bored nobles might well have gone to Versailles without so much as a by-your-leave. Now, however, before the King's departure, Richelieu was appointed Commander-in-Chief, outranking Marshals Angoulême, Bassompierre, and Schomberg.

In April, after Métezeau's dam was completed, the unexpected happened: Louis XIII kept his promise and punctually returned to camp, on the very day agreed on at his departure.

In La Rochelle, food was running low. Harsh punishment could not halt speculation on black markets. There were cases of scurvy. When a request of the burgomaster's for permission to evacuate some of the women and children was turned down by Richelieu, attacks on town councilors followed. The prospect of aid from the southern Huguenots grew fainter by the day. And the English fleet—when would it come? It was the last hope, the only hope.

A letter from King Charles was smuggled through the blockade: he promised help if they concluded a definite alliance with him. The townsmen saw no way out; they must sign although the alliance was aimed at their King. Their signature was odd: they accepted the conditions of His Majesty, the King of Great Britain, but averred they would remain loyal and obedient subjects of their rightful lord, His Most Christian Majesty of France.

On April 30 they elected a new burgomaster. Jean Guiton—his statue still stands in the town—was a seaman, a robust, burly citizen, plain, kind, pious, at the same time diplomatic and intrepid. His heart was in the right place;

he seemed built to make others stand their ground; always cheerful, he let no man see the worry gnawing at his heart. When he walked through the streets, dressed in black, everyone greeted him; he knew them all. When he preached, he told them how often God, to whom they prayed, had sorely tried them—but had He not always saved them at the eleventh hour? Starving, they clung to the certainty that one day the English fleet would arrive, smash the barrier, and bring meat, fat, and vegetables. At windows high up in the gables the women kept watch from dawn to dusk, staring out to sea. When would the white sails come? Had not five white swans passed over the roofs only yesterday, heralds of the white sails of the King of England?

And in fact, two days later the new rescue fleet, commanded by the Duke of Buckingham's brother-in-law, hove in sight. The English people had forced its dispatch from the cowardly, twisting and turning, ever-indecisive Buckingham. Afraid of the man in the street, he quickly had put these old ships to sea—badly manned, and loaded, for want of money, with rotten foodstuffs. As they appeared off La Rochelle, sailors climbed the masts of the ships in the harbor to wave to them; the entire population poured out of the houses, shouting, sobbing, waving, praying. Guiton had the bells rung, and then called on the Duchess of Rohan. The opposition, he told her, was suggesting negotiations with the King: perhaps, now that England really was sending help, he would grant better terms. The old lady shook her head. "The King, perhaps; not Richelieu."

But the day passed and the night passed, and while the French fleet filled up with volunteers wanting to fight the

English, Buckingham's brother-in-law did nothing. On his ships were men of La Rochelle, who had been in London and were coming back with him. They entreated him, knelt before him, kept up their pleas until three in the morning, but every hour found him more discouraged. Those in La Rochelle were seized by a terrible uneasiness. Why did the sails not come nearer? And in the afternoon, they did come nearer—but then, slowly, the ships veered about, grew smaller, leaving naked horror behind.

Guiton aged visibly. He grew thin in his dark clothes, but kept his fists clenched. "And if just one of us stays alive, he'll keep the gates locked."

In May, when the siege had lasted almost a year, a pale group moved from one of the gates toward the royal positions, imploring hands uplifted. They were women and children, and they were driven back with naked swords. Then the deaths began. At first it was two hundred a day, then three hundred, then four hundred. The survivors, no longer strong enough to remove the bodies, left them lying where they died. The soldiers were too weak to hold their weapons. But they did not capitulate.

Guiton still could not believe that the English would fail him. In his simple sermons he talked of Paradise; that would be a happy reward for the dead, there the women and children were already waiting. Opposition to him grew among the older councilmen, who asked that he surrender. But he won out, for the citizens credited the rumors current about the eerie Cardinal, rumors that he had sworn to put the male population to the sword and turn the women over to his soldiers. They remained in awe of Guiton; a man who followed him with murder in his heart dropped his arm under the burgomaster's glance. When-

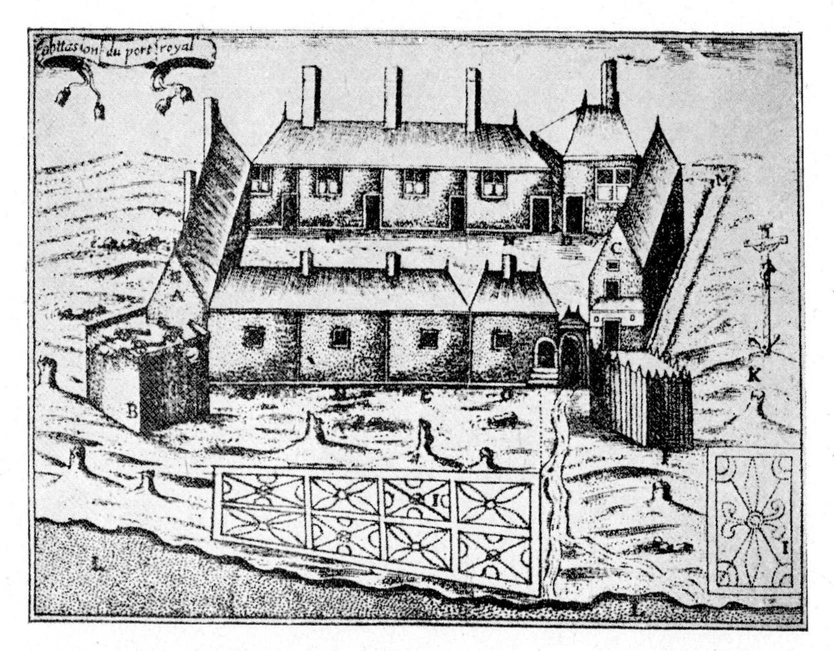

A Logemens des artisans.
B Plate forme où estoit le canon.
C Le magasin.
D Logemét du sieur de Pontgraué & Champlain.
E La forge.
F Palissade de pieux.
G Le four.
H La cuisine.
O Petite maisonnette où l'on retiroit les vtansiles de nos barques ; que de puis le sieur de Poitrincourt fit rebastit & y logea le sieur Boulay quand le sieur du Pont s'en reuint en France.
P La porte de l'abitation.
Q Le cemetiere.
R La riuiere.

PORT ROYAL, L'ACADIE
1605

N ij

Drawing by Champlain

Engraving by Tiebout

JOHN JAY

ever Guiton preached now, he fainted from hunger; but when he came to, he laughed broadly. His untiring helper was the old Duchess of Rohan, who went from house to house with her unmarried daughter to distribute scant rations of food; she herself lived on soup cooked from scraps.

In September, Guiton sent two envoys to the Cardinal to ask terms of surrender. Richelieu's answer was that it was not too late, the town could still hope for royal mercy.

Perhaps La Rochelle would have decided to capitulate on this vague, ambiguous promise, if word had not reached the town that a new English fleet was approaching. The report was founded on fact. Mutinous sailors in Portsmouth had forced Buckingham to start equipping another expedition. He delayed the work—not for spite but because he had no money—until, on August 23, he was murdered by a destitute cashiered officer, John Felton. The third English fleet appeared off La Rochelle, but was pounded by French cannon and then dispersed by a storm. The next day its commodore, Lindsey, tried to rally. He sent word into the town that he was bringing food, that his ships would smash the dam. But when a new obstacle paralyzed the fleet—the captains of several ships refused to carry out orders—Lindsey had to turn back.

Eight thousand people in La Rochelle died of hunger in the last six months, two thousand in the last two months. On October 26, the burgomaster called the council, but the gentlemen were so weak that the meeting lasted only a few minutes. They decided to send an intermediary to the King: they were ready to surrender unconditionally, and humbly beg for mercy.

The King's Council was so nervous that all dignity was thrown off. Bassompierre ran around between the tents, snapped at the soldiers, was laughed at, laughed back. Wild excitement reigned everywhere. A majority in the Council called for pitiless severity, for a terrible example to be made of the rebels; others wanted only the ringleaders executed. Richelieu was silent until the King asked for his views.

"Sire," said the Cardinal, "never before has a prince had such opportunity to shine in the eyes of present and future generations. If we are created in God's image, the King, above all, must prove it—by clemency and mercy, by the joy he takes in doing good; never by destruction, unless he is forced to destroy. Punishment? I think La Rochelle has been punished enough. At the beginning of the siege it numbered 25,000 souls; today, according to reliable intelligence, 5000 remain. I am of opinion that the King's greatness of heart will appear all the purer the more purely he forgives."

The King stared before him. He was moved, perhaps aware that they, too, were his country's children, whose fate he had to decide. Then his eyes darkened. "Forgive? How can I let these criminals . . ." He became confused. He hoped the others would speak; but when all began to talk at the same time, he interrupted them and again turned to the Cardinal. A quick discussion ensued in which Richelieu asked for full amnesty, but the King insisted that at least Guiton and ten leading councilmen be banished for life and that the walls be razed.

"I submit to your judgment, Sire," said Richelieu. "I should have preferred unbounded mercy, which would have disarmed Rohan and the Southern Protestants. . . ."

The Fall of La Rochelle

When the deputation of La Rochelle appeared before the King, they were too weak to dismount from their borrowed horses. They were informed that everyone's life would be spared, that religious freedom would be permitted as before. But the town's independence would cease with the day of surrender. Privileges, elective authorities, burgomasters, councilmen—all that would cease. Royal officials would govern. The fortifications would be razed, except for those facing the ocean. The Catholic faith would be dominant in the town, with Protestant worship restricted to churches which would be tolerated outside the town limits.

For the first time in European history since the Middle Ages, a town was occupied with iron discipline, without an act of violence, without so much as a derisive word. Silently the troops marched in; only the shouts of command echoed in the deserted narrow streets. On the heels of the troops followed food wagons, herds of cattle, butchers, spits. Anyone asking more than the fixed prices was hanged on the spot. On November 1, King Louis rode in with his generals and his government, to the ringing of bells, the roar of cannon, and the rattle of muskets. The English fleet, which had remained on the horizon, disappeared during the night of November 10. The leveling of walls and towers had already begun, with a host of workmen quickly recruited. Where breastworks had been, fields were to ripen in future. For weeks, masses of townspeople continued to die of malnutrition, and a regiment of engineers had to be brought in to bury the dead.

La Rochelle of old, the free, stubborn fortress by the sea, had ceased to exist.

29

EXIT FROM HISTORY

THE fall of La Rochelle marked the end of political Calvinism. In Guyenne and Languedoc civil war continued for some time, but the very cruelty with which it was waged helped shorten it. The Peace of Alais was signed in July, 1629, followed in a month by the Pardon Edict of Nîmes. The Protestants received a promise of full civil rights and freedom of religion, and a general amnesty. But the name of the edict was significant. It was no longer a pact between two parties, but an act of judicial leniency toward a criminal. The strongholds and castles of the Huguenots were razed, their military formations disbanded, their Assemblies placed under guard. Their fate, henceforth, hung on the constancy of royal favor.

And though for decades they went on living and laboring, tolerated and persecuted by turns, they were merely Protestants now, members of a church different from the official one. Huguenot history as such came to a close with the Pardon Edict. For the Huguenots, by definition, were a compound of interdependent religious and political forces; their end as a political force—destroying the will as well as the way to further resistance—removed them from the stage of French history, where for nearly a hundred years they had initiated essential reforms, forced changes in the social structure, leavened feudalism with *bourgeois* ideas. What remained was a multitude of Protestants, still large, but now fitted into the framework of the state and dependent upon governmental tolerance. The defense of their religious, civil, and social rights lay no longer with themselves but with the King.

Time and again, chiefly by the Roman Curia, Richelieu was urged to stamp out the Calvinist heresy and repeal the Edict of Nantes. He was too much of a statesman to comply. His eyes were on France, not on Rome. He was waging European war and needed money; and the Calvinists, if left to do their work in peace, were abler and consequently wealthier than the rest of the nation. The Cardinal had enemies in plenty and did not propose to make new ones of people with capital, who were of the greatest importance to French industry.

To be sure, he did little about the widespread highhanded disregard of the Pardon Edict. Foreign affairs kept him too busy to pay much attention to the domestic religious issue once it had ceased to be urgent. And the country was not as yet sufficiently well organized for all lower functionaries to have been caught up by centralization; thus, local officials were still more or less at liberty to administer the law as they saw fit. They were rarely called to account for violating its spirit.

Hardly a year passed without the closure of some Calvinist church or school on a flimsy pretext or without the imposition of some new restriction. If a house of worship was found to occupy ground that had originally belonged to an abbey, it was expropriated. In the old Huguenot town of Sancerre the Protestant form of worship was suddenly forbidden, and no appeal ever obtained rescinding of the measure. The Protestant high school in Loudun was turned over to the Ursuline nuns, because their convent had become too small for them. The Bishop of Valence forbade the Protestant clergy to preach outside their towns of residence, depriving the dependent parishes of divine service. In Poitiers, the town council resolved that no Protestant could be a master. The list could be extended to include a few more grotesque injustices—such as, for instance, the Paris decree that Protestants could bury their dead only at sunset—but the cases cited adequately illustrate the situation. Although Protestant officials, of whom Richelieu thought highly, kept their posts, and although the government affirmed repeatedly that the Edict would stand, the Calvinists were still regarded as second-class citizens. Even nobles and upper *bourgeois* among them were in bad odor as an inferior sort, at whom it was quite *bon ton* to look down your nose.

Their party was weakened further by the defection of the aristocrats. Failure of the attempts to upset Richelieu's authoritarian power had left the feudal nobility facing a devil's choice: either to perish in a last, lost fight for independence or to let themselves be transformed into a Court set. In the new social structure they were lost without government subsidies; it became essential to their very existence to be employed and salaried by the Court. But since the King's religion was the Court's as well, the Protestants, in dismay and grief, soon saw members of the great families who had been their pride and support, whose forebears had given their blood for their convictions, returning into the fold of the Apostolic Church. The apostates, to name but a few, included Philip Duplessis-Mornay's brother, Peter; Sully's son, Maximilian de Béthune; Coligny's grandson, Charles de Châtillon; also Lesdiguières, the Duchess of Condi, and famous scholars such as Du Perron and Palma Cayet. Many preachers abjured, too; whenever the Holy See took Richelieu to task for failing to re-establish religious unity, the Cardinal replied with figures: tabulations of the sums paid out in bribes to Reformed clergymen.

The skill with which he made his eel's way among the parties—fundamentally of equal indifference to him, doubtless—remains astounding. To pour oil on the stormy Roman waves, he deprived the Protestant clergy of the right to travel abroad, to transfer to other parishes, even to call themselves priests. But at the same time, to please his Protestant German and Swedish allies, he made extensive concessions to them in the dogmatic field, especially as regards the concept of transubstantiation. It is one of the most absurd paradoxes of European history that the very man who crushed Protestant political power in France saved Protestantism in Germany: the aid he rendered to Gustavus Adolphus of Sweden and to Bernhard, Duke of Weimar, preserved the Reformed Church to the east of the Rhine from the fate it suffered to the west of it. Side by side, Richelieu's Catholics and Bernhard's Protestants fought the imperial troops in Alsace and in Lorraine; after the battle of Wittenweiler, Weimar vowed brotherhood-in-arms to the French commander, Guébriant, and after his death the French Duke of Longueville took over part of his command.

Nothing shows better how religion had yielded to politics than this war against the Habsburgs from 1638 to 1641. It was far more important to Richelieu to stand in well with Protestant Germany and Sweden than with Rome; accordingly, he distributed money and honors among Calvinist nobles and preachers in France to attract them to Catholicism, but refused consistently to convert them by force. Besides, it was now more and more apparent that Calvinism would remain a matter for the little man and the urban trader. The flame of the older generation had petered out. In sad resignation the elders had withdrawn from public life, and their retirement was hardly noticed by the state. Soon the great names of French Protestantism would be no more than historic memories.

There was old, very old Agrippa d'Aubigné, once Henry IV's conscience, the swashbuckler with the scarred body, the poet. How long ago since a boy had promised his father to avenge the hanged ones of Amboise! Improbable past—forgotten epics . . . How long, too, since he had persuaded Henry of Navarre to flee from Court! This intransigent Huguenot had often clashed unpleasantly with his beloved King's Catholic airs; and Henry had made him Governor of Maillezais, just to keep him honorably at a safe distance. There he sat, a growling, outspoken bard, he who had once lauded the Huguenots as "men encased in their armor like tortoises." He could not get used to the new times; when he came to Court to vent his spleen, the King would embrace him tearfully and yet be glad when he left. D'Aubigné lived on the fame of having penned the *Tragiques*, the great epic of Calvinism, seven volumes of eleven thousand alexandrines altogether, singing the tragedy of French Protestantism which to him was the tragedy of France. After Henry's death, he acutely discomfited his party by the scathing wrath with which he denounced their timid, lower middle-class compromises; they called him "*le brouillon*," and he explained his refusal to attend any more of their Assemblies by describing them as public prostitutes. Under Louis XIII he sold his fortress, resigned his offices, retired to a private house, and wrote his *Histoire Universelle*. But the ever-recurring persecution of the Protestants was more than the old man could stand. He went into voluntary exile to Geneva, where he was received with the highest honors, and began a new life—marrying, finally, at the age of seventy-one.

Philip Duplessis-Mornay died in November, 1623. His last years had been filled with a quiet, pious serenity. He looked on smilingly as his end approached, and his smile radiated such strength that family and friends, standing about his bed, were made calm and glad with hope. He admitted that he had been given much and made little of it; when someone protested that few had so faithfully used their gifts for the common good, he replied: "My gifts? Why mine? Don't say they were mine. God worked through me." Duplessis was the last representative of the great, strong generation which had been formed by Calvin's teaching and Coligny's example. By his life he bore witness that even in the degradation of civil war man can keep his character stanch and his name unblemished.

There remained Sully. He too grew very old, so old that he outlived himself. Notorious as an eccentric throughout Paris, he had his revenge on his former foes when he wrote his memoirs. His contemporaries fared badly therein—all but the King, who fared magnificently, and the writer, who fared most magnificently of all. When talking with people, his only topic was his merits. When he walked on the street, urchins ran after him noisily; for he was dressed after the fashion of thirty years before, in the taste of stopped thinking of the past or mourning the victims of St. Bartholomew's and the religious wars, whom each family had to lament.

But their rigid discipline also made the Protestants a prime factor in the public life of the nation. It was chiefly thanks to them that trade and industry prospered in France during the seventeenth century—the very period in which Spain became impoverished.

It was the Protestants who promoted colonization, and supported the East and West India Companies. Protestants founded the great merchant firms of La Rochelle, Bordeaux, Dieppe, Nantes, Calais, and Rouen. They established the big textile mill in Abbeville, the biggest in France, employing 1200 workers, and the smaller ones in Reims, Rethel, Mézières, and Caudebec. They developed the silk industry of Lyon, the paper factories of Auvergne, the tanneries of Touraine, the iron foundries of Sedan, the weaving mills of Gévaudan, the lace-making plants of Paris. Their strong and capable Huguenot spirit made France into an active, rational, *bourgeois* state. It prevented the degeneration then advancing irresistibly in Italy and Spain. To the solid mixture of Catholic *joie de vivre* and Calvinist discipline of labor the French nation owes the character which weathered all storms and that capacity for shifting from one extreme to the other, according to the exigencies of the situation, which in a spiritual but very real sense made it the center of Continental Europe.

30

EPILOGUE

THE war of annihilation against French Protestantism was not resumed until the reign of Louis XIV—not until after Richelieu's successor, Cardinal Mazarin, who continued to protect the minority, had died in 1661. Then it broke out everywhere in full fury.

The first blow fell upon churches and other places of public worship, which were dissolved wholesale. Next, the right of private individuals to hold services in their own homes was restricted by means of countless chicaneries. Thereafter the number of Reformed priests was reduced, and the performance of their duties made virtually impossible. So it went on, with schools closed, theological seminaries abolished, high schools turned over to the Jesuits, synods prohibited, conversions to the Protestant faith prohibited, claims of dissidents to government positions ignored.

All this is no longer part of Huguenot history. But perhaps the horror which now began in 1680, with the so-called "conversions"—when a show of hands would be forced at the point of the sword—perhaps this horror cries even louder to Heaven than all the outrages of the religious wars. For this was done to peaceful, unarmed citizens. A the refugees; since most of the Huguenots arrived penniless, they took up extraordinary collections for their support, in England, Scotland, and Ireland. In the revolution of 1688, when William of Orange landed in England to defend the threatened Protestant faith against the hated King, the Huguenots naturally sided with him. They flocked to his army and became his most valiant partisans; the main credit for his victory has often been given to their famous general, Armand Frédéric de Schomberg. Now, under William, the French immigrants at last were allowed to show what they could do. Their methods of producing silk, linen, batiste, carpets, and paper were so highly perfected and so astoundingly modern that it became a sought-after distinction for English boys to be taken into their shops as apprentices. Denis Papin, the man who conceived the first steam engine, was among the Huguenots who made England their home.

The largest number of refugees came to the Netherlands—about 100,000 all told. The reason is obvious. The Dutch government was so lavish in its hospitality that retirement pensions were paid to French noblemen, officers, and pastors—a generosity unequaled in the history of mankind. But the entire population took part in this great humane effort. In Amsterdam not only the Jews collected money for the alien Protestants but the Catholics as well! Here, again, paper and hat manufacturing, printing, and the ceramic industry were the principal beneficiaries of the Huguenots' arrival. And one odd fact ought to be mentioned: a French preacher, Jacques Saurin—who in Geneva had already stirred up such enthusiasm that people fought in the streets to force their way into the cathedral, who later in London had transformed British phlegm into its opposite—this Saurin, in 1705 called to The Hague for life, set the style not only for Dutch sermons ever since, but in many respects for Dutch literature in general.

Huguenots went to Switzerland and to Sweden; they went to Hungary; they even went to Russia; and some went as far as the Cape of Good Hope. Wherever they settled, they brought not only their proverbial zeal and capacity for hard work, but also a mature experience in most fields of commerce and industry—and again not alone experience but trade secrets heretofore jealously guarded for France. Yet in all these countries they formed small, closed communities. They were tiny minorities in the midst of alien majorities, clinging to their native language, to their French customs, to their own peculiar forms of worship. They prospered everywhere, and because of their ability and industry soon came to exert a considerable weight, economically and culturally, but everywhere their anxious self-segregation prevented their absorption by the people who had given them asylum. It took them centuries really to become one with their hosts, and nowhere did they play any great part in the body politic—except in one of their numerous countries of refuge.

That exception was America.

Huguenot emigration overseas, both to French Canada—until it was closed to Protestants in 1633—and under foreign flags, had continued steadily during the first half of the seventeenth century. At times, when government policy at home was tolerant, it was a mere trickle. At other times, under the spur of renewed mistreatment, it was a stream. When the first measures of Louis XIV convinced all who did not deliberately shut their eyes that it was

Y

wiser to prepare for worse days than to hope for better ones, the exodus became a river; and after 1685, when the Edict of Nantes was repealed and Protestantism in France finally, officially wiped out, it rose to a torrent.

America, by then, was no longer the continent of uncertainty, mystery, and adventure. The Huguenots knew that there across the Atlantic, expecting them, were their co-religionists. They knew of the groups that had crossed on the earliest ships, to New Amsterdam, Virginia, and other places; they knew of the hapless French Protestants who had open up La Nouvelle France in 1604, only to be expelled again thirty years later and driven south in headlong flight, to the English and Dutch possessions. In neighboring New England, the Puritans had not forgotten their own escape from similar troubles in England under the Stuarts; they lived the same moral lives as the Huguenots and sought the same direct relation with the Heavenly Father, without intercession by any priest or Pope. They had welcomed the Acadians; they would welcome other French Protestants, too, with complete religious sympathy.

Furthermore, the Huguenots had been in close, constant commercial contact with the colonies. From La Rochelle, Nantes, Bordeaux, St. Malo, Dieppe, their merchantmen had sailed to Massachusetts Bay, to New Amsterdam, to the Antilles; they were thoroughly familiar with American conditions and opportunities. They even had the right to feel that they were needed in the settlements. All colonial agencies—the companies which sold the land; the other companies which organized soil cultivation, which bought up the harvests and made the arrangements for export, which marketed the products of trapping and hunting; even the governors themselves—made every effort to attract capable European immigrants. An increase in the population was decidedly in the best interest of the colonies. Both in America and in England money was collected to pay the passage for those who could not pay it themselves.

The Huguenots knew that in the New World they would find no overwhelming, firmly rooted majority, set in its ways and presenting them with the alternative of radical absorption or an insular existence as a minute foreign cell. The English strain, to be sure, would outnumber the French one; but this numerical superiority would not be immense and crushing, as in England proper or in other Old World countries. In America the French would come as settlers to other settlers, as founders to other founders; although they were few, the others were not many, either. Here the arrivals would not need to cling to their own narrow circles; they would be able to retain their traits and traditions even while mingling freely with the rest. Here the fact that they were Huguenots, and proud of it, by itself would not brand them as an alien element, unable to share in the civic activities of the *terre d'asile*. On the contrary, they would be welcomed the more warmly for this inherited character, so valuable as a component of Colonial community life.

The first large, compact Huguenot group came to fast-growing Boston, the "Puritan capital," in 1662: merchants of La Rochelle, who petitioned the governor and magistrates for permission to settle among the English colonists. Permission was granted, and new refugees followed in short order. Two years later a group arrived in so horrible a state of exhaustion and destitution that the entire colony was moved to pity; the subscription lists traveled from house to house and from farm to farm. Large tracts of arable land were given gratis to the Huguenots; those wholly without means were taken into homes until they became self-supporting.

About this time, Gabriel Bernon settled in Massachusetts: a great, daring merchant, an organizer and leader, who ceaselessly, undaunted by reverses and aspersions, fought for the idea of Huguenot colonization until he died at the age of eighty-one. Another great man who reached Boston toward the end of the century, to work there the rest of his days, was the Reverend Pierre Daillé—one-time professor of divinity at the famed Protestant seminary of Saumur—who not without reason has been called the real founder of the French Reformed Church in America.

Daillé came to Boston from New York, where he had been active for thirteen years. In that city, grown out of Huguenot-settled New Amsterdam, the French at first had worshipped in the Dutch church, for which, whenever possible, pastors were engaged who could speak both languages. On Sundays, they preached two sermons, first Dutch and then French; and year in and year out, like the circuit riders of later days, four of them wandered from congregation to congregation, preaching in Manhattan, Staten Island, Long Island, Wiltwyck (Kingston), Rondout, and New Rochelle. After 1659, the French congregation in New York was independently organized, with a minister of its own, but services were still held in the Dutch church, as were the English ones. In 1682, Daillé arrived from France. He re-organized the church, stressing the rôle of laymen, such as the *anciens* (Elders)—who were elected by the congregation, had the oversight of the flock, and, with the pastor, formed the *consistoire* of the church—and the *lecteur* or *chantre*, who read chapters of Holy Writ before services and sang the hymns. Daillé personally founded the French churches in Hackensack, Staten Island, and New Paltz, and from time to time visited all the Huguenot settlements in the region.

It was during his term in office, in 1688, that the French in New York first built a house of worship for their exclusive use, a humble chapel in Petticoat Lane—later known as Marketfield Street—near the Battery, on a site occupied today by the New York Produce Exchange. Soon this chapel became too small for the congregation, especially since every Sunday worshippers came into town from twenty miles around, from Long Island, Staten Island, New Rochelle, and other points. In 1704 a stone building, large for the time, was erected on Pine Street, opposite the Custom House. The name which the church then received —L'Eglise du St. Esprit—it has borne to this day, although it changed its home several times and once even its affiliation, being now Episcopalian. Its records are among the outstanding Huguenot-American documents extant. The names of the founders, too, are still familiar: De Lancey, Girard, Vincent, Fresneau, Jay. The last-named was Augustus Jay, who came to New York in the 1690's and whose grandson, perhaps the greatest American of Huguenot descent, became the author of the Constitution of the State of New York and its governor for six years, president of the Continental Congress and secretary for foreign affairs, Special Minister to England with which he concluded a treaty named for him, finally the first chief justice of the United States Supreme Court: John Jay.

Of the Huguenot settlements in the vicinity of New York, New Rochelle deserves particular mention. Built on

6000 acres purchased in 1689 on behalf of a band of refugees—local tradition still points out their landing place at Bonnefoy's Point, known today as Davenport Neck—its very name attested to the founders' love for their birthplace. Yet their letters to France—at least those that have been preserved—tell the persecuted brethren of God's mercy that made America, urging them to flee and join the ones already here. New Rochelle built its first church in 1692, and later welcomed the many Protestants who had to leave the French Caribbean islands—Martinique, Guadeloupe, St. Christopher—when the dragonnade laws of the mother country were extended overseas. It became the outstanding compact Huguenot settlement on American soil.

There were others, such as New Oxford in Massachusetts, founded by a small French group, which became quite important but had to be abandoned when the Nipmuck Indians, together with Canadian tribes, went on the warpath; its inhabitants later found permanent homes in Connecticut and Rhode Island. There were solid Huguenot settlements in up-state New York—such as the New Paltz mentioned at the beginning of this book—and in Pennsylvania, where several hundred arrived at one time, led by a brave woman, Madame Ferrée.

In 1666 Maryland naturalized all French Protestants, no matter how long or short their period of residence in the colony. Five years later Virginia followed suit; there the end of the century saw one of the largest organized Huguenot migrations. One ship brought 300 French immigrants, another 200; some groups settled near Jamestown, others in Norfolk County, still others joined the Huguenot colonists around Manakin; it was then that the largest number of refugees ever to come to American shores arrived: about 11,000 in four years. Again they received donations of money, land, and supplies, and the governor took up a subscription for their benefit. All taxes were waived for several years. When they did not succeed in raising grain crops, the English colonists gave them credit so that they might try their hands at more accustomed pursuits, such as viniculture, tailoring, shoemaking, or the silk industry. Soon their prosperity was astonishing.

Then there were the Carolinas—the Huguenots called them Canaan—which suited them so well and were so like their native France in latitude and vegetation, and in the character of the soil. Especially was this true of South Carolina, where the first Frenchmen since the unfortunate Coligny-sponsored expedition of Ribault and Laudonnière arrived immediately after the repeal of the Edict of Nantes. They immediately planted vineyards and olive groves, went about raising silkworms, built a tiny church. But their first years were years of cruel hardship. They had not expected this Canaan to flow with milk and honey; they had wished for no more than daily bread to still their hunger; but often we can read in their reports that days of toil did not earn them even that bread. Strife soon added to their troubles: they had difficulty with the English, who sought to force their conversion from Calvinism to the Episcopal Church and forbade marriages between members of the two denominations. Still, the Huguenots held out. They succeeded in founding and maintaining several fairly large *établissements:* before 1700, principally, in Charles Town, the Goose Creek area, St. John's Berkeley, the "Orange Quarter" on the Cooper, and Jamestown on the Santee where about eighty French families had settled by 1690. Later they founded Purysburg on the Savannah and New Bordeaux in Abbeville County. Within half a century, in South Carolina, social, financial, and political leadership was equally and amicably shared by families and men of English and French descent.

In the decades following the repeal of the Edict of Nantes—when emigration from France became a general flight and the number of arrivals in this country grew into the thousands, scattered over the entire Atlantic seaboard—a correlated picture of their activities became an impossibility. But whatever pursuits they followed, these noblemen, bankers, tanners, hatmakers, physicians, printers, vintners, factory laborers, weavers, and musicians, they never abandoned the first principle of their ancestors: to let their faith, and their generous philosophy with its libertarian and egalitarian ideas, guide their daily lives. Nor did they change when for America, too, the "critical and formative period" arrived.

If it is true that man is the worst beast on earth—the story of the Huguenots appears to prove it, and who, in any event, will doubt it today?—it is also true that no beast can rival his courage. An animal, hungry or cornered, will sometimes charge at a foe ten times its strength; its act is instinctive, not preceded by desperate reflection. But the perils which man has time and again defied in the thousands of years of his sorrowful history—often for gain, but as often for an idea, for an inner conviction, for a higher moral law within him—these perils bear witness to a courage, an intrepid magnitude, raising him far above all more primitive creatures. It is something else, too, to risk one's life in the exaltation of war, and to walk to the wheel or the torture, fully aware, without illusions, clearly foreknowing every horror to come. Yet millions of men have trod this path who need not have done so. A simple abjuration, a signature set quickly to a document, would have saved them and might have opened up a life of honor and prosperity; this tiny signature, which need not have altered their convictions, they refused to give. No virtue of man is so august and admirable as his courage, just as human cowardice is lower than animal fear.

The one fact most firmly rooted in our consciousness is that we must pay for every least step forward. We know we must pay in blood or, worse, in nameless, lifelong anguish; we know that to fight for our fellow-men means to be stoned by them. Hand another your loaf of bread; he will return it, poisoned. But man has never counted the cost of standing by his convictions. Stretched on the rack, no longer able to speak, he has shaken his head in silence when asked if he would save himself by a little conversion. All the countless generations of fighters have not exhausted this courage. It has not decreased. It is alive, unchanged, our greatest warrant that man was not placed senselessly into this world although his doings often may seem senseless, that the very fact of his unending suffering conceals the fact of his growth. And this is not altered one whit by the complacent smiles of the majority, who smugly withdraw from the contest.

The struggle of mankind continues uninterrupted; it began with the Creation and has never been waged in vain. He who gives himself to this struggle knows that the courage of man is his best hope, perhaps his only one.

Bibliography

Charlevoix, Pierre F. X. de. *Histoire et description générale de la Nouvelle France*, 3 vols. (Paris, 1744).

Chinard, Gilbert. *Les réfugiés huguenots en Amérique, avec une introduction sur le mirage américain* (Paris, 1925).

Davila, Enrico Caterino. *Historia delle Guerre Civile di Francia*, 4 vols. (Venetia, 1638).

Delaborde, Jules, comte. *Gaspard de Coligny, amiral de France* (Paris, 1879–1882).

Documentary History of the State of New York, 4 vols. (Albany, 1849–1851).

Documents inédits pour servir à l'histoire de la réforme et de la ligue (Paris, 1875, edit. Jean Loutehitzki).

Documents Relative to the Colonial History of the State of New York, 15 vols. (Albany, 1853–1887).

Félice, Guillaume de. *Histoire des protestants de France, depuis l'origine de la réformation jusqu'au temps présent* (Paris, 1856).

Fosdick, Lucian J. The French Blood in America (New York, 1906).

Gilman, Theodore. The Huguenots as Founders and Patriots (An address delivered before the New York Society of the Order of the Founders and Patriots of America, on March 27, 1913; New York Soc. No. 32).

Goulart, Simon. *Mémoires de la Ligue*, 6 vols. (Amsterdam, 1758).

Hanotaux, Gabriel. *Etudes historiques sur le XVIe et le XVIIe siècle en France* (Paris, 1886).

Harper, Lillie Du Puy. The Huguenots; in: Colonial Men and Times (Philadelphia, 1916).

Henry IV, King of France. *Lettres intimes* (Paris, 1876, ed. L. Dussieux).

Hotman, François. *Franco-Gallia, seu Tractatus isagogicus de regimine regum Galliae et de jure successionis* (Genève, 1573).

Huguenot Memorial Association. The Huguenot (Official publication of the Huguenot Memorial Association, Huguenot Park, Staten Island, 1931–1934).

Huguenot Society of America. Abstract of Proceedings, No. One (New York, 1884).

———. Collections of the Huguenot Society of America (New York).

Jameson, J. Franklin (editor). Narratives of New Netherland 1609–1664 (New York, 1909).

La Ferrière, Hector de. *Le XVIe siècle et les Valois* (Paris, 1879).

———. *Lettres de Cathérine de Médicis* (Paris, 1880).

Lavisse, Ernest. *Histoire de France depuis les origines jusqu'à la Révolution;* Vol. 5 by H. Lemonnier, Vol. 6 by J. H. Mariéjol (Paris, 1904–1911).

L'Estoile, Pierre de. *Journal des choses mémorables advenues durant tout le règne de Henry III, roy de France et de Pologne* (Cologne, 1663).

Martin, Henri. *Histoire de France, depuis les temps les plus reculés jusqu'en 1789*, 17 vols. (Paris, 1838–1885).

Michelet, Jules. *Histoire de France*, 11 vols. (Paris, 1855–1867).

Molinier, Auguste Emile L. M. *Les sources de l'histoire de France depuis les origines jusqu'en 1815;* Part II, *Le XVIe siècle*, by Henri Hauser (Paris, 1906–1915).

Palm, Franklin Charles. Politics and Religion in Sixteenth-century France (New York, 1927).

Parkman, Francis. Pioneers of France in the New World (Boston, 1865).

Poirson, Auguste Simon J. C. *Histoire du règne de Henri IV*, 4 vols. (Paris, 1862–1867).

Puaux, N. A. F. *Histoire de la Réformation française*, 7 vols. (Paris, 1859–1863).

Ranck, Rev. Henry H. The Huguenots and American Life (The Reformed Church Review, 1924).

Ranke, Leopold von. *Französische Geschichte vornehmlich im sechzehnten und siebzehnten Jahrhundert*, 6 vols. (Stuttgart and Augsburg, 1856–1862).

Relazioni degli ambasciatori veneti al Senato (Firenze, 1839, ed. Eugenio Albèri).

Richelieu, Armand Jean du Plessis. *Mémoires du Cardinal de Richelieu*, 5 vols. (Paris, 1907).

Romier, Lucien. *Les origines politiques des guerres de religion*, 2 vols. (Paris, 1913).

———, *Catholiques et Huguenots à la cour de Charles IX* (Paris, 1924).

Schaeffer, A. *Les Huguenots du XVIe siècle* (Paris, 1870).

Bibliography

Thompson, James Westfall. The Wars of Religion in France, 1559–1576 (Chicago, 1909).

Thou, Jacques-Auguste de. *Histoire universelle;* Vol. IV (Paris, 1740).

Valois, Marguerite de. *Mémoires et lettres* (Paris, 1842, ed. F. Guessard).

Wassenaer, Nicolaas van. The First Settlement of New Netherland, from "Wassenaer's *Historie van Europa*"; in: Papers Relating to the First Settlement of New York by the Dutch, 2 vols. (Edinburgh, 1888).

———. *Historisch verhael alder ghedenck-weerdichste geschiedenisse* . . . (Amsterdam, 1622–1635).

Weiss, Charles. History of the French Protestant Refugees, 2 vols. (New York, 1854, translated from the French by H. W. Herbert, with an American appendix, by a descendant of the Huguenots).